Civil D[illegible]ience

Civil Disobedience

A Philosophical Overview

Piero Moraro

ROWMAN &
LITTLEFIELD
INTERNATIONAL
London • New York

Published by Rowman & Littlefield International, Ltd.
6 Tinworth Street, London SE11 5AL
www.rowmaninternational.com

Rowman & Littlefield International, Ltd. is an affiliate of
Rowman & Littlefield
4501 Forbes Boulevard, Suite 200, Lanham, Maryland 20706, USA
With additional offices in Boulder, New York, Toronto (Canada), and London (UK)
www.rowman.com

British Library Cataloguing in Publication Information
A catalogue record for this book is available from the British Library

ISBN: HB 978-1-78660-716-4
ISBN: PB 978-1-78660-718-8

Library of Congress Cataloging-in-Publication Data

Moraro, Piero
Civil disobedience : A philosophical overview
Description:
Identifiers:
Subjects:
Classification:
LC record available at

∞™ The paper used in this publication meets the minimum requirements of American National Standard for Information Sciences Permanence of Paper for Printed Library Materials, ANSI/NISO Z39.48-1992.

To Samu and Tilly.
Disobey Well.

Contents

Acknowledgements

I would like to express my thanks to the Centre for Law and Justice at Charles Sturt University, for providing invaluable support and encouragement during my work at this manuscript.

I am also grateful to Rowman & Littlefield International for offering me the opportunity to write this book, and for their professionalism in assisting me during my work at the manuscript.

I am grateful to John Wiley & Sons, Oxford University Press and Sciences Po Press for having granted me permission to use some of the material I have previously published with them.

Thanks to my family in Italy, without whom this book would have never been written.

Finally, I thank my wife, Jacqui, and our two kids, Samuele and Matilde, for cuddles, laughter and constant reminders that there is more to life than writing a book.

Introduction

> A society in which there was no possibility of murder would be a better one, but a society in which there was no possibility of civil disobedience would be much worse.
> —Green (2003, 383)

The topic of civil disobedience began to attract philosophers' interest (at least in the Anglo-Saxon tradition) in the 1960s, in the wake of the civil rights movement and of anti–Vietnam War protests in the US. In those years, the philosophical debate focussed on the 'definition' of civil disobedience, and on the attempt to identify the 'necessary conditions' an illegal act should fulfil in order to be labelled 'civil'; for example, nonviolence, and a willingness to accept the punishment after the breach of the law, were treated as sine qua non of civil disobedience. After this spike in academic interest, the topic began to lose relevance in the philosophical literature in the late 1980s, and by the mid-1990s few academics were writing on civil disobedience. At the start of the new century, civil disobedience was deemed 'a faded subject' belonging 'in a curio cabinet of topics destined never again to be topical' (Edmundson 2006, 7). And yet, in those same years, there was a resurgence of academic interest in civil disobedience, thanks to the work of a new generation of philosophers. These younger academics were less interested in clear-cut definitions and necessary conditions of civil disobedience, and rather centred on its communicative nature and its capacity to empower citizens and promote rights. Furthermore, these authors tried to make sense of new forms of protest – the No-Global Movement, Occupy Wall Street and Edward Snowden's whistleblowing – which did not fit the earlier (and outdated) accounts of civil disobedience.

In this book, I offer an overview of these new contributions, focussing on the period from the early 2000s to the present. The book is organised around themes rather than individual authors, and is mainly (though not exclusively) concerned with philosophers working in the analytic tradition. Where I present the work of earlier authors (e.g., John Rawls, Ronald Dworkin, Jürgen Habermas and Joseph Raz), I do so in order to provide context for the more recent contributions to the debate. In the last chapter, I provide my own account of civil disobedience, aiming to address some of the issues discussed in the recent literature on the topic. Central to my account is an approach grounded in virtue ethics, which shifts the focus from *the act* to *the agent*. I start from the assumption that labelling a disobedient 'civil' implies something praiseworthy in her conduct, something that sets her apart from the 'uncivil'; therefore, to make sense of civil disobedience, we need first to make sense of what it means for an agent who disobeys the law to display 'civility'. This shift addresses the shortcomings of earlier authors who, as already mentioned, focussed on the act, not on the agent, in search of a list of 'necessary conditions' for civil disobedience. The problem with this approach is that there is no specific 'civil' act, as there is no specific 'benevolent', 'courageous', 'kind' act: judgements about an action's value must be made from within the context in which the act is performed. For example, giving money to a needy person may be a 'benevolent' act, yet may fail to be so if done with the goal of receiving others' approval rather than of helping the needy person. Similarly, earlier theorists upheld the willing acceptance of punishment as signalling respect for the law (and therefore as 'civil'): yet this cannot be established without looking at the specific circumstances, for the agent may accept the punishment in the attempt to manipulate public opinion, or even to show her *dis*respect for the law.

I begin by placing the problem of civil disobedience within the broader debate on political obligation (chapter 1). Civil disobedience is, first of all, *disobedience*, hence the problem of its justifiability arises only if there is something wrong with disobeying the law per se. I survey the major arguments in support of a *pro tanto* moral duty to obey the law, and show that they fail to establish the pro tanto wrongness of illegal conduct: under some circumstances, an agent may fulfil the underlying values of those accounts (e.g., fairness) through an act of disobedience rather than obedience to the law. This signals the need to reframe the debate on political obligation in terms of the agent's dispositions rather than specific actions (i.e., obedience), a task to which I return in the final chapter. Having discussed the broader notion of disobedience, in chapter 2 I narrow the focus on *civil* disobedience, aiming to highlight its nature as a 'constrained' form of communication. First, I advance an account of civility, which I define as a disposition to treat others with the respect due to their status as autonomous agents; that is, as self-legislators. I do not present this as a new account of civility, but rather argue that it is the one implied by most authors writing on the topic. I then survey some recent accounts of civil disobedience against the background of

John Rawls's seminal account (1999), to which most contemporary authors refer; I discuss the case of Edward Snowden, which has received significant attention from academics working on civil disobedience. In the last part of chapter 2, I consider issues concerning the justifiability of civil disobedience; that is, the conditions under which citizens may resort to it. One main implication of my account is that the specific cause of the protest has an impact on its civility (or lack thereof): for example, a racist protest cannot be 'civil', for it lacks a commitment to the equal value of people as autonomous agents.

In chapter 3, I consider the role of civil disobedience within democratic societies. First, I discuss two different conceptions of civility within the public sphere, namely, Rawls's 'duty of civility' and Habermas's 'performative attitude', and argue that the latter is better equipped to capture how agents can approach each other, within the democratic arena, in ways that show respect for autonomy. After that, I consider some recent accounts of civil disobedience as a democracy-enhancing, rather than democracy-limiting, practice. First, I present Markovits's notion of 'democratic disobedience'; then, I return to Habermas, presenting his conception of civil disobedience as 'guardian of legitimacy'; I then consider Iris Marion Young's critical stance on deliberative democracy and Archon Fung's notion of 'deliberative activism'; that is, of a commitment to deliberative ideals which, nonetheless, is open to the use of coercive measures.

This leads into chapter 4, where I consider in more detail how a commitment to the 'performative attitude' may be compatible with the use of force in civil disobedience. I briefly review some of the early arguments describing civil disobedience as inherently 'nonviolent', and find them unconvincing. After that, I discuss Nathan Adams's claim that civil disobedience may employ physical violence as long it is not directly aimed at other people. I then consider a broader view, according to which civil disobedience cannot involve violence (physical or psychological) against other people's *dignity*. Finally, I present my own version of this view, arguing that an act of civil disobedience may not use force (either physical or psychological) which targets people's *autonomy*.

In chapter 5, I offer an overview of the recent debate on a moral right to civil disobedience. I present the work of David Lefkowitz, Kimberley Brownlee and William Smith, who have each offered their own argument in support of such right. I also consider the implications these views may have on the claim, discussed in chapter 2, that a civil disobedient should be willing to accept the punishment for her law-breaking conduct.

In the conclusive chapter, I return to some of the issues previously discussed, aiming to offer a way to address them. First, I outline an account of political obligation based on virtue ethics, according to which citizens are under a moral obligation to respect, rather than merely obey, the law. This obligation arises from a natural duty to respect fellow citizens as autonomous agents which, in turn, may give rise to a duty to engage in civil disobedience. I then return to the issue of violence in civil disobedience, and argue that, under some circumstances, using a degree of force may be necessary in order to address others as autonomous agents. Third, I consider the requirement to accept the punishment for civil disobedience, arguing that a civil disobedient may have a pro tanto duty to answer to her fellows, during the criminal trial, for her choice to breach the law; however, she may have no duty to accept the punishment merely for engaging in civil disobedience, for she may have committed no wrong. If citizens have not merely a moral right but also a political duty to engage in civil disobedience, then the mere illegality of their conduct may not warrant punishing them.

Chapter One

What's Wrong with Disobedience?

To make sense of the philosophical problem civil disobedience poses, we must acknowledge first of all that there is a philosophical problem with disobedience in general: We must assume there is something wrong with illegal conduct *tout court*. As Candice Delmas has pointed out, 'The only feature that poses a problem is civil disobedience's illegality' (Delmas 2017, 198). Hence, the first step in this inquiry on civil disobedience involves identifying what, if anything, makes law-breaking wrong; in order to assess whether citizens may *justifiably* disobey the law, we need to first establish why disobedience requires a justification. This task involves addressing one of the central questions in political philosophy; namely, the problem of political obligation. The problem concerns whether citizens are under a *pro tanto*, comprehensively applicable, universally borne, and content-independent reason to obey the law (Kramer 2005, 179).[1] The term *political* seeks to capture the idea of an obligation applying to the individual qua citizen; that is, as member of a political community.[2] In this chapter, I present the major accounts employed to defend the existence of a moral duty to obey. My goal is merely descriptive, and by no means do I intend to provide an exhaustive critical assessment of these accounts.[3] Rather, I seek to highlight that none of these accounts, despite their appealing features, succeeds in establishing a pro tanto duty to obey the law. They do not show that disobedience per se is wrong.

There is an obvious sense in which we may be said to have a duty to obey the law. It is part of the very nature of any legal system that it imposes duties on its subjects, and that it backs those impositions of duties with the threat of punishment. Insofar as states have *legal* jurisdictions over their subjects, those subjects have a legal duty to obey the laws of their own governments. From this standpoint, a citizen's duty to obey the law is akin to a member's duty to follow the rules of the club or association: the existence of these duties is simply a function of what is required by the rules according to which the club or association operates (Wellman and Simmons 2005, 93). However, legal duties are not moral duties, for one may not be under a moral obligation to obey these legal requirements. As John Simmons writes, the goal of the philosophical inquiry on political obligation is to find out 'whether there is an external, neutral moral duty (or obligation) to discharge the internal duties imposed by law' (ibid., 94). There are obvious cases where law defiance is indeed morally wrong, as with laws forbidding sexual assault. Yet there are *extra-legal* reasons to obey these laws, having to do with our duties as moral agents. Sexual assault is *malum per se* – that is, is wrong in itself – we do not need to refer to the law to explain why this act is wrong. In fact, a malum per se is wrong regardless of what the law says (consider the oddness of telling a would-be rapist 'You cannot rape that woman! It's against the law'!). But what about cases that are not so obvious? To cite a famous example in the literature on the topic (Smith 1973), we should be able to explain why someone is supposedly under an obligation to stop at a red light in the middle of the desert with nobody around.[4] A successful account of political obligation should articulate why the fact that the law tells one to stop at a red traffic light should make a difference to the individual's decision as to whether or not to stop (apart from the desire to avoid being fined). This requires focusing on cases where an agent would do X but for the law's command not to do X – that is, cases where the forbidden act is *malum prohibitum* – wrong because the law says so (Dimock 2014). The problem of political obligation concerns what reason people have to obey the law: we may obey out of self-interest (e.g., to avoid the punishment) or, as in the case just mentioned, our compliance with the law may be a mere matter of coincidence between what we already had reason to do and what the law demands that we do. But this would not show that we ought to obey the law because it is the law.

> When I put food in front of [my dog] and command her to 'Eat'!, she eats. Every time. But of course she is not obeying my command. She would eat the food placed before her even if I said nothing at all. And it is the same with the commands of the law. When the law tells me to do what I would have done anyway, the law's commands are no more causally consequential than commanding my highly food-motivated dog to eat. Our interest in law is largely an interest in law insofar as it is causally consequential, and for that purpose *the distinction between law that makes a difference to behavior and law that makes no difference* is of central importance. If we are interested in obedience to law, we must focus on law's effect on people who, but for the law, would have done something other than what the law commands. Or, to put it differently, we are interested in the cases in which what the law commands differs

from what a subject of the law would have done for law-independent reasons. (Schauer 2015, 49; added emphasis)

This inquiry is important in order to make sense of what will be a central concept of my discussion in later chapters; namely, the idea that a citizen is answerable to the rest of the community for the breach of the law. This refers to the fact that we tend to disapprove of people who cheat on their taxes, drive in the emergency lane, park in the disabled spot without a permit, and so on; we demand that they do something – that is, pay a fine, compensate the victims, go to prison. Sometimes we make these demands not just as human beings, but as fellow citizens: we feel that *we* are being wronged when one of our co-nationals breaks the law, even if we may not be the victims of their crimes. However, if the law breakers are not breaching any moral principle (i.e., not committing *mala per se*), then we may not blame them unless there is something wrong with breaching the law. The search for a moral duty to obey the law seeks to provide an explanation of these feelings, and of why the law breaker may be the appropriate target of moral condemnation. This raises a further question: *To whom* does the law breaker have to answer for her conduct? Is the duty to obey the law owed to the institutions of government – that is, to the members of Parliament – or rather to fellow citizens, in whose name the government acts? In one sense, it is obvious that citizens are answerable to the state prosecutors, and to the law makers, for their failure to comply with the law; however, as I just mentioned, it also seems that a law breaker should answer to the community at large – that is, to the other citizens – for her breach of the law.[5] As an Australian citizen, I am answerable to other Australians, not to American, French or Chinese citizens. As I mentioned above, this is what makes the problem of political obligation 'political': it should fulfil a 'particularity requirement' by explaining the special bond among members of a political community (Simmons 1979, 30–35).

I begin by focusing on utilitarian accounts of political obligation. Though marred by the same problems facing its underlying moral theory, the utilitarian account of political obligation correctly points out that a citizen's conduct cannot be assessed without considering the agent's specific circumstances. I then outline the consent-based view, which claims that citizens ought to obey the law, for they have consented to state authority; ironically, critics have seized upon this account to show that one who does not consent to state authority has no duty to obey its laws. I will then move to more promising non-voluntarist accounts of political obligation. First, I will discuss the natural duty–based view, highlighting the problem it faces with reference to the particularity requirement mentioned above. After that, I will focus on the fair-play theory of political obligation, which addresses the particularity requirement yet faces further objections. Then, I will present the so-called

Samaritan account, which hinges on a natural duty of Samaritanism and on the fair-play principle. Although, I will argue, it falls short of providing a satisfying account of the duty to obey, it correctly signals the need of a multi-principled account of political obligation. Finally, I will present the associative view, according to which the duty to obey the law arises from the special relation between fellow citizens. I will claim that this account, while appealing, fails to show that disobedience is wrong per se: in some cases, it may provide citizens with reasons to disobey rather than to obey the law.

Before I start, I should specify that no account of political obligation aims to defend an absolute duty to obey all laws at all times. It is generally acknowledged that the duty to obey, if it exists at all, applies only to not-outrageously-unjust laws, and arises under political regimes that satisfy a minimum threshold of justice. Any successful defence of the moral duty to obey must be consistent with other moral duties that apply to us (Edmundson 2004, 224). In fact, under conditions of serious injustice, arguments for a duty to obey may not apply (Lyons 1996), or they might even lead to a duty to rebel against the unjust regime (Delmas 2018a).

Most of the discussion in this chapter is instrumental to the chapters that follow. I highlight some of the strengths of existing arguments for the duty to obey, while also stressing what I take to be their main shortcoming – namely, their inability to establish the wrongness of disobedience per se. For this reason, the comments I make in this chapter should be seen as conducive to my argument, in the final chapter, for a conception of political obligation based on a duty to *respect*, rather than to *obey*, the law. This will enable me, in turn, to present civil disobedience as fulfiling the agent's political obligation, despite its illegal nature. I leave that account to the last chapter, for it will involve other assumptions (concerning, for example, the value of individual autonomy) that I will spell out in the central chapters of this book, where I will focus on the nature and role of civil disobedience.

1.1 UTILITARIANISM AND POLITICAL OBLIGATION

The utilitarian approach to political obligation hinges on the principle of Utility, according to which an action's moral rightness depends on its tendency to maximise overall utility. Utilitarianism occupies a central place in moral philosophy, and it is not possible to do justice to the debate around its viability (or lack thereof) in this context (Darwall 2003a).[6] It suffices to say that there are at least two features that make it an attractive moral theory; namely, (a) it upholds the equal value of each person (though, as we will see later, this also gives rise to one main problem; namely, its seeming inability to account for special relationships); and (b) it acknowledges that, since our actions have an impact on the world and on others' lives, we must pay great attention to our actions' outcomes. Thus, from a consequentialist perspective, the choice to obey the law is to be assessed by reference to the consequences it brings about. We may identify different accounts of the 'goodness' produced by citizens' obedience to the law, having to do with the coordination of citizens' different life plans and daily activities (imagine the chaos, and danger, if people stopped following traffic regulations). Obedience has, in this context, an instrumental value, due to its capacity to bring about good consequences, but this also implies there is nothing valuable per se in obeying the law, apart from the outcome it produces. As Simmons has pointed out, a consequentialist account of political obligation does show that we ought to obey, but also that we ought to disobey (1979, 48). If I am the only one who fails to pay taxes, my defection would cause no harm to society, and I would be better off by not paying. As a good utilitarian, I should then disobey the law and cheat on my tax return; it would be my duty to do so. From a consequentialist standpoint, there is nothing wrong with disobeying the law per se; the reasons to comply with legal directives depend on the overall 'goodness' produced by the general compliance with a system where actions are coordinated by rules. On the one hand, consequentialists correctly point out that the choice to obey the law cannot be made in a vacuum, but rather has to be based on an assessment of the act's consequences; this is, indeed, a central premise of this book.[7] However, they also dispose of the idea of a duty to obey the law, for the only duty we have, according to consequentialism, is the duty to maximise utility. We should disobey the law where the consequences of compliance would be inferior to those of non-compliance; in fact, under such circumstances we would be morally blameworthy for failing to act according to our moral duties.

The problem persists in more articulated utility-based approaches, like R. M. Hare's attempt to give an account of the specific 'moral obligations that we have because we are citizens', and of how they arise (Hare 1998, 8). Hare's account, built on a more refined *indirect* consequentialism, does no better than defending the existence of a 'more or less unbreakable' principle according to which we ought to obey the law (ibid., 11).[8] Hare identifies the wrongness of disobedience with the fact that 'if I break the law, I shall be taking advantage of those who keep it out of law-abidingness although they would like to do what it forbids, and thus harming them by frustrating their desire not to be taken advantage of' (ibid., 18). As John Horton has pointed out (2010, 68), this is an odd account of 'harm', for people who obey the law are not harmed, in the case Hare discusses, by those who break it. Rather, 'the desire not to be taken advantage of' seems to rest on an independent moral principle; namely, a requirement of fairness 'masquerading as a desire' (ibid.). As we will see below, fairness-based accounts of political obligation have little, if anything, to share with consequentialist views of the duty to obey. From a *rule*-consequentialist perspective, it could be argued that utility is best promoted when people adopt law obedience as a rule of thumb: obedience would make it more likely for people to go about their own business in life without encroaching on each other's liberties. But there are problems with this approach too. First, arguing that the law should be obeyed 'as a rule of thumb' falls short of capturing the normative force the law claims to have (Soper 2002). When we say that the law has 'authority' over us, we mean more than the simple fact that obeying the law is a useful rule of thumb: we mean that the fact that X is a law is, in itself, a reason to X. Yet from a rule-consequentialist perspective, we should not be blamed for breaching the law in circumstances where doing so would lead to 'better outcomes'. In this way, rule consequentialism fails to capture a crucial aspect of law's alleged normativity; namely, its power to generate exclusionary reasons for action: the fact that X is a law is a reason for me to X, and one that excludes other countervailing reasons I may have for not X-ing (Raz 1999).

The consequentialist account of political obligation is particularly ill suited to the case of the individual act of disobedience. Although widespread disobedience may lead to less 'utility', in comparison to general compliance with the law, 'the net effect of one instance of law-breaking will almost always be negligible in the context of the preservation and maintenance of a system of law and order' (Horton, ibid., 67). As already mentioned, a citizen's failure to pay taxes would go unnoticed, and would have hardly any effect on society's stability and survival; a group of citizens' decision to smoke marijuana in public, to campaign for the legalisation of cannabis, may not harm anyone. It is true that objections to illegal protest are often framed as a slippery-slope argument, stressing that these protests would encourage widespread lawlessness: when citizens start disobeying the law as part of their protest, they set an example that others may follow. However, the available evidence of the effect of civil disobedience on social order does not support this slippery-slope argument; rather, many political theorists, as we will see in chapters 2 and 3, argue that this form of protest enhances the life of democratic societies. Furthermore, sometimes disobedience does lead to positive outcomes (e.g., the end of a despotic regime or, more modestly, the repeal of an unjust law). Once again, utilitarianism may at best tell us that disobedience is sometimes wrong, not that it is wrong per se.

A final point to notice concerns the nature of interpersonal relationships, and the particularity requirement. Consequentialism centres on the claim that each individual counts for 'one and no more than one'; from this standpoint, the aggregation of overall utility is the best (and only) action-guiding criterion. No one has priority over others in the decision-making process; rather, we do the maths and identify which course of action will benefit 'the highest number'. This is how majority rule works: the option that satisfies the highest number of voters is selected. However, this egalitarian perspective on morality fails to capture the idea of 'special relationship'; namely, the fact that, from an individual perspective, someone's needs may have priority over someone else's. For example, it seems plausible to claim that parents should place the interest of their children above those of strangers; while our family members are certainly equal (in terms of dignity) to other people, we may have reasons to prioritise the former's happiness and well-being over the latter's. Similarly, as we will see below with reference to the associative account of political obligation, we may have pro tanto reasons to prioritise our fellow citizens over foreigners: the utilitarian view, with its emphasis on aggregate utility, runs afoul of the particularity requirement, and hence is unable to ground a satisfying account of political obligation.

1.2 CONSENT

The problem of political obligation, as we saw above, focuses on whether citizens have a moral duty to abide by legal requirements. If such duty exists, then disobedience of the law is not only legally, but also morally, wrong. Its wrongness goes beyond the mere breach of a procedural rule, and rather involves some deeper failure. The case of promising offers a good analogy of this form of moral wrongdoing: one who breaks a promise may not cause harm to others, yet may be still blameworthy for the broken promise; for example, because of the breach of trust that conduct involves. Some theorists have, in fact, treated *law* breaking as a form of *promise* breaking, and advanced a consent-based account of political obligation. According to the latter, the duty to obey the law originates from an individual's acceptance, either explicit or implicit, to submit to the rule of law. The paradigmatic case is offered by the Social Contract view, which describes political societies as based on an agreement among individuals, who accept to follow shared rules in order to avoid the dangers of the state of nature (Morris 2000).

The underlying idea of consent is that we may be compelled to follow a certain scheme's rules if and only if we have accepted to be part of that scheme. Thus, employees usually sign a contract with their employers, whereby they acknowledge the latter's right to demand that they perform certain duties in the workplace; when travelling by plane, we consent to aircraft regulations forbidding us to use mobile phones during take-off and landing; upon signing a mortgage agreement, we give our consent to the bank exacting a certain sum of money from us, every fortnight (and for decades). Through our consent, we give the employer, the airplane crew, and the banks the right to demand a certain conduct from us: our consent gives legitimacy to these demands. Once we accept X's authority over us, we grant X a right to coerce us into following its directives and, correspondingly, we acquire a pro tanto duty to comply with X's directives. As an account of political obligation, this view holds that citizens' duty to obey the law stems from the fact they have consented to subject themselves to the state's authority. Disobeying the law, in this context, represents a breach of contract.

It is an interesting and, probably, unintended effect of this theory that it has been used to prove that most citizens are *not* under a moral duty to obey. Thus, John Simmons enthusiastically writes that 'only the voluntary giving of a clear sign that one finds the state acceptable (and is willing to assume political bonds to it), can ever obligate one to support or comply with the commands of that state's government' (1979, 69). Yet, he argues, few citizens, if any, have expressed their acceptance of the rule of law. Most of us are simply born within our political communities or, as Simmons argues, 'dropped into' the state (2001, 24); we find ourselves bound by the law of our state, regardless of our 'acceptance' or lack thereof. The problem with a consent-based account of political obligation is that there is no act of consent, strictly speaking, through which we may be said to have accepted the rule of law. In reply, consent theorists have appealed to the idea of tacit consent, to argue that, although there may be no official way to consent to state's authority, we may infer from other factors that the subject has consented. One way to defend this claim has an old pedigree, having made its first appearance in Plato's *Crito.* In that dialogue, Socrates claims that his acceptance of 'the Laws of Athens' is implied by his decision to live in Athens rather than move somewhere else. This view, later echoed by John Locke, takes continued residence on a state's territory to signal acceptance of the state's right to rule. We may refer to this as the Like It or Leave It view. Other supporters of the consent theory of political obligation accept that citizens have not uttered their acceptance in any specific way, yet would certainly do so if asked. We may refer to this as the Where Do I Sign? view.

The Like It or Leave It view places an unreasonable burden on the non-consenter by demanding she leave her home and relationships because of others' choices. Clearly, the onus should be on others to elicit my consent before starting the scheme, rather than imposing the scheme upon me. How realistic is it to demand that one willingly abandon family, friends and loved ones to avoid being coerced by the state? And where exactly should the non-consenter go? Every habitable corner of the earth is under some form of political authority; hence one would be doomed to a nomadic life under the auspices of the Like It or Leave It view, in the effort to eschew the rule of law.[9] On the other hand, the Where Do I Sign? view does not succeed in establishing the existence of a general duty to obey the law. It shows, at best, that *some* people – that is, those who would consent if asked to – are under a duty to obey; yet it is those who would *not* consent to the state who require an argument as to why they ought to obey its laws. This would apply also to the view that takes *voting* as signalling tacit acceptance of the state (Plamenatz 1968): those who do not vote would then not be morally bound to obey the law. Yet many people do *not* vote; that is, they fail to turn up at the polls; in some countries (e.g., Australia), citizens are legally required to vote, whether or not they want to. Also, one may turn up at the polls yet decide to cast a 'spoiled vote' to express frustration at the state's coercive apparatus. In all these cases, it would follow that those citizens have not consented.

To summarise, the attempt to ground the duty to obey the law on an act of consent cannot succeed, for it implies that those who do not consent are under no duty to obey. A more promising account may focus not on the fact that citizens have accepted the state's authority, but rather on the fact they have accepted the state's benefits. This approach moves from the idea of consent to that of fairness.

1.3 FAIR-PLAY THEORY

One central assumption of the consent-based theory discussed above is that life without the state is so bad, people would accept state coercion in order to avoid living in the State of Nature. There are, undeniably, some benefits in living under the rule of law, having to do, first and foremost, with personal safety: we are less likely to be robbed or attacked by others if there is a system that punishes those who commit such acts. The provision of this benefit, however, is possible insofar as enough people obey the law. From this standpoint, law defiance may be deemed wrong not as a breach of promise, but as a form of unfairness over those who comply with the law. This view of political obligation hinges on the so-called principle of fair play, first formulated in an oft-cited passage by Herbert Hart:

> When a number of persons conduct any joint enterprise according to rules and thus restrict their liberty, those who have submitted to these restrictions when required have a right to a similar submission from those who have benefited by their submission. (Hart 1955, 185)

The idea behind this fairness-based account of the duty to obey the law is that disobedience is akin to free riding.[10] The law breaker is like the passenger who fails to pay the bus fare: she shares in the benefits the system produces, yet refuses to also share the costs the scheme's maintenance requires. The failure to contribute may cause no harm to others, nor compromise the scheme's subsistence; it is, nonetheless, wrong because of the way it treats others (ibid.).[11] The other passengers could justifiably complain that the fare evader is acting unfairly, for she exempts herself from the costs they willingly bear in return for the benefit of a reliable public transport system. As Simmons explains, the wrongness of this form of conduct lies in the 'unfair self-selection', whereby the agent 'selects herself' for the privilege of doing the amount of free riding that will not undermine the cooperative scheme (Simmons 2001, 30). In this way, the free rider takes advantage of the good faith of others, exploiting their sacrifices to her own advantage.

Let us consider in some more detail what benefits the state is meant to provide to its subjects. As already mentioned, there is personal protection: few would enjoy living under conditions of total lawlessness. Thomas Hobbes's words still ring true today, warning us of the 'short, brutish and nasty' existence humans would lead without the state: the fear of constant threats would certainly be an unwelcome element of life in the State of Nature. The law acts as a fundamental deterrent against harmful conduct, thus the risk of suffering at the hands of others would undoubtedly be higher in the absence of law enforcement.[12]

However, the alleged benefits the state affords to (the majority of) its subjects go beyond personal safety. If mere survival was our only advantage in joining a political community, we would have no special reason to live under a dictatorship rather than a democracy, as Hobbes thought. However, as human beings we aim for more than just surviving: we aim to do something with our lives, to develop our skills and acquire new ones, to realise our projects, and more. These goals cannot be achieved without an overarching institution able to coordinate our different plans. Only by following a shared system of rules can we live together and benefit from the limited amount of resources at our disposal. This is not due to the fact that humans are intrinsically evil and would start killing each other if there was no punishment in place. The problem, according to Wellman, is that without a state that establishes, enforces and adjudicates 'a clear and uniform set of rules that everyone must follow', conflicts would be inevitable (Wellman and Simmons 2005, 6). As Gregory Kavka argues, even if humans were 'morally perfect agents', they would end up in disagreement about practical matters (Kavka 1995). First, they would still be affected by cognitive limitations: their different intellectual capacities, experiences and information would inevitably lead to disagreements about values (e.g., what constitutes a *just* outcome), which in turn would lead to practical disagreement. For example, they may disagree about 'whether smoking in public violates others' rights to life and well-being, because they have different beliefs about the health effects of breathing the fumes of other people's cigarettes' (ibid., 4). Secondly, morally perfect agents could still have reasonable moral disagreement, holding irreconcilable and yet reasonable moral beliefs (a point we will discuss at length in chapter 3). Finally, there would be classical 'Prisoner's Dilemma' scenarios, where a group of agents, even 'morally perfect' ones, would be more likely to realise their individual goals if 'mutually coerced' by the government, rather than if acting independently based on their 'flawless moral beliefs' (5).[13]

I will return to the benefits provided by the state in the next chapters, with reference to the notion of individual autonomy. For now, let us consider the second step in the fair-play theory of political obligation, which highlights that the state can fulfil its role only if enough citizens follow its directives. As in the case of public transports, the benefit of state protection comes with a price; namely, the submission of one's own will to the directives of the law. The state could not perform its coordinating function if citizens refused to be coordinated – that is, to follow its commands. Of course, for the state (as for the transport system) to remain in place, it is sufficient that *enough* people obeyed its rules; as already noticed in the previous section on consequentialism, the individual defection may have no significant impact on the scheme's survival. Yet as with the case of the free rider on public transports, the individual law breaker would be morally blameworthy for engaging in that 'unfair self-selection' mentioned above; that is, for exploiting her fellow citizens' sacrifices to her own advantage. Through her disobedience, the law breaker has gained 'something others have – the benefits of the system – but by renouncing what others have assumed, the burdens of self-restraint, (the law breaker) has acquired an unfair advantage' (Morris 1968, 487).

A crucial difference between this view and the consent-based theory of political obligation, discussed in the previous section, lies in the fact that the former does not rely on the notion of a voluntary act of acceptance. The reason why other passengers may justifiably complain about the free rider's conduct is not that the latter has broken a promise she previously made to contribute to the transport system: she never made such promise, nor would she if asked! The reason to blame the free rider is that she is benefiting unfairly from others' efforts: since she is enjoying the benefits of the scheme, fairness binds her to do her part to contribute to it. If she does not want to be part of it, she should not reap the scheme's benefits. The fairness-based account of the wrongness of law breaking seems closer to our own experience: it is plausible, for example, to blame the tax evader, first and foremost, for acting unfairly towards all other citizens who pay their share of taxes, to support of the provision of benefits the tax evader enjoys as well.

However, this account faces a series of objections no less troubling than those faced by the consent theory. To begin with, some have challenged the idea of the state as a cooperative enterprise, in which people work together towards the achievement of common benefits. Two groups engaged in a social practice may be 'cooperating' by following the same rules (e.g., two teams engaged in a football game), but would this be a case of 'social cooperation' producing mutual benefits? As John Horton has argued (2010, 90), even two individuals engaged in a duel might be said to be part of a cooperative enterprise, although clearly only one would 'benefit' from it. Horton claims we should distinguish 'participating in a socially constructed practice' from 'engaging collaboratively in a common endeavour for mutual benefit': both may impose obligations on their participants, yet only the latter would fit the account of cooperative scheme at the core of the fair-play theory of political obligation.

More relevant is the objection that obligations of fairness may not be imposed in cases involving non-exclusionary goods; that is, goods one cannot avoid. Suppose my neighbours decided to take turns at cleaning our communal driveway, regardless of my open refusal to partake in the joint cleaning enterprise; the alleged benefit of a clean driveway would then be bestowed upon me, through my neighbours' cooperative efforts, despite my unwillingness to be part of that scheme. It would not be possible to provide the clean driveway only to *some* of its users. However, I should not be accused of free riding on my neighbours' efforts: the mere receipt of benefits may not generate an obligation, for the recipient, to reciprocate (Simmons 2001, 34). When applied to the political context, the fair-play account faces objections similar to those raised against the consent theory of political obligation: the citizen may be deemed under a fair-play duty to obey the law only if she has accepted the benefits she has received. There is no way for the citizen to opt out of the state's benefits – for example, police protection, public health, garbage collection and more – under such circumstances, the citizen may not be *blamed*, on grounds of fairness, for her failure to obey the law.

George Klosko has replied to this objection by focusing on the concept of 'presumptively beneficial goods' (Klosko 2004). For Klosko, the objection fails, for the kind of benefits the state provides are different from the ones employed in the critics' example, which usually involved (as in the one I mentioned) clean streets, free books or musical entertainment (Nozick 2013, Simmons 1979). These cases are all trivial, for they focus on goods that people may well find irrelevant; yet, according to Klosko, the state provides goods that are extremely relevant; namely, indispensable to any worthwhile life, and hence we may presume all members of the community would want them (Klosko, ibid.). As we saw above, the state provides personal safety and, Klosko claims, everyone wants be safe: without the protection of the rule of law, we would not be able to lead a meaningful and rewarding life. The state does not merely offer us *some* service, which we may or may not want. It provides us with crucial goods 'without which people could not live' (Klosko 2004, 40). And if we thought that we do not need these goods, we would be mistaken.

We might worry about the paternalistic overtones of Klosko's account. From its standpoint, the state provides benefits it presumes we want, regardless of what *we* actually want, and forces us to obey its directives on that ground. This may well be a non-voluntarist account of political obligation – that is, one that avoids the problem faced by the consent theory, concerning the agent's acceptance – however, the underlying *infantilisation* of citizens, deemed unable to choose for themselves, may be in tension with the conception of citizens as *autonomous* agents that I will spell out in the next chapter. We may feel underwhelmed by the claim that we ought to obey the state in order to reciprocate for the 'presumptively beneficial goods' it provides us, despite us not wanting these goods, us not deeming them beneficial, and perhaps us not even wanting to obey the law. The analogy between law breaking and free riding also provides some odd results when applied to the case of *mala per se.* It is indeed implausible to treat crimes such as rape or murder as cases of 'free riding', as acts where the rapist or murder takes an unfair advantage over others' 'cooperative effort' not to rape or murder (Duff 2008).

It is beyond the scope of this book to assess whether the fair-play theory can overcome this problem; for our purposes, it suffices to note that this theory offers a promising way to understand at least the wrongness of some *mala prohibita*; for it is undoubtedly true that the state plays a crucial role in enabling people to live 'meaningful and rewarding' lives. Without the state, individuals could not lead a flourishing existence, due to the coordination problems mentioned above. It is also important to note that this account can satisfy the particularity requirement: the duty of fairness is owed to our fellow citizens, from whose cooperation we benefit. These are notable strengths of this account, to which I will return in chapter 6.

As already mentioned, all accounts of political obligation acknowledge that a *pro tanto* duty to obey may not arise where the law is immoral and/or the political regime is deeply unjust.[14] However, even in contests that fulfil these basic requirements of justice, we may not conclude that a law breaker is ipso facto a free rider. Specifically, it might be unwarranted to treat civil disobedience as form of free riding merely based on its illegal nature. This is because the label *free rider* indicates that the person is unwilling to do her part in return for the benefits she receives: she tries to exploit others by evading her share of the costs. However, as we will see in detail in the next chapter, the choice to engage in civil disobedience may not be described as the agent's attempt to evade her obligations as citizen; treating the civil disobedient akin to a free rider grossly misrepresents what motivates the former to resort to illegal protest. We may accept the underlying assumptions of the fair-play theory of political obligation (concerning a citizen's duty to do her part to support the cooperative scheme of the state), while remaining open to the possibility that, under some circumstances, this duty may be discharged through an act of civil disobedience (Moraro 2019b). This paves the way for a radical change in our understanding of some forms of law breaking; rather than interpreting them as a *justifiable* breach of the agent's duty to obey, as acts that are pro tanto wrong though *all-things-considered* justified, we may conceive of civil disobedience as pro tanto right – that is, as fulfiling our political obligation. This, however, involves abandoning the exclusive focus on *obedience*, a task I will face in the last chapter.

1.4 NATURAL DUTY

One problem we saw above, concerning the fair-play theory of political obligation, is that obligations cannot be imposed on someone without the latter's acceptance. If Y has no way to avoid the benefits provided by X, then Y cannot be held under a duty to reciprocate to X for the benefits received. The natural duty–based account of political obligation avoids this problem by focusing not on the benefits the state provides to the duty bearer, but rather on the fact that the state provides benefits to others. The duty to obey the law, from this different standpoint, arises out of a natural duty we have qua moral agents: 'natural' duties apply independently from the agent's consent. For example, we have a duty not to kill innocent people, even if we have not given our consent to this rule: in fact, our consent plays no role in such case – even if we 'refused' to obey the 'thou shalt not kill' principle, we would be morally blameworthy for engaging in murder. Natural duties explain why some crimes are *mala per se*: they are wrong because they violate basic requirements of morality. In this and the next section, I will consider two major attempts to ground the duty to obey the law on these premises; however, as in the case of the fair-play view discussed earlier, I will stress that, despite some attractive features, the natural duty–based account fails to establish the pro tanto wrongness of disobedience. In some cases, an agent may fulfil her natural duty by breaching the law; for example, as part of an act of civil disobedience.

An influential formulation of this account of political obligation comes from John Rawls, who identified two core elements of what he calls a 'natural duty of justice':

> First, we are to comply with and to do our share in just institutions when they exist and apply to us; and second, we are to assist in the establishment of just arrangements when they do not exist, at least when this can be done with little cost to ourselves. (1999, 293–94)

As already mentioned, this view of political obligation avoids voluntaristic requirements that burden both the consent and the fair-play theory. It claims that our duty to obey the law arises from our nature as human beings, rather than from a transactional agreement: where political institutions satisfy a basic threshold of justice, we should do our part to support them by complying with the law. Our duty to obey, from this standpoint, derives from our duty to respect other's rights as free and equals. Thus, the person who disobeys the law fails to live up to this moral requirement; her failure to comply with the directives of an institution that promotes justice is also a failure to uphold others' rights. This applies also in cases where the law is less-than-ideal: as Buchanan (2003) has argued, a legitimate political institution may impose imperfect laws on citizens through force. As we will see in chapter 3, this is the underlying reason why we usually have to accept democratic decisions with which we disagree: if we resist these decisions through force, we disrespect our fellow citizens by seeking to impose our own preferred outcome in ways that deny their right to an equal say in deliberative democratic law making (Christiano 2008, 249–55, Lefkowitz 2007, 207–11). This is indeed a plausible idea, one that I will employ in the last chapter, when advancing the claim for an autonomy-based duty to respect (rather than obey) the law. For the moment, however, I should point out two major problems with a natural duty–based account of political obligation framed along the Rawlsian model.

The first problem refers to disagreements around what constitutes a just or nearly just institution. Rawls defended a conception of justice as fairness and understood a just society along those lines; however, many disagree with his conception of justice. A libertarian may deem the welfare state intrinsically unjust, describing redistributive policies as a form of institutionalised theft; a social democrat, on the other hand, may see market-driven, capitalistic regimes as the epitome of injustice. Could citizens of either group be deemed to have a natural duty of justice to obey the law of their (in their own view) unjust societies? The second, and more pervasive, problem with this account concerns its seeming inability to establish an obligation to obey the law of one's own state; that is, to satisfy the particularity requirement. Suppose two states, A and B, both satisfied some account of 'justice': Would A's citizens have specific reasons to obey A's laws rather than B's? Or suppose that state A was less just than state B: Should A's citizens, therefore, obey B's rather than A's laws? The natural duty of justice seems unable to address this crucial element of political obligation. William Smith (2013, 30–31) has attempted to address this problem by employing Jeremy Waldron's 'Kantian approach' (Waldron 1993). Smith argues it is plausible to limit the application of the natural duty of justice to certain people; namely, those who are in close proximity to the agent. In fact, problems of coordination between people's lives will be more pressing with reference to those who are closer to us, those with whom we will be more likely to experience conflicts. Therefore, people should settle upon an effective institution capable of solving the coordination problems within the territory. Against this background, Smith claims, a political institution may be said to 'apply to us' if (a) we fall under its territorial jurisdiction; (b) it performs tasks that are necessary for the realisation of justice in our territory; and (c) if it is a 'legitimate and salient agent of justice' in our territory (i.e., if it enjoys 'popular support').[15]

This reply is also meant to address a second, related problem with Rawls's account of natural duty, concerning the 'application objection' (Smith, ibid.). What is it for an institution to 'apply' to someone? The most straightforward way to interpret this idea involves the notion of membership:

the institutions that apply to us are those of which we are members. However, we are members of different institutions: To which should we give priority? Simmons famously wondered whether he would be bound to support an 'Institute for the Advancement of Philosophers' (IAP) given that, in some loose sense, such institution would 'apply to him' as a philosopher (1979, 148). Smith argues, in reply, that the IAP would not be a 'salient administrator of justice': the fact that it may promote the interests of its members is not sufficient for considering it as *promoting* justice. For this reason, Simmons could refuse to comply with the directives of the IAP, but not with the directives of the state.

We do not have to settle this issue here. An account of political obligation grounded on a natural duty is, indeed, quite attractive, and will be central to later discussions in this book. However, this account, like the fairness-based one discussed above, falls short of establishing that disobedience is pro tanto wrong. As we saw above, Rawls claims that 'we are to assist in the establishment of just arrangements when they do not exist', yet he remains silent as to what this implies. It seems compatible with his view that the natural duty of justice may prescribe disobedience of the laws of an unjust regime with the aim to re-establish justice. On closer examination, the natural duty of justice does not entail a duty to obey the law; it places a significant emphasis on the government's pedigree, and may support disobedience when the latter falls below a certain threshold of basic justice. Compared to other accounts of political obligation, which argue that citizens should obey the laws of not-unreasonably unjust governments, the natural duty account goes further, suggesting that citizens *should disobey* unreasonably unjust governments. We may have identified a surprising (though by all means accidental) analogy between the utility-based account, discussed earlier, and this natural duty–based view of political obligation: from both standpoints, citizens may have a duty to obey or to disobey, depending on the specific circumstances. As I will argue later, this might be more than a mere coincidence, for a viable account of political obligation should also encompass acts of disobedience of the law.

1.5 SAMARITAN DUTIES

Suppose you are on a small boat on a pond, with your best friend. It is a nice afternoon, and you, wearing your favourite shirt, are enjoying the peace and the pleasant breeze. All of a sudden, you hear someone crying for help; as you turn around, you see a person struggling in the water, just a few metres from you. You could easily use one of the oars in your boat to help that person get out of the water and onto your boat. In the process, you would probably get wet and muddied and ruin your shirt; it would probably also be the end of your pleasant cruise with your friend, at least for that day. Few would claim that, in such scenario, you could ignore that person and continue to enjoy the breeze: it is obvious that you ought to do something; namely, use the oar to help that person out of the water. Although this would cost you your shirt and your pleasant afternoon with the friend, this would usually not justify a failure to rescue the person in the pond. It would be a very reasonable cost for you to bear, under the circumstances (your shirt may be hardly worthier than a human life). This is the gist of the so-called Samaritan principle: we ought to rescue or help rescue people from serious perils when we can do so at no unreasonable cost to ourselves or others. The Samaritan principle locates the source of the duty to rescue in the rights of the imperilled person; that is, the latter has the right to demand that *you* rescue her. Like the duty of justice, the Samaritan duty is a natural duty: it is grounded in our nature as moral beings and binds us all equally, regardless of our relations or voluntary acceptance.[16]

Christopher H. Wellman has advanced an account of political obligation based on these very premises, claiming we have a Samaritan duty to assist in the rescue of people from what he labels the 'perils of the State of Nature' (Wellman and Simmons 2005). The latter is a direct reference to Thomas Hobbes's account of human life in the absence of political institutions, as 'solitary, poor, nasty, brutish and short'. As we saw earlier, Wellman contends, like most political theorists, that it is not possible to have a minimally rewarding and meaningful life in those circumstances due to the constant threat of attack from others: only under the authority of a sovereign power can humans exercise their moral rights. It is in this sense that, for Wellman, the state *rescues* people: he claims that the coercive authority of the state is '*the only* viable solution to the perils of the State of Nature' (ibid., 38).[17] However, the state cannot accomplish its rescuing function if its citizens do not comply with its directives – that is, if they do not obey the law. Hence, Wellman concludes, 'The only way to explain a citizen's duty to obey the law is as the correlative of others' Samaritan rights' (ibid.); our failure to obey would be tantamount to a failure to assist in rescuing others from the perils of the State of Nature. Like the person in the water in the previous example, our fellow citizens have a right to demand that we rescue them. This is because, for Wellman, the costs of submitting to the law are 'relatively trivial' compared to the benefits derived from the political community. Hence, Wellman concludes, we ought to obey the law. However, we may struggle with accepting that by running a red traffic light, when no one is in sight, I fail to rescue people from the perils of the State of Nature. My individual act of disobedience would mostly have no impact at all on the state's capacity to execute its 'rescue operation': all that is needed is *general* compliance; that is, that enough citizens follow the state's directives. It is for this reason that Wellman further invokes the principle of fairness: while it may be true that my individual defection would not compromise the state's capacity to rescue people from the State of Nature, this would be due to the fact that the majority of my fellow citizens do submit to the law. I can enjoy discretion over whether to obey the law because my fellow citizens have relinquished the freedom to make that kind of choice, as part of their Samaritan duty. My act of disobedience, while inconsequential to the state's rescue operation, is unfair to my law-abiding fellows.

Thus, Wellman advances a multi-principled account, comprising a natural duty to rescue people when this can be done at no unreasonable cost, and a duty of fairness to do so by obeying the law of the state. In the background, there is Wellman's attempt to address the particularity requirement which, as we saw in the previous section, poses serious problems to accounts of political obligation based on natural duties. However, Wellman's account faces pressing questions too, as Massimo Renzo (2011) has highlighted. Renzo focuses on cases where there is *more than one* endangered person. Suppose that, in the imaginary boat case described above, there were two persons in the water: one of these is able to swim and, albeit struggling, will manage to eventually reach the shore; the other person cannot swim and will most likely drown. Many of us would agree that, in this case, you should rescue the second person, who is facing a more pressing danger. However, if we applied this reasoning to the political context, it would follow that the state should use its resources to help people in Third World countries, who face death through disease, starvation, and civil unrest, compared to citizens of Western societies who generally face less serious (though by no means trivial) dangers. If, in circumstances where we cannot rescue everyone, we should rescue those who are most at risk, then Western democracies should use their resources to help the citizens of more disadvantaged countries rather than their own, less endangered ones. As Renzo points out, a successful account of political obligation should capture not only the special relationship between citizens and their state, but also that *between the state and its citizens*: it should explain why a state should treat its citizens differently from the way it treats other people. Yet the Samaritan principle would require country A to use its resources to help the citizens in country B, if the latter faced more pressing dangers than those of country A. This seems to be an odd implication of Wellman's view, for many believe that a government should prioritise the well-being of its own citizens over that of foreigners (not vice versa). By grounding the duty to obey the law on the Samaritan principle – that is, on a duty to help *others*, Wellman may forego a basic assumption in the debate on political obligation; namely, the special ties between a citizen and *her* government.

Renzo also considers cases where the demands of the Samaritan duty may conflict with those of the principle of fairness. Suppose that, instead of paying my taxes, I sent my money to an NGO that relieves poverty in a Third

World country. In doing so, I would discharge my Samaritan duty, given that (a) I would be devoting my resources to helping people who face a more serious danger than my compatriots and (b) my defection will have no tangible impact on my government's capacity to rescue its citizens from the State of Nature. However, while my tax evasion may fulfil my Samaritan duty towards imperilled people, it would contravene my fair-play duty to my fellow citizens. If my action is wrong *because it is unfair* to my fellows, then the Samaritan principle is not doing the work – in fact, it seems to be redundant (215). The same issue arises if we treat my defection as *all-things-considered* justified; that is, as a justified violation of my duty of fairness to my fellow citizens. If, on the other hand, I should prioritise my Samaritan duty and my obligations *to imperilled people in the Third World*, then my tax evasion would be the right thing to do; that is, an all-things-considered fulfilment of my *political* duty, or my duty *as citizen.* My failure to pay my share of taxes would be morally equal to my fellows' paying their share, as we would all fulfil the same Samaritan principle, which, in Wellman's view, grounds our political obligation. Once again, this account of political obligation, like most of those previously discussed, may uphold both a duty to obey *and* a duty to disobey the law, depending on the circumstances.[18]

Candice Delmas has recently claimed that 'if the Samaritan duty holds at all, then it does so even if fulfilling it forces an agent to break the law' (2018a, 141), including by resorting to civil disobedience. Her main target are laws that 'prohibit Samaritan rescue', an example of which would be the Fugitive Slave Act 1850, which famously forbade helping runaway slaves and imposed a duty to return them to their 'owners'. A more recent example, in her view, is France's law L622-1, which forbids facilitating, or attempting to facilitate, the illegal entry, movement or residence of a foreigner in France; sanctions include up to five years of imprisonment and a fine of €30,000 (142). However, this seems an odd reading of the Samaritan duty which, as we saw above, prescribes rescuing others at no unreasonable cost for the rescuer: few would consider five years in prison as a 'reasonable' cost, thus we may not think there is a Samaritan duty to disobey law L622-1 (Moraro 2019a). There appears to be a shift from a Samaritan duty to a duty of justice, as Delmas points out that the laws she discusses are 'inherently unjust': if the reason to disobey that law is that it is unjust, however, then the Samaritan principle is redundant. Furthermore, it is not obvious why the French law she mentions is 'inherently' unjust, as it seems only fair that a state should prevent 'the illegal entry' of foreigners.

Delmas claims the duty to disobey is a political duty. She seeks to offer an account of political obligation; that is, of the specific obligations of citizens as members of the political community. Yet it is unclear how the duty to save others can be interpreted as political; that is, as linked to our status as citizens. We saw above that a successful account of political obligation must satisfy the particularity requirement: it must explain why members owe an obligation specifically to the community of which they are members, rather than to another community (Horton 2010, 10; Simmons 1979, 31–35). However, Samaritan duties are owed *to the imperilled ones*, not necessarily to one's own fellow citizens, and Delmas does consider *transnational* cases of rescue, such as disaster relief (149). I may have a Samaritan duty to rescue the victims of 2017 Hurricane Maria in Puerto Rico, but that is a duty I owe to the Puerto Ricans, not to my fellow citizens. The former, not the latter, could justifiably complain if I failed to disobey the law as part of my rescue operation. Hence, Renzo's objection to Wellman applies also to Delmas's view: an account of political obligation based on the Samaritan duty cannot capture the special relation between fellow citizens. It certainly highlights an important moral duty we have, yet not one we bear as members of a polity.

Both Wellman and Delmas ground their argument on the Samaritan principle and the principle of fairness (Delmas 2018a, 162–63). This project is doomed to fail, for the two principles target two different groups of people: the former is owed to imperilled people, whoever (and, according to Delmas, also wherever) they are; the latter is owed to the members of one's own polity. And as we saw already, when the two conflict, we either prioritise fairness, which makes the Samaritan principle redundant, or we prioritise Samaritanism, which may fall foul of the particularity requirement. This does not undermine the project of a multi-principled account of political obligation: it signals, however, the need for a different account of natural duty, one able to fulfil the particularity requirement. I will focus on the task of providing such account in chapter 6.

1.6 ASSOCIATIVE OBLIGATIONS

Natural duties are universal and non-voluntary: they apply to all human beings, and do not require an act of acceptance from the duty bearer. The associative account of political obligation that we are about to consider preserves the non-voluntary element, yet claims that political obligations are owed to a specific group of individuals; namely, to one's own co-nationals. In this way, the associative account is better placed to address the particularity requirement; that is, the idea that political obligation should explain why a citizen must obey the law of her own state.[19]

The associative view starts from the claim that membership to a group generates obligations for its members. If I join a sports club, I am thereby required to follow its rules: the other members of the club can make demands on me (e.g., that I pay my fee, attend meetings), and I owe it *to them* to act upon these demands. However, not all groups of which we are members are joined voluntarily. Consider the family: we owe something special to our family members, even if our membership to the family differs, in important respects, from membership to a sports club. We do not choose our parents, siblings and others; however, the fact that they are our parents or siblings gives us a reason to prioritise their interests over those of others. To return to the case mentioned in the previous section: suppose that two persons were drowning in the pond, and you could save only one; suppose, further, that one of them was your father, the other a stranger. It would be plausible to claim that, under those (horrible) circumstances, you should rescue your father. It would make perfect sense for you to explain your choice by stating 'I saved *him* because he is my father'. The special relation between the two of you gives you a (very weighty) reason to address his needs rather than those of the stranger. This appears to overcome one of the main problems with the Samaritan principle, discussed earlier; namely, that it cannot capture the special relationship between citizens.

According to the associative theory of political obligation, an individual's relationship to her fellow citizens mirrors, to some extent, that to her family members. 'For we are, after all, born to parents we did not choose at a time we did not choose; and we land in some region we did not choose of a social world we did not choose' (Schaffler 2001, 64).[20] These relationships, while non-voluntary, define to a serious degree our identity, and subject us to claims by fellow members. We cannot opt out of these relationships as easily as we could opt out of a voluntary one, for

> the verdict of common moral opinion seems to be that we can never wipe the slate entirely clean. Our specific historical and social identities, as they develop and evolve over time, continue to call forth claims with which we must reckon, claims that cannot without distortion be construed as contractual in character, and which are not reduced to silence by general considerations of need. (ibid.)

Some versions of the associative account are framed in communitarian terms and focus on the shared identity of a group's members (Horton 2010); others seek to reconcile the associative account with the demands of a liberal view (Dworkin 1986; Tamir 1993). Either way, the associative perspective claims we owe something special to our co-nationals *because* they are our co-nationals. This means that, as we have reasons to prioritise the interest of our family members and friends over those of strangers, we also have reasons to prioritise our co-nationals over foreigners; for example, by redistributing our resources to support our fellow nationals rather than the people in Third World countries. The crucial assumption of the associative account is that the relation underlying a political community gives legitimacy to the community's norms: these norms have authority on us as long as we are members. We are, therefore, under an obligation to abide by these norms by obeying the law of our state: the latter defines the terms of association within a polity (Vossen 2011a).

An obvious objection to this view is that the mere fact that something is an association does not entail a moral obligation to follow its rules. A person born into a Mafia group does not acquire a moral duty to follow the group's rules, which involve killing, kidnapping, threatening and the like. One's parents might be morally wicked individuals, with whom one should not 'associate' at all, not to mention cooperate. And one may be born in a seriously unjust political regime, where racism, violence and exploitation are rife: it seems odd to say that this person has a moral duty to obey the laws of that state because it is *her state*. Some theorists try to circumvent this problem by stressing the pro tanto nature of political obligation: notwithstanding our special ties with the Mafia group, with our morally wicked parents, or with our seriously unjust government, we also have weightier reasons to not follow their rules (Tamir 1993, 101–2).[21] Others claim that only *moral* communities can generate associative obligations for their members. Thus, Michael Hardimon contends that the obligations arising from unjust political communities are 'void *ab initio*' (Hardimon 1994, 350). For Ronald Dworkin, only membership to 'true', rather than 'bare', communities may generate genuine moral obligations for their members.[22] Horton criticises Dworkin's 'highly idealised' conception of community; however, he too acknowledges that the polity must meet a 'minimal standard' in order to generate obligations for its members (177–78). Richard Dagger, in response, has argued that these provisos show that 'membership' per se is insufficient to ground a duty to obey; rather, 'something extra must be added – an appeal to justice or to the nature of a true community – to supply what a straightforward appeal to membership lacks' (Dagger 2000, 110). Renzo has also questioned the non-voluntarist nature of the associative account of political obligation, focussing on John Horton's claim that 'at least a minimal sense of belonging to, or identification with' the political community is *necessary* for political obligation to exist (Renzo 2012, 117–18). In fact, Horton outlines a 'subjective' requirement in his account of political obligation, according to which a person who, for whatever reason, does not identify at all with her polity is *not* bound by an associative duty to obey its laws (2010, 183). The problem is that arguing that the acknowledgement of a common authority is one of 'the conditions of political obligation' (187) may lead to the conclusion that, where there is no acknowledgement, there is no political obligation.[23]

Once again, I do not aim to settle these issues. Let us grant, for argument's sake, that the associative account has the means to address these objections. What is relevant to our discussion is that, although the associative account can successfully address the particularity requirement, it is less able to establish the wrongness of disobedience (recall the goal of this chapter is to capture the pro tanto wrongness of disobedience; that is, to show that illegal conduct is per se wrong, though sometimes all-things-considered justifiable). While we might agree (perhaps with some effort) that the obligations we owe our compatriots are akin to those we owe our family members, more needs to be said as to whether this entails a duty to obey the law. Claiming that we owe something special to our co-nationals is compatible with the idea that, in some cases, we should disobey the law of our state. Candice Delmas has pointed out that associative theorists like Margaret Gilbert and Andrew Mason acknowledge that citizens' political obligations go beyond mere obedience to the law (2018a, 171). John Horton makes a similar concession at the end of his book, where he mentions that political obligation 'is not reducible simply to obeying the government or law' (191).[24] I suppose these authors mean that citizens should also play an active role in the political life of their community (e.g., voting, being engaged, etc.); but then, in some cases we may have an associative duty to *engage in civil disobedience*. A concern with our community may require us to take action to protect the interests and well-being of our fellow members, yet our action may also take a law-breaking form, if necessary. In some cases, we may have to criticise, or even upset, our family members if we think they are doing something unwise, irresponsible or just plain wrong: the same may be said in relation to our fellow citizens. This is a point I will explore in detail in chapter 4, where I will consider the role of non-violence in civil disobedience. In that chapter, I will also discuss the notion of *respect* for one's own fellow citizens, an attitude which, in some circumstances, may be displayed through acts of civil disobedience. A refusal to obey the law may stem from a concern with the overall justice of our community and the well-being of our fellows. I contend that, like most of the accounts considered above, the associative view of political obligation fails to establish a pro tanto duty to obey the law; rather, it defends a (potentially plausible) duty to prioritise the interest of our co-nationals over those of foreigners which, *under normal circumstances*, is discharged through obeying the law of our own country. Under different circumstances, our special obligation to our fellows may require us to break the law; for example, by engaging in civil disobedience.

The accounts discussed in this chapter do, in the best case, establish a *presumption* that citizens should obey the law. This does not signal the defeat of political obligation at the hand of *philosophical anarchism* (Simmons 2001, 102–21); rather, it highlights the need for a conception of political obligation that, rather than centring on compliance with the law, focuses on the *disposition* an individual should have, and act upon, as a member of the political community.[25] This chapter has covered the general issue of disobedience of the law. In the chapters that follow, I will narrow my focus on the concept of *civil* disobedience. I begin, in the next chapter, by offering an account of civility as a disposition to respect fellow citizens as autonomous agents. This will establish the conceptual framework for the issues to be discussed in later chapters; namely, the role of civil disobedience in democratic regimes, the permissibility (or lack thereof) of *violent* civil disobedience, and the debate around a moral right to civil disobedience. After that, I will return to the problem of political obligation in the last chapter, to provide a different account of the moral duties arising from one's membership to the political community.

Chapter Two

The Concept of Civility

As already mentioned, it is somewhat surprising that most authors have discussed the conditions for an illegal act to qualify as civil, without explaining what it means for an illegal act to be civil. The general tendency has been to start from a conception of 'uncivil' disobedience, usually described as violent, secretive, subversive, and then to identify 'civil' disobedience as that which is not uncivil. That is to say, most theorists have specified a list of external conditions with which the law-breaking act must comply, and used it as the benchmark separating the civil from the uncivil.[1] This approach has proved unhelpful, for various reasons, including the risk of neutralising the political power of civil disobedience by labelling most disruptive or disorderly forms of protest as uncivil *merely because* they are disruptive or disorderly (Celikates 2016; Delmas 2018). As the discussion in the next chapter will reveal, civil disobedience is a valuable strategy to counter power imbalances in democratic societies; it represents a group's attempt to force others to engage in further deliberation over important issues concerning the common good. Demanding that it be 'civil' by fulfiling certain specific external constraints may fatally undermine its capacity to further the political debate.

Firstly, the term *civility* indicates a virtue that is, a character trait in the agent: an act is civil if it displays the agent's civility. Talking of acts of civility is akin to talking of acts of generosity, kindness, courage. It focuses on the agent's inner dispositions in performing that act (Baron, Pettit and Slote 1997). When we define an act as civil, we are implicitly praising the agent for her good character. Like most virtues, civility does not single out any particular action; despite its popularity in political theory, it remains a somewhat vague label, loosely used to indicate 'the moral and political qualities that make a good citizen' (Walzer 1974, 693).

Civility is usually associated with attitudes such as politeness, courtesy and tolerance; we praise the civil person for her good manners at the table, for her conversational skills and capacity to listen, while we criticise the uncivil conduct of those who talk on their mobile phones inside libraries, use foul language, do not clean after themselves and so on.[2] Narrowing the focus onto the political arena, we deem uncivil those who resort to insults, threats, not to mention physical violence; we praise, on the other hand, the civility of those who are willing to listen to others, who accept criticisms, who follow the rules and so on (Kingwell 1995).[3]

Hence, at the core of a civil disposition, there is a willingness to get along with others on good terms, to follow common rules and, overall, *to show respect and consideration for others*. One main reason we approve of those who act civilly (and, conversely, disapprove of those who act uncivilly) concerns the way they treat others: their behaviour shows respect for others' feelings, interests, needs and more. The person who keeps talking on her mobile phone in the library, uses foul language in public, does not clean up after herself and so on fails to show proper regard for others *and therefore* acts uncivilly. From this standpoint, civility is intrinsically *relational*, for it centres on the manners in which agents relate to each other. As Cheshire Calhoun has argued, civility is a disposition that 'communicates basic moral attitudes of respect, tolerance and considerateness', or, more specifically, that acknowledges 'the value of others' lives' (Calhoun 2000, 258). This value, I argue, refers to people's status as autonomous agents: an agent acts civilly when, through her conduct, she shows respect for other's autonomy.

The idea of autonomy at the core of this discussion refers to a person's ability to shape the course of her life by choosing and pursuing her own conception of the good. It involves 'the self-determination of what happens to one' (MacCallum 1993), the capacity to *choose the kind of person one wants to be*. Described in this way, autonomy represents a character ideal; namely,

> the ideal of people charting their own course through life, fashioning their character by self-consciously choosing projects and taking up commitments from a wide range of eligible alternatives, and making something out of their lives according to their own understanding of what is valuable and worth doing. (Wall 1998, 128)

An autonomous person can shape her life by adopting projects and commitments in accord with her values.[4] Thus, the defining feature of this conception of autonomy lies in the agent's capacity to make choices about her life (Feinberg 1989a, 28–43).[5] Raz (2001) identifies individual autonomy with the capacity to 'engage with value' through the action of choosing. This capacity is *of value in itself*; more specifically, the capacity to set one's own goals, to choose one's conception of the good life, to attribute value to some things over others, has a non-instrumental value.

> The very idea of something which is of value in itself is the idea of someone who can relate to value in the appropriate way. . . . Just as the fact that an object has intrinsic value marks a potential in it, the potential of being engaged with in the right way, so the status of being someone of value in oneself marks a potential in one, the potential to engage with value in the right way, and be thereby enriched or improved, etc. Therefore, valuers are of value in themselves. (Raz 2001, 157)

It is because of this capacity to engage with value, by choosing one's own ends in life, that we respect each other as autonomous agents (158). In this way, autonomy sets both a descriptive and a prescriptive standard of human agency: it identifies what is distinctively human – the capacity to make rational choices – and also posits a normative requirement about *respecting* autonomous agents.[6] An autonomous agent has a right that her choices be respected; I will refer to this as a person's *right of autonomy.* This right generates a duty for others to treat the right bearer with the respect due to her status qua autonomous. This is a natural duty, which we owe each other simply in virtue of our human nature; it is on this specific natural duty that I will ground my account of political obligation in chapter 6.

Let me expand on this notion of respect. As Raz further explains (ibid.), respect is due independently of the choices others make: their dignity, qua autonomous agents, is not jeopardised when they do not engage with value as they should. That is to say, we respect others as autonomous agents even when they act wrongly; this warrants, and even requires, certain attitudes and actions towards them; for example, disappointment or resentment. The crucial point is that 'these reactions can only be appropriate when directed at people who are ends in themselves, and do not show that they have lost this status'.[7] Hence, the attitude of respect with which we are concerned is not grounded on the agent's merit or *demerit*; we respect others' dignity not because of what they have achieved, but because of who they are (i.e., an autonomous person).[8] Respect is owed *regardless* of our own inclinations towards them, as when we have to respect our enemies or someone's opinions we may find morally reprehensible. It is not based on a *subjective* evaluation of the person to whom respect is due; rather, it hinges on that person's *objective* worth or dignity (Rawls 2000, 153).[9]

I need to stress this point, for it is central to my analysis of civil disobedience: our duty to *respect* others as autonomous agents applies *unconditionally*, yet is fulfilled in very different ways depending on the circumstances. Respect for autonomy centres on disposition rather than outcome. Thus, Stephen Darwall claims we should not confuse 'respect' with 'care' (2006, 126–27). When we 'care' for someone, we focus on that person's well-being;

respect, on the other hand, involves *responding* to a person's dignity; that is, to her *authority to make claims and demands of us*. Treating a person in accordance with her right of autonomy is not identical with providing for that person's well-being, and there may be cases where we show our respect for a person's dignity in ways that may inconvenience her, as I will argue in chapter 5, where I discuss the possibility of using violence in civil disobedience. Calling to account, blaming or even punishing a wrongdoer may express respect for her status as an autonomous person (Duff 2007). This will be a central assumption throughout this book.

The notion of a right of autonomy also requires further discussion. What kind of claims does it generate – that is, what corresponding obligations do others have towards the right bearer? A common approach separates 'negative' from 'positive' rights, and then identifies corresponding duties; however, many find the negative/positive dichotomy unsatisfying, since many rights have both a positive and a negative side (Shue 1996; Raz 1986; Fredman 2008; Möller 2009). Consider the right to migrate from one country to another, or the right of a linguistic minority to preserve its own language: both rights demand that others not interfere, but also require the provision of some goods (e.g., transports, in the former case; language schools, in the latter).[10] This is a traditional point of contention in the debate between socialists and libertarians; namely, what kind of claims can citizens make upon their state. Should resources be invested in enforcing negative rights only (e.g., protecting property rights), or also in providing services (e.g., public education) to help subjects realise their goals in life? As I argue below, it is implausible to limit the realm of the right of autonomy to negative claims: someone who is merely free from interferences 'will have attained a perfectly useless state if she lacks intelligence, skills, knowledge, and emotional health' (Berofsky 2007, 2). Respect for others' autonomy involves also taking positive action to support others in the exercise of the capacity to make choices (Gilabert 2018; Möller 2009).

This is due to the fact that, while sharing the same capacity (i.e., the same dignity as autonomous agents), individuals differ as to whether they are in the actual condition to make autonomous choices (Feinberg 1989b, 31). One who is kept as a slave by another would not be able to exercise her capacities to make autonomous choices (Raz 1986, 373–74). Similarly, a person born and raised in a strictly controlling environment, who is taught to abide by strict religious requirements and to not question authority, may have the same capacity for autonomous choice, yet not be in the condition to make such choices. This reveals a central element of this conception of autonomy; namely, its *social* dimension: *a person needs other people* in order to be autonomous (Dagger 1997). When we exercise our capacity to make autonomous choices, we apply standards that are not entirely determined by ourselves but are partly the product of the context we have grown into (Anderson and Honneth 2005). We have not determined these standard *ex nihilo*: we have acquired them, at least in part, from others' examples and teachings.[11] From this standpoint, autonomy requires both a degree of distance from and of proximity to others – that is, both independence and support. It is something that must be learned, and such learning requires a background of shared values against which autonomous choices may be made (Mendus 1989, 96–97). While being autonomous implies achieving a degree of independence of choice, the latter can be realised only from within a life shared with others. An effective ability to make choices involves the power to revise or reject our own projects according to criteria determined, in part, by the context in which we grow up.

We can now return to 'civility' and to civil disobedience. I contend that what separates a civil from an uncivil act of disobedience is the agent's disposition to respect others' autonomy. Citizens act civilly when they seek to avoid undue infringements upon others' autonomous choices; for example, coercing, intimidating or undermining others in the public arena. An *uncivil* act disrespects others as self-legislators. Within the context of civil disobedience, as I will discuss in the next section, this implies that, for an act of disobedience to be civil, it must *persuade* rather than *coerce* others, for coercion is inherently disrespectful of others' status as autonomous agents.

2.1 ON CIVIL DISOBEDIENCE

For the purposes of this discussion, I start from the following 'conceptual specification' of civil disobedience as 'a constrained, communicative protest, contrary to law, that people engage in to support a change in governmental or nongovernmental practices' (Smith and Brownlee 2017, 3). The first feature of this practice is, obviously, its illegality: engaging in civil disobedience implies breaching a law. The act of disobedience, however, intends to communicate a concern about a certain law or policy (more on this below), and the need to further discuss the possibility of legislative change. The disobedience may be direct or indirect, for the law being disobeyed may not be the one targeted by the protest (Rawls 1999, 320; Edmundson 1998, 58; Brownlee 2012, 19). For example, smoking marijuana in a public space, in open defiance of laws prohibiting recreational drug use, constitutes a direct act of disobedience; the law being disobeyed is the very target of the act of protest. These are often called test cases, whereby citizens openly defy a certain law or policy in order to challenge its constitutionality (Falcon Y. Tella 2004). Occupying a public space to protest the government's unjust treatment of asylum seekers, on the other hand, may represent a case of indirect civil disobedience; here, protesters breach a law to which they do not object (concerning public spaces and traffic regulations) in order to draw attention to a certain policy (e.g., the indefinite detention of asylum seekers in off-shore detention centres). Sometimes, the choice between these two forms of protest may be purely strategic – for example, one may be more effective than the other, under some circumstances, at drawing public attention to the specific issue – however, sometimes it is simply impossible to directly violate the law in question, as the example just mentioned shows. Anti-war and environmental protests, in most cases, take this indirect form: citizens breach a law they deem legitimate in order to denounce a different law or policy which is the target of their protest. Indirect civil disobedience often faces more challenges, in terms of its justifiability, compared to direct disobedience, for in the former case the agent knowingly breaches a law she accepts as reasonably just.[12] The problem lies in the fact that the argument often employed to justify direct disobedience (i.e., there is no pro tanto obligation to obey a seriously unjust law) may not be employed to justify indirect civil disobedience. This is one major reason why, I argue, political obligation should not be framed exclusively in terms of obedience to the law. Furthermore, while for earlier authors such as Joseph Raz (1979, 264), civil disobedience does not include breaches of law in protest against morally unacceptable actions or policies of private agents (trade unions, banks, private universities, etc.), Brownlee argues that 'the policies and practices of nongovernmental institutions [e.g., a university's discriminatory policies] are matters of law', and may be the legitimate target of a campaign of civil disobedience aiming to challenge 'the legal framework that accepts these policies and practices as lawful' (2012, 19, fn.8).

Traditionally, civil disobedience has been associated with Henry David Thoreau, often hailed as 'the most notable American exponent of civil disobedience' (Herr 1974, 87). He is also usually acknowledged as the first to use the term *civil disobedience*, as per the title of one of his famous works. However, there is no evidence that Thoreau himself ever employed the expression; even his essay known as 'Civil Disobedience' was originally entitled 'Resistance to Civil Government', and it received its more familiar title only four years after Thoreau's death, and not because of the author's desire (Perry 2013, 65). Thoreau famously refused to pay taxes in protest against the US invasion of Mexico in 1846. However, as will become more evident throughout this chapter, his law-breaking conduct falls short of the requirements of civil disobedience, and is closer to what is commonly considered *conscientious objection*. Similar considerations will apply to Gandhi and King, who alongside Thoreau are often hailed as the epitome of a civil disobedient: We will see that their commitment to non-violence did not rest on a commitment to persuasion.

The first academic accounts of civil disobedience appeared in the 1960s and 1970s, by authors such as Hugo Adam Bedau, Carl Cohen and John Rawls. Rawls's account has had the more lasting influence, and it is indeed a rare occurrence for an academic source on civil disobedience not to mention it (Rawls 1999, 319–23). It is also, true, however, that most recent authors have taken issue with Rawls's view, mainly due to its controversial attempt to provide a checklist of necessary conditions an act must fulfil to qualify as civil disobedience. Most recently, philosophers have abandoned the search for such necessary conditions, and rather have highlighted the *communicative* nature of this form of protest.[13] As Tony Milligan (2013, 18) has pointed out, Rawls's account of civil disobedience marked 'a turning point' in the philosophical discussion on the topic. On the one hand, it 'secularised' civil disobedience by grounding it in political principles, rather than (as Gandhi and King) on religious ideals. On the other, Rawls was the first to emphasise the communicative nature of civil disobedience, presenting it as a form of address: for Rawls, the breach of law constitutes a speech act, through which a minority seeks to address the majority's sense of justice to communicate a concern that the conditions of free cooperation are being violated (1999, 321). After Rawls, most accounts of civil disobedience have adopted this 'communication thesis', despite having 'picked Rawls apart on other matters' (Milligan, ibid.). Milligan expresses scepticism about a conception of civil disobedience centred on communication; referring to earlier work by Hugo Bedau (1961), he emphasises the disruptive, rather than merely communicative, nature of this form of protest, which in Bedau's view aimed at 'frustrating' a government's laws or policies. For Milligan, sometimes 'the point of an action may be to frustrate and obstruct but to do so in as civil a manner as possible' (ibid., 20). In such circumstances, focusing on communication may be irrelevant to our judgement as to whether that action constitutes civil disobedience. Milligan contends the main reason to be sceptical about the 'communication thesis' is that it portrays civil disobedience as overly deferential to authority, as aiming to persuade political elites who stand in need of coercion rather than persuasion' (2017, 296).[14] However, based on the account of civility sketched above, and on the ensuing discussion in this and the next chapters, there are indeed good reasons to treat communicativeness as one of the criteria separating civil and uncivil disobedience.

One reason to resist Milligan's scepticism concerns the risk of blurring the line between civil disobedience and direct action, which is a similar, though distinct, practice. The similarity lies in the principled nature of the breach of law: agents engaging in either conduct use law breaking to target a perceived wrong in a law or policy. The difference, however, is that 'direct action' aims to stop the perceived wrong from occurring, rather than simply to communicate opposition to that wrong (Smith 2018, 13). There is indeed a thin line separating these forms of protest since, for example, they often employ similar strategies; for example, blockades. However, while the civil disobedient seeks to promote a debate as to whether the perceived wrong warrants a change in legislation, those engaging in direct action are less concerned with debates, and rather want results; that is to say, they are less concerned with being civil than they are with averting the wrong they are protesting. Anti-abortion protesters may try to shut down a hospital where abortions are carried out; animal welfare activists may secretly free animals from a slaughterhouse to prevent their killing; anti-war activists may damage military equipment to prevent airplanes from bombing innocent civilians. These are all forms of direct action; nonetheless, while certainly admirable, their main goal is not to call for further deliberation.[15] For this reason, they should not be treated as civil disobedience.

2.2 COMMUNICATION AND PERSUASION

It is therefore important to preserve the 'communication thesis'; that is, to understand civil disobedience as, first and foremost, a communicative act.[16] Following Kimberley Brownlee's seminal work on the topic, communication constitutes an other-directed activity, through which the speaker seeks to engage the hearer in a rational exchange concerning a certain issue. In a communicative exchange, the speaker seeks to transfer some data or information onto the hearer, and to elicit the latter's reply. The person who communicates intends to have an effect on others through her message; she aims to generate a certain belief in the hearer. As opposed to acts of expression, communication thus requires an audience. We may successfully express our rage by screaming from the top of a mountain, with no one hearing us, but we may not communicate that same feeling without someone to acknowledge it (ibid., 140; Duff 2001, 79). William Smith identifies a 'vertical' and a 'horizontal' dimension of the communicativeness of civil disobedience (2013, 32). On the one hand, he argues, citizens address the state, asking that it reconsider a certain law or policy; on the other, they address their fellow citizens, to draw their attention to issues deemed highly relevant to the community as a whole.[17] Thus, the communication in civil disobedience is intentional. We do not always intend to communicate our feelings to others. A person biting her fingernails during a job interview may have no intention to communicate to others that she is feeling anxious; that is, no intention that they acknowledge her anxiety. Yet the choice to engage in civil disobedience is based on the intention to communicate to others a serious and sincere concern with a certain law or policy. Brian Smart (1978) identified three separate, though related, intentions grounding an act of civil disobedience. The first is the intention to bring about a change in the hearer by communicating to her a certain belief; for example, 'law X should be reconsidered'. The second intention is the intention that the hearer recognise the previous intention. This rules out cases of deception or manipulation, where the speaker may try to bring about a change in the hearer by communicating a false belief. When Iago warns Othello 'Beware, my lord, of jealousy'! he intends to plant the seeds of jealousy in Othello's mind, yet he does not intend Othello to realise that Iago has that intention. Iago seeks to manipulate Othello into distrusting Desdemona; his act fails to be communicative, in the way discussed here. In civil disobedience, the agent does not simply intend to generate a certain belief in her audience; she also intends that the audience understand she has that intention. She wants her fellows to notice that her resort to law breaking indicates her attempt to lead them to reconsider a law or policy. Finally, Smart highlighted a third intention characteristic of civil disobedience: the agent intends that the audience form the belief (that a certain law or policy should be reconsidered) *as a result of* the agent's second intention just mentioned. Upon realising how far the protesters have gone (to the point of openly breaching the law) to denounce a possible injustice in the legal system, the hearer may become persuaded that the law or policy in question should indeed be reconsidered. Crucially, this does not imply that the addressee will also *accept* the protesters' demands for legislative change: having heard the protesters' reasons, the addressee may still conclude that the law or policy does not need further discussion, for it should not be modified. This brings to light another crucial aspect of civil disobedience as a communicative act; namely, its *persuasiveness.*

For our purposes, it suffices to understand a persuasive act as one that seeks 'to lead a person to the performance of an act by argument', while a coercive one aims, on the other hand, to 'forcibly constrain or impel [a person] into doing something' (McArthur, Lam-McArthur and Fontaine 2018). As we will see in detail in chapters 3 and 4, in a persuasive exchange, A seeks to convince B to *share* A's reasons for acting in a certain way; on the other hand, A acts coercively when aiming to *impose* her own reasons upon B, regardless of B's own will. The concept of persuasion is the backbone of my discussion of civil disobedience throughout this book, for it plays a central role in the account of civility I sketched above. By addressing others in persuasive manners, we respect them as autonomous agents; that is, as self-legislators with a right to act upon principles they have chosen themselves. Coercion fails to do so; hence, it is incompatible with the communicative nature of civil disobedience.

If I point a gun at your head and ask you to 'Do X', I engage in a communicative act. I intend (1) that you do X; (2) that you understand that I am pointing a gun at you because I want you to do X; and (3) that you do X upon realising that I am pointing a gun at your head because I want you to do X. This is indeed how terrorism works: terrorists kill innocent individuals to communicate a specific message, expecting others to 'acknowledge' it and to act accordingly. That is to say, threats are communicative acts. Terrorists do not intend to engage others in a rational exchange, for their goal is simply to force them to yield to their demands. They have no interest in respecting others' equal right to have their say and to defend their own interests in the deliberative arena; in fact, they are not interested in *deliberation* either. Civil disobedience, on the other hand, is a persuasive act, characterised by a forward-looking attitude. Brownlee argues that civil disobedience, as opposed to other forms of non-persuasive acts such as direct action or terrorism, fulfils a 'dialogic' requirement that involves the effort to engage others in reasoned deliberation about the merits of the protesters' own convictions. Note that, for Brownlee, this does not impose restraints on the kind of beliefs the protesters may advance, but rather on the means through which they may communicate their position (ibid., 44). I will discuss this issue in detail in chapter 5.

Andrew Sabl (2001) has offered an influential reading of Rawls's account, focusing on the notion of forward-looking civil disobedience: the latter represents a form of communication which is also cooperative; that is, grounded on a desire to work with others to better society, to improve the legal system by identifying potential risks to its underlying values. Sabl agrees that *civil* disobedients do not aim to impose their views through brute force; herein lies their *civility*, as discussed above. For Sabl, the underlying motivations of civil disobedience is the capacity to 'look forward' towards future cooperation with the authorities in power. Focusing on the civil rights movement, Sabl points out that the serious injustice of Jim Crow laws may have warranted an armed revolution against that racist regime (309).[18] A government that enacts serious violations of human rights – for example, Jim Crow laws – does not appear a suitable partner for a cooperative enterprise. Yet Sabl argues that what motivated the civil rights movement to resort to civil disobedience was the regard for future possibilities:

> There was evidence that cooperation with former oppressors was both desirable and possible. More specifically, because ruling groups had shown themselves capable of being relatively cooperative and fair *within their own group*, there was reason to believe that they could extend this habit to their relations to other groups. Civil disobedience was based not on current obligations but on the desire not to foreclose future cooperation. (2001, 310)

On this same point, Michael Blake (2016, 171) writes that King 'believed fervently that the Constitution and the government it had created were worthy of allegiance'.[19] For this reason, there is a tendency to distinguish civil disobedience from revolution. Revolutionaries do not see the government in place as a partner for future cooperation, and have no intention to establish a rational exchange with it; rather, their goal is to overthrow that regime and to replace it with a new one. Revolutionaries do not aim to engage their government representatives in a persuasive enterprise due to their conviction that things will not change as long as those people remain in power. Like saboteurs or hackers, they are mainly concerned with ends rather than means. While revolutionaries aim to overthrow a government they see as unjust and abusive, civil disobedients are hopeful that the government in place is able and willing to further the cause of justice. Throughout this discussion, I will work on the assumption that civil disobedients accept their government as satisfying a minimal threshold of legitimacy and justice; they also acknowledge that, qua citizens, they have specific political duties.[20] This need be no more than an assumption, for, as I discuss in more detail below, there may be no inconsistency in a campaign of civil disobedience aiming not just for legislative but for governmental change.

However, there is also a tendency amongst recent authors to overstate the transformative power of civil disobedience, by describing it exclusively as a practice to further social change (Cooke 2016; Celikates 2016; Delmas 2018a). Contrary to this view, civil disobedience may also play an important conservative role by preventing basic rights from further breaches; that is, by opposing a legislative change. For example, protesters may draw attention to the risks of a new anti-terrorism legislation, which would unduly violate fundamental civil liberties in the interest of an elusive 'war on terror'.

2.3 A CONSTRAINED FORM OF ACTION

We saw above that the civility of civil disobedience lies in the agents' motivation to respect others as autonomous agents. Civil disobedience is a constrained form of law-breaking communication, for it remains within the limits set by others' autonomy, while uncivil disobedience may not.[21] However, the academic debate on the topic has been characterised by disagreement around the specific constraints of the act of civil disobedience. As already mentioned, it seems safe to argue that one reason why Rawls's account, after almost fifty years, is still widely cited lies in his attempt to provide an exhaustive list of necessary conditions for civil disobedience, which has attracted countless objections. Rawls sought to identify criteria enabling us to judge whether a certain illegal act could be considered an instance of civil disobedience. He highlights three such criteria; namely, *publicity*, *nonviolence, and willingness to accept the punishment*. It is important to notice that, despite the amount of objections Rawls's 'list' elicited, most authors tend to acknowledge at least a presumption that civil disobedience satisfies such description.[22] First, civil disobedience is performed publicly, not in secret. This stems directly from its communicative nature: for the action to be a successful form of address, a plea for further discussion, it is important that the speaker reveal their identity. A forward-looking communicative enterprise cannot proceed insofar as the participants act secretly. Once again, the comparison with direct action is helpful here, for citizens who engage in direct action often act covertly, without revealing their identities.[23] By the same token, hacktivism should not be considered a form of civil disobedience, given its inherently anonymous nature. Rawls seemingly stretched this requirement too far by adding that civil disobedience be carried out 'with fair notice' (321): He thought protesters should inform the local authorities beforehand about the planned disruption in order to minimise the disruption to innocent bystanders; for example, commuters. This appears to place unreasonable burdens on the civil disobedients, since many acts of protest could not even take place if the police were given advanced notice of the protesters' plan. It seems sufficient, for an act of civil disobedience, that the protesters reveal their identity and motives upon, or shortly after, committing the illegal act (Raz 1979, 265; Smart 1978; Brownlee 2012, 23).

The importance of acting openly relates to Rawls's other requirement for civil disobedience; namely, the agent's *willingness to accept the punishment*. Following from Gandhi's and King's examples, Rawls held that a civil disobedient should not avoid the legal consequences of her deliberate choice to break the law; she accepts that, despite the principled nature of her act of disobedience, she remains subject to law's authority to punish law breakers. Submission to the punishment, for Rawls, was necessary evidence of the disobedient's 'fidelity to the law', notwithstanding her disobedience.[24] By stressing this requirement, Rawls was attempting to address the seeming paradox of a law-breaking act that seeks to be, at the same time, law respecting (Bulman-Pozen and Pozen, 2015). Political philosophers have devoted a significant amount of their attention to this specific issue, and in chapter 5 I will consider some of the recent contributions in light of the debate concerning the existence of a moral right to civil disobedience. Earlier commentators worried about the consequences of allowing civil disobedients to go unpunished. For example, Kent Greenawalt claimed that, even if the judges rightly acquitted acts of justifiable civil disobedience, 'citizens may draw mistaken inferences, and restraints of deterrence and norm acceptance may be weakened for unjustified acts that resemble the justified ones' (Greenawalt 1987, 273). Yet, as already mentioned, earlier thinkers were heavily influenced by the examples of Gandhi and King, whose campaigns were characterised by a willingness to suffer the legal consequences of law defiance. In his famous *Letter from Birmingham Jail*, King explained that 'an individual who breaks a law that conscience tells him it is unjust, and willingly accepts the penalty by staying in jail to arouse the conscience of the community over its injustice, is in reality expressing the highest respect for the law' (Bedau 1991, 74). However, there is some ambiguity in King's words, for it is not clear whether the willing submission to the penalty (even in the face of a seriously unjust law) serves the consequentialist aim of 'arousing the conscience of the community', or rather expresses an (at least partly) non-instrumental attitude of respect for the law. According to David Lyons (1996, 40), Gandhi's and

King's acceptance of punishment 'signified a strategic, not a moral, judgment'. The same ambiguity about the rationale for the willingness to accept the punishment in civil disobedience persists in Rawls's view. While he explains that 'the militant' (as opposed to the civil) disobedient escapes the punishment to avoid 'playing into the hands of forces he believes cannot be trusted' (Rawls 1999, 323), the acceptance of punishment 'demonstrates a belief that current powers can be "trusted" . . . and that the disobedient can be trusted as well' (Sabl 2001, 318). Hence, Rawls explains that accepting punishment in this way represents 'a bond of one's sincerity, for it is not easy to convince another that one's acts are conscientious'. Once again, based on this argument, submission to punishment plays a merely *strategic* role:

> King talks about 'staying in jail to arouse the conscience of the community over its injustice'. He does not speak of staying in jail because he *owes* that to the government, and that . . . he has a duty to obey whatever the government tells him to do. Not at all. The staying in jail is not for philosophical or moral reasons, but for a practical purpose, to continue his struggle in a different way, 'to arouse the conscience of the community over its injustice'. (Zinn 1991, 915–16)

William Scheuerman has objected to this claim. In his view, 'King's acceptance of punishment was not exclusively or even mainly strategic' (Scheuerman 2015, 432). Scheuerman reiterates the importance of showing respect for the law, 'even if in some instance such fidelity paradoxically demands disobedience'.

> Only laws embodying the quest for *generality* typically are just and worthy of respect. By accepting the possibility of legal penalties disobedients concede that they, in principle, are subject to the same legal rules as other members of the legal community. (433)

Scheuerman might be correct in his judgement of King's conduct, but he does not show that *therefore* a civil disobedient must accept the punishment. As mentioned above, *civility* is *in the agent*, as a character trait: hence we cannot conclude that one is acting civilly by simply pointing at the external features of the act, for we must consider the agent's disposition. Revolutionaries may be willing to accept the punishment for their illegal actions, yet they may not do it to show respect for the law. Similarly, Brownlee points out that Gandhi's willingness to accept the punishment was hardly born of the attempt to show 'fidelity to the law', given his attempt to overthrow the British regime.[25] 'Militant' disobedients may simply go through the motions of being punished, to bear witness to the unjust regime that punishes them. Or they might engage in 'jail solidarity', by appearing in court and pleading guilty en masse, demanding a full trial, thus forcing prosecutors to abandon the case due to lack of resources (Lovell 2009; Starr, Fernandez and Scholl 2011). Contrary to the idea that accepting punishment shows respect for the law, many have pointed out that 'breaking the law and accepting the punishment, with plans to break it again, simply instantiates the belief that the law has no moral force' (Levine 2004, 375): deliberately breaking the law, and then submitting to the punishment, signals a very shallow kind of 'respect' for the law (Moraro 2012; Storing 1991). As Michael Sandel points out (2005, 94), the penalty may be treated as a mere 'fee' to then be able to break the law, rather than a 'fine' signalling wrongful conduct.[26]

In chapter 4, I will discuss reason for scepticism over treating Gandhi and King's campaign as an instance of civil disobedience, with reference to the fact that the use of nonviolence was aimed at coercion rather than persuasion. However, although we may question King's and Gandhi's reasons for accepting punishment, this does not entail that civil disobedients have no obligations following their deliberate breach of the law. That is to say, Rawls's underlying assumption about accepting the consequences of civil disobedience is plausible, insofar as it is not interpreted strictly as a willingness to accept the legal punishment; for example, a requirement to plead guilty. In fact, Rawls acknowledged that the protesters may challenge the prosecution and plead not guilty in court, although he further adds that 'there comes a point after which dissent ceases to be civil disobedience' (322); from this perspective, the attempt to avoid punishment when facing the court – for example, by invoking a legal defence – would be compatible with civil disobedience. Many have challenged this possibility, however, holding that the appeal to legal defences is incompatible with the disposition of a civil disobedient, for it would impoverish the principled nature of the disobedients' message by casting doubts over their sincerity and selflessness (Bauer and Eckerstrom 1987; McEwen 1991). More recently, Brownlee has argued for a 'non-evasion' condition in civil disobedience, which requires the protesters to 'bear the risks' of defending their conviction through illegal conduct. This does not necessary require undergoing imprisonment: to satisfy this condition, it is sufficient that the disobedients 'take the risk of being arrested or punished or socially censured' (2012, 37).

A third requirement in Rawls's account of civil disobedience is nonviolence. Rawls claimed that engaging in violent acts 'likely to injure and to hurt is incompatible with civil disobedience as a form of address', and that 'any interference with others' civil liberties' may weaken the principled nature of civil disobedience as a form of address. Others before him, most notably Hugo Adam Bedau, had upheld the same view. As we will see in detail in chapter 4, contemporary authors tend be less prescriptive about nonviolence in civil disobedience, using it as a rule of thumb for a constrained form of law breaking rather than as a strict requirement. A more realistic approach tends to separate violence that is permissible from that which is impermissible: instead of defending a blanket denial of 'any interference' with others' liberties, authors have sought to identify what *kind* of violence should not be part of an act of civil disobedience. One assumption in this debate is that the specific circumstances (e.g., the seriousness of the injustice, or power imbalances in the deliberative arena) may justify employing some violence as part of the protest. However, for the act to display the agents' civility, it must remain within the limits of respect for others as autonomous agents (Moraro 2014).

It is important to notice that, as opposed to Gandhi and King, Rawls was not committed to pacifism, as he had no issue with granting that, against a tyrannical regime, the use of violent means of protest may be necessary to overthrow the tyrants. This is why Rawls deemed civil disobedience an appropriate form of address only in 'nearly just' societies. As Simmons notices (2010, 1806), Rawls's account is unclear, as he describes a nearly just society as one that makes 'due allowance for what it is reasonable to expect in the circumstance' and has 'some form of democratic government, though serious injustices may nevertheless exist' (Rawls 1999, 335). However, King's America seems a far cry from a society that is *nearly just*. On this point, Sabl (2001, 311) points out that Rawls seemingly deems 'nearly just' regimes that

> are prone to deprive people of voting rights or persecute them on religious grounds – the latter a paradigm case of deep injustice for Rawls. . . . The injustice is not merely blind or due to apathy but 'more or less deliberate over an extended period of time in the face of normal political opposition': those practising injustice are 'immovable and apathetic' despite repeated appeals. . . . The injustices involved are 'serious' and the enforcement of them by law amounts to nothing less than 'illegitimate force'.[27]

Rawls's concern with nearly just societies reflected his attempt to preserve the non-revolutionary nature of civil disobedience.[28] However, there is no inconsistency in thinking of a campaign of civil disobedience that aims for governmental rather than legislative change. Citizens may start a campaign of civil disobedience to draw attention to the fact that elected politicians have become extremely corrupt and incompetent, and to persuade others of the necessity of holding new elections to replace them. This is exactly the approach that characterised Gandhi's campaign for independence, if we are to think of him as a civil disobedient.[29] There would be nothing per se *uncivil* in this approach. In my view, the only reason why civil disobedience may be unsuitable to a revolution is that it is time-consuming: the plea for reconsideration, the appeals to further debate, the effort to persuade others to join in a communicative exchange may not match the urgency and the complexity of a change in government (Moraro 2019a). But there is nothing conceptually wrong in civil disobedience that calls for a new government.

2.4 CIVIL DISOBEDIENCE, CONSCIENTIOUS OBJECTION, HACKTIVISM

Most accounts of civil disobedience follow Rawls's conception of the latter as a political act, which focuses on the community's interest or what is often called the common good. Citizens who engage in this sort of protest do not advance a cause specifically based on their own interest; civil disobedience is other-oriented not only as a form of communication, but also as it is concerned with the interests of the community as a whole. Rawls himself acknowledges that considerations of personal interest may be part of what grounds the disobedients' action, but only insofar as they stem from a general concern with the principles of justice. For example, when single parents engage in a protest against budgetary cuts to social welfare, they communicate their concern that such cuts may undermine a commitment to helping the worse-off in societies, while also drawing attention to their own predicament.

Focusing on the political element brings to light an important difference between civil disobedience and another oft-cited form of dissent; namely, *conscientious objection.* The latter is not inherently 'political', in that the conscientious objector seeks, first and foremost, a personal exemption from a law she perceives as unjust or incompatible with her own values. In Hannah Arendt's famous account, conscientious objection is *unpolitical*, for conscience 'is more interested in the self than in the world' (Smith 2010, 151; Petherbridge 2016). It motivates agents to dissociate themselves from the injustice being perpetrated, without necessarily drawing public attention to the need to remove the injustice altogether. A conscientious objector need not engage her fellows in a rational exchange over whether the law should be changed or removed; her goal is to 'keep her hands clean' by not partaking in the injustice. Thus, a doctor who refuses to conduct an abortion may accept that a colleague with different views on the (alleged) right of the foetus could perform it in her place; what matters to the doctor, in this case, is exemption from conducting the abortion, rather than the criminalisation of abortions altogether. In this sense, conscientious objection may well be 'public and conscientious', in that it is performed publicly and is based on the agent's sincere convictions; yet it lacks the political aim to bring about a change in legislation which, on the other hand, is characteristic of civil disobedience. Brownlee has cast some doubts over the 'conscientiousness' of those who engage in conscientious objection (which she prefers to call 'personal disobedience'), pointing out that 'to remain silent [in the face of others' wrongdoing] necessarily casts doubt on the sincerity of our conviction that the conduct is seriously unjust' (2012, 29). A main contention of her book is that civil disobedience may be *more admirable* than conscientious objection because, as opposed to the latter, it satisfies her 'non-evasive' condition discussed earlier. As William Smith writes, while the conscientious objector aims for personal exemption, the civil disobedient has 'an active interest in what goes on within the world and, crucially, a willingness to safeguard its durability and integrity. Civilly disobedient minorities aim to defend and develop the stable worldly structures that house political life' (Smith 2010, 152).[30]

The same idea of non-evasiveness helps draw the line between civil disobedience and other forms of activism that occur online, usually grouped under the label *hacktivism*. As Candice Delmas has pointed out, we should not commit the mistake of classifying this form of acts, which may as well be political and communicative, as civil disobedience. First, she argues, the analogy between off-line and online protest is untenable:

> Protesting against a company on one's personal blog is akin to shouting from one's living room; there is no lawful online equivalent of protesting outside a company's storefront or headquarters. To do the latter, hacktivists have to digitally trespass on private property (e.g., through website defacement or DdoS actions), which already raises the stakes for disobedients, compared with their offline analogues. (2018b, 66)

Second, Delmas continues, the attempt to portray hacktivism as civil disobedience ignores the fact that many hacktivists *do not* want to be seen as civil disobedients, for many members of Anonymous, for example, 'embrace their status as rebels or villains of the Information Age' and 'are not committed to the standards of civility' (ibid., 70). From this standpoint, to conceive of guerrilla warfare as 'civil' disobedience 'is to tame its aesthetics and radical disruptiveness' (76). She identifies this attempt to broaden the concept of civil disobedience, to the point it may encompass also these new forms of online activism, as characteristic of *radical democrats*, who seek to 're-inject the concept of civil disobedience with the disruptiveness that made it powerful and attractive in the first place, but which the ordinary, sanitised and stale understanding of civil disobedience has much diluted' (ibid.). While we may sympathise with its underlying concern, this approach targets the very idea of civil disobedience as a 'constrained' form of protest; in fact, it is this very idea that radical democrats identify as 'ordinary, sanitised and stale'. For example, Robin Celikates presents an extremely broad account of civil disobedience, which he describes as

> an intentionally unlawful and principled collective act of protest . . . , with which citizens – in the broad sense that goes beyond those recognized as citizens by a particular state – pursue the political aim of changing specific laws, policies, or institutions . . . in ways that can be seen as civil (as opposed to military). (2016, 4)

From Celikates's standpoint, for an illegal act to count as civil disobedience, it is sufficient that it aim for legislative or institutional change; none of the constraints mentioned earlier are of particular significance. It is somewhat ironic that this definition, while aiming to be more inclusive than others, seemingly excludes cases of civil disobedience that *oppose* legislative change. Celikates is interested in political contestation and 'struggles for democratisation (from below)' (10), which explains his belief that civil disobedience is 'not reducible to an ethical or legal understanding either in terms of individual conscience or of fidelity to the rule of law' (2). As a critical theorist, he is wary of attempts at identifying the philosophical underpinnings of civil disobedience, which in his view may hamper (perhaps even deliberately) the power of this form of protest as an instrument to challenge constituted power. However, his proposal takes us to the opposite extreme, for we may have lost any reason to use the label *civil* at all (except to separate it from 'military'), for it is obvious that Celikates is not interested in the agents' disposition in disobeying the law. This may be too high a price to pay for the political philosopher, and an unnecessary one: Celikates's concerns about the risk of 'sanitising' civil disobedience may be accommodated without sacrificing the search for some necessary, though context sensitive, moral constraints.

2.5 WHISTLEBLOWING

Whistleblowing is usually treated as a form of hacktivism, yet it should be kept separated from it, at least in those instances in which the whistleblower does not act anonymously but rather reveals her identity. According to Ceva and Bocchiola (2018, 1), whistleblowing refers to 'the practice of reporting immoral or illegal behaviour by members of a legitimate organization with privileged access to information concerning an alleged wrongdoing within that organization'.[31]

One of the most famous cases involves Edward Snowden's revelation, in 2013, about National Security Agency (NSA) dragnet surveillance of citizens' communications. The Snowden case has received a fair amount of attention by philosophers working on civil disobedience; while many admire Snowden's selflessness and courage in bringing to light what were later acknowledged as illegal breaches of citizens' privacy, others question whether his act should be treated as civil disobedience or as a different form of principled disobedience. Amongst the points of contention is whether Snowden's act adhered to the constraints that characterise a communicative and conscientious breach of the law.

During his time as a contractor at the National Surveillance Agency (NSA), Edward Snowden realised that the US government collected and stored and incredible amount of information about civilians' private conversations. Although the US Congress had authorised a degree of surveillance of private conversation, as part of the 2001 Patriot Act, Snowden soon discovered the NSA had gone far beyond the limits set out in the US Constitution concerning respect for individual privacy. In June 2013, he leaked secret files to journalists from *The Guardian*, whom he met in a hotel in Hong Kong. The files documented the extent of the NSA dragnet surveillance programme. *The Guardian* did not initially reveal the identity of its sources: Snowden agreed to come out publicly two days after the first revelations were published. He then went into hiding, while seeking asylum in over twenty countries (all requests were accepted), and eventually he settled in Russia, where he is still residing (in a secret location) at the time this book was written.

Snowden's action was illegal, as it breached the US Espionage Act.[32] Snowden also conceded that he signed the standard obligatory government 'classified information non-disclosure agreement', and that, therefore, his actions might be considered a violation of a 'civil contract' with the US government (Scheuerman 2014, 611). It seems safe to argue that Snowden's act was done *publicly*, in the sense discussed above, despite the fact he did not provide 'fair notice' to the authorities of his intention of leaking the documents. This is controversial, however, since, as Kimberley Brownlee has pointed out,

> Snowden gave no notice to his society and its authorities that he would leak documents about NSA programs that gather information about millions of Americans and foreigners. Indeed, before his disclosures . . . became public, Snowden removed himself from Hawaii to Hong Kong. (Brownlee 2016a, 966)

Obviously, it would have been self-defeating for Snowden to inform the NSA of his intention to leak classified documents revealing government misconduct; nevertheless, this does not show that whistleblowing cannot qualify as *civil* disobedience. We saw above that Rawls's requirement of 'fair notice' is too demanding, and that a more realistic approach to the issue of publicity should involve demanding that the agent's identity be revealed *at least* shortly after the breach of the law. From this standpoint, Snowden's conduct may certainly be characterised as a public (as opposed to a covert) act. Thus, William Scheuerman (2014) has offered a heartfelt defence of Snowden's action as an example of 'Rawlsian' civil disobedience, highlighting its political and conscientious nature. Scheuerman stresses Snowden's selfless behaviour, epitomised by the choice to forsake a 'life in paradise with his family (i.e., a job reportedly earning him US$200,000 per year in Hawaii, where he resided with his partner)' in order to tell society about a surveillance regime that affects all citizens. Snowden's statement that he *had to* inform the public about mass surveillance policy bears witness to the conscientiousness of his conduct: his choice to leak classified documents was not intended to provide him with any personal benefit (quite the contrary, as we will see).

> I believe in the principle declared at Nuremberg in 1945: 'Individuals have international duties which transcend the national obligations of obedience. Therefore individual citizens have the duty to violate domestic laws to prevent crimes against peace and humanity from occurring. (quoted in Scheuerman 2014, 623)

We need to be clear as to how Snowden intended to 'prevent crimes against peace and humanity from occurring'. He could have worked from within the NSA, trying to undermine the dragnet surveillance by, for example, sabotaging or damaging key infrastructures. Instead, he decided to leak classified information to the public, to make them aware of the extreme and (as it turned out) unwarranted level of governmental surveillance over civilians' lives. He resorted to reveal document available to the public, 'so what affects all of us can be discussed by all of us in the light of day' (Lewis 2013). Thus, his action should not be confused with direct action: his goal was to lead society to consider whether those surveillance policies should be reconsidered. As he explained in a later interview at the *Washington Post*: 'I didn't want to change society. I wanted to give society a chance to determine if it should change itself' (Gellman 2013). In this sense, his act was inherently communicative. It is obvious that Snowden's communicative act was intentional, as he carefully planned all stages leading to his revelations, and offered a full account of his motives. He also resorted to leaking documents after having exhausted other legal avenues, as he claims to have reported his concerns 'to more than ten distinct officials, none of whom took any action to address them' (quoted in Delmas [2016b]). In fact, there were no *legal* avenues he could have reasonably pursued, for US legislation does not protect Intelligence Community contractors; hence, he had no legal protection for following institutional channels. As Candice Delmas has pointed out (in an essay aiming to distinguish whistleblowing from civil disobedience),

> before Snowden, four NSA whistleblowers had done the same without success and suffered serious legal reprisals. The last one, Thomas Drake, followed the protocol set out in the Intelligence Community Whistleblower Protection Act by complaining internally to his superiors, the NSA Inspector General, the Defense Department Inspector General. He also presented unclassified documents to the House and Senate Congressional intelligence committees. Four years later, he leaked unclassified documents to the *New York Times*. The NSA went on to classify the documents Drake had leaked, and he was charged under the Espionage Act in 2010. (Delmas 2016b)

It is more controversial, however, whether Snowden's conduct fulfiled the requirements of non-violence and acceptance of punishment. Snowden's critics contend that, by revealing top-secret information about the US surveillance system, he posed a serious threat to public safety, exposing the US to the threat of terrorism. In the aftermath of the 2015 Paris terrorist attacks, the head of the CIA, John Brennan, lamented that

> because of a number of unauthorized disclosures and a lot of hand-wringing over the government's role in the effort to try to uncover these terrorists, there have been some policy and legal and other actions that are taken that make our ability collectively, internationally, to find these terrorists much more challenging'. (Davidson Sorkin 2015)

Regardless of the accuracy of such statement, one may agree that Snowden acted irresponsibly by leaking top-secret documents about anti-terrorism strategies, for in doing so he exposed the community to unreasonable risks. Three points should be made in response to this. First, given Snowden's special position as insider to the NSA, it may be expected that he knew his action would not have exposed the community to direct or indirect danger. He knew what should and should not be revealed; namely, he made public the *abuse* of surveillance powers by the state, yet did not provide measures to neutralise those powers, nor did he reveal specific details concerning the US anti-terrorist operation.[33] Furthermore, Delmas (2016b) mentions a report by the online intelligence monitoring firm *Flashpoint*, which rebuts the claim that Snowden's whistleblowing alerted terrorists to US surveillance policies.[34]

Second, even if we accept that Snowden's conduct exposed people to some harm, we also need to consider that it did so to protect them from a very significant threat to their right to privacy. As we will see in more detail in chapter 5, the presence of a degree of force or violence may be allowed in an act of civil disobedience, in ways that should at least be proportional to the harm to be averted (Raz 1979). Thirdly, as discussed above, non-violence may be as coercive as violence; a boycott or a strike may be as 'coercive' as, or possibly even more coercive than, smashing the windows of a McDonald's. Rather than pondering over the potential risks of physical violence, we need to ascertain whether Snowden's act should be deemed 'coercive' or 'persuasive'. If we are to trust Snowden's own account of his choice to blow the whistle on the NSA (and there seems to be no major reason why we should not do so), there is an undeniable 'persuasive' aim underlying his tactic, as he has stated several times that his goal was to make the public aware of the amount of surveillance to which it is subjected, and then to decide whether to accept it or not.[35] Snowden did not try to force or manipulate people into accepting his ideas; notwithstanding the magnitude of his revelations, his whistleblowing can and should be interpreted as a forward-looking communicative action. Based on his own account, he aimed to make the public aware of the level of surveillance it is unknowingly subject to, and then leave it to others to decide whether those practices were justifiable. In this sense, Snowden's act was not only a forward-looking, persuasive form of address, but a successful one at it, for the US Congress was forced to reconsider the Patriot Act and to revise some of its provisions in light of Snowden's revelations.

It could be replied that the previous statement confirms that Snowden's act was coercive with respect to the NSA and the US government at large, as it forced them to answer for their conduct, to reveal details of their own policies and to reconsider those very policies. However, as I will argue in chapters 5 and 6, forcing others to answer for their conduct may not be considered a form of coercion, as there are obligations to answer to members of special groups (e.g., that between a government and its own citizens); in fact, calling the NSA to answer for the breach of civil liberties does, in an important way to be explored in the final chapter, respect NSA members as autonomous agents. For this reason, Snowden's whistleblowing should not be considered a form of 'coercion'.

The most troubling aspect in treating Snowden as a civil disobedient concerns the requirement of accepting the legal consequences of one's act of disobedience. There are three ways to interpret Snowden's conduct in light of this requirement. First, we may claim that he was unwilling to accept the punishment, since he escaped arrest and went into hiding. From this perspective, we may conclude, with Delmas (2016b), that Snowden did not engage in civil disobedience, and rather performed some other form of (allegedly justifiable) law breaking. Second, we may adopt Scheuerman's view. Scheuerman contends that, although (at least in Rawls's account) the willingness to accept punishment is considered a sign of 'fidelity to law',

> a person who accepts the legitimacy of criminal proceedings which are secret, irregular, arbitrary, or unduly brutal does not, in fact, necessarily uphold legality. On the contrary, by participating in them she risks becoming complicit in the regime's attack on the rule of law. Precisely such attacks, as Snowden astutely grasped, are what politically motivated conscientious disobedients have to avoid if they are to demonstrate their very 'highest respect for the law'. (2014, 963)

Despite escaping the legal consequences of his conduct by going into hiding, Snowden did show 'fidelity to the law'. His refusal to submit to criminal proceedings that may well have been irregular or arbitrary, if not purely brutal, was a refusal to be complicit in the regime's alleged attack on the rule of law. For this reason, argues Scheuerman, Snowden's action should be considered a form of civil disobedience nonetheless.

A third way to assess whether Snowden can be considered a civil disobedient involves Brownlee's 'non-evasion' condition discussed earlier. According to Brownlee, civil disobedience, as a form of conscientious communication, requires a willingness to 'bear the risks of honouring our conviction, which means that we do not seek to evade the consequences for reasons of self-protection, and, in some cases, take positive action when appropriate to support our conviction' (2012, 37).[36] Brownlee argues that Snowden satisfied this condition, for

> after he succeeded in passing documents to reporters, he exposed his identity. Both through his disclosures and through his self-exposure, he showed that he was willing to bear the risk of being punished as well as to endure the substantial losses of his citizenship rights and residence rights in the USA. (2016, 967)

It may be objected that Snowden went into hiding and later applied for asylum in various foreign countries, eventually settling in Russia. Hence, contrary to what Brownlee argues, he did indeed escape prosecution 'for reasons of self-protection'; that is, to avoid the disproportionate punishment the US would have inflicted upon him. Snowden later explained he did not want to face the undoubtedly severe sanction the US would have imposed on him, for he did not want to be used as 'a bad example' to deter other would-be whistleblowers who see something happening and think they need to say something about it (Delmas, ibid.). However, I would argue that 'non-evasion' is not to be conceived exclusively in *legal* terms, as risking to face a legal sanction, for it would be hypocritical to discount the facts that Snowden (1) was aware of the broader consequences of his choice to blow the whistle of the NSA would have had on his own, private life and (2) accepted these consequences as part of the price of honouring his convictions. Snowden has not been able to return to the USA since 2013, and he lives in a secret location in Russia, under extremely uncertain conditions, as he is at the mercy of the Russian, and the American, governments. Hence, while he perhaps did escape the legal consequences for reasons of self-protection, he should not be treated as a free rider, a coward, or a 'narcissist'.[37] In this sense, his action appears to satisfy also the 'non-evasion' condition: it should therefore be conceived as conscientious, communicative and a forward-looking breach of the law; that is to say, as *civil* disobedience.

2.6 ISSUES OF JUSTIFIABILITY

The above discussion aimed to draw the contours of civil disobedience by providing criteria distinguishing civil from uncivil forms of illegal protest. To sum up, the account sketched above centres around a conception of civility as a disposition to respect fellow citizens as autonomous agents. This disposition guides the choice to resort to a constrained act of protest; an uncivil act of disobedience, on the other hand, does not abide by the constraints posed by others' autonomy. A civil act of disobedience seeks to persuade others of the necessity of reconsidering a certain law, policy or governmental practice; an uncivil act of disobedience may often coerce others into yielding to the protesters' request. Civil disobedience aims for cooperation with the rest of society; uncivil disobedience, on the other hand, often stems from distrust in the government and in future cooperation with it.

Rawls also outlined circumstances in which the resort to civil disobedience may not be justified. For example, there is a general presumption, mentioned already in the previous section on Edward Snowden, that the resort to illegal protest must be a 'last resort'; citizens may engage in civil disobedience only after

> the legal means of redress have proved of no avail. Thus, for example, the existing political parties have shown themselves indifferent to the claims of the minority or have proved unwilling to accommodate them. Attempts to have the laws repealed have been ignored and legal protests and demonstrations have had no success. (Rawls 1999, 327)

Rawls acknowledges that 'this condition is, however, a presumption', since legal channels are never, strictly speaking, exhausted ('free speech is always possible', ibid.); we could always write yet another letter to our MPs, organise yet another event, distribute yet another round of leaflets and more. Furthermore, some cases might be 'so extreme that there may be no duty to use first only legal means for political opposition' (ibid.). This 'last resort' condition, therefore, may be better interpreted as requiring the would-be civil disobedients to give due consideration to the context in which they are acting. It places the onus on them to assess whether the specific circumstances warrant the decision to disobey the law. I would argue that resorting to law breaking in cases where, for example, legal alternatives may still be expected to succeed would display a fault in the agent's character; rather than constituting a case of unjustified civil disobedience, in my view this conduct would fall short of the requirements of civility – that is, it would not be *civil* disobedience.

The *last resort* requirement highlights that the choice to engage in civil disobedience hinges partly on the seriousness of the injustice: the wrong targeted by the protest should be serious enough to warrant escalating to illegal measures. Citizens may not engage in law-breaking protest any time, for frivolous or non-urgent causes; civil disobedience should aim at a significant wrong. Rawls, once again, set out very strict criteria for the conditions warranting the resort to civil disobedience: his argument focuses on his two principles of justice:

1. *Principle of Equal Liberty*: Each person has an equal right to the most extensive liberties compatible with similar liberties for all.
2. *Difference Principle*: Social and economic inequalities should be arranged so that they are both (a) to the greatest benefit of the least advantaged persons, and (b) attached to offices and positions open to all under conditions of equality of opportunity. (1999, 266)

Rawls deemed civil disobedience justifiable only in response to serious infringements of the first principle, and to 'blatant violations' of part (b) of the difference principle (326). In his view, violations of the first principle constitute obvious injustices; for example, the denial of a minority's right to vote, to hold office or to practice its religion. In such circumstances, the resort to civil disobedience would draw attention to a serious departure from society's commitment to equal liberty; in Rawls's words, the principle of equal liberty 'lies at the basis of the political order. When it is fully honoured, the presumption is that other injustices, while possibly persistent and significant, will not get out of hand' (327).[38] Things are less clear, according to Rawls, when it comes to violations of the difference principle. This is because while, in the previous case, the violations are deemed 'obvious', with the difference principle there is 'usually a wide range of conflicting yet rational opinion as to whether this principle is satisfied' (ibid.). Judging whether a certain law or policy is in breach of the difference principle involves complex analyses, comprising statistical data and other information, 'all of this seasoned with shrewd judgment and plain hunch' (ibid.). For this reason, Rawls believes that engaging in civil disobedience against, say, a perceived unjust taxation policy should be avoided, for the appeal to the shared conception of justice would not be sufficiently clear. The latter might be the wrong cause to illegally protest, due to the probability of reasonable disagreement rather than of a clear injustice.

Let us return then to the case Rawls deems less controversial, that of civil disobedience against 'obvious' injustices; namely, violations of his *principle of equal liberty*. Two immediate problems with Rawls's account of justifiable civil disobedience seem evident. First, Rawls is too optimistic as to how 'obvious' violations of this principle may be. Peter Singer (1991) has considered the use of hallucinogenic drugs by some 'religious groups' in the USA as part of their rituals, and asked whether a ban on these rituals would constitute an 'obvious' violation of the principle of equal liberty (i.e., an infringement on freedom of religion). Singer also questions Rawls's assumption that civil disobedience should be based on an appeal to the society's 'shared conception of justice', but not on personal morality or religious doctrine. In later works, Rawls explored in great detail the problem of pluralism and disagreement, arguing that we could not expect citizens to agree on nonpolitical issues, for each individual should be able to choose and pursue her own conception of 'the good'. As we will see in the next chapter, Rawls worried that appealing to private rather than public reasons in the political arena, especially through illegal measures, could pose a serious threat to the liberal commitment to neutrality; hence, he postulated the existence of a 'shared' conception of justice, one which, in his view, all members could reasonably accept. This view has been the object of intense scrutiny in political philosophy, and this is not the place to engage with that body of literature. It suffices to say that a theory of civil disobedience based on these premises appears unnecessarily restrictive, and inadequate to account for the communicative nature of this kind of protest. For we cannot ignore that civil disobedience is a valuable deliberative instrument in cases where people *disagree* as to whether a certain law or policy conflicts with the underlying values of the political community. A libertarian and a communitarian, a progressive and a conservative, will defend different conceptions of justice, and hence will inevitably disagree, for example, over whether a certain taxation policy is 'just' or 'unjust'. Rawls's account overly simplifies the reality of civil disobedience by granting it legitimacy only in cases of 'blatant' violations of basic equality, while overlooking the fact that, as we will see in more detail in the next chapter, it can constitute an important instrument to allow some groups within society, usually a minority, to communicate their disagreement.

In criticising Rawls's over-reliance on a shared conception of justice, I am not gesturing towards some form of relativism or moral nihilism. In fact, as I argue in the last chapter, I endorse Rawls's claim that democratic societies are indeed built around a core set of values centred round the equal dignity of citizens as autonomous agents; yet, as already mentioned, the disagreement hinges on whether the laws or policies these societies implement are compatible with this commitment to individual autonomy. On this point, I should stress two central elements of my conception of civil disobedience, which will receive further attention in chapters 5 and 6. First, the civility of this form of protest does not require that the protesters be necessarily right, for the primary goal of civil disobedience is communication, not legislative change. Even if the protesters' claim was rejected – that is *even if they turned out to be wrong* about the alleged incompatibility between a certain law or policy and the underlying values of the liberal community – their act may not lose its *civil* nature. That is to say, even if they mistakenly saw a 'blatant violation' of the values underlying their political community, they may still justifiably engage in civil disobedience; that is, in a forward-looking communicative act. Second, this does not mean that everything is up for grabs: I will argue that some instances of illegal protest in support of *unreasonable* causes, such as racism, do not qualify as instances of civil disobedience, for they fail to display a *civil* attitude in the agent resorting to them.

2.7 STATIC VERSUS DYNAMIC CONCEPTIONS OF JUSTICE

The above remarks highlight one last problem with Rawls's account; namely, its reliance on a *static* conception of justice. For Rawls, once we have 'discovered' the basic principles of a just society, we then proceed to model our institutions upon them; this gives us a clear benchmark of what may constitute an injustice. After the constitution has been ratified, the society's conception of justice is institutionalised once and for all. From this standpoint, civil disobedience is justifiable only to *defend* the existing conception of justice from violations. However, this presupposes that said conception is self-evident; in Rawls's account of justifiable civil disobedience, there is no room for issues of legal interpretation. Writing shortly after Rawls, Ronald Dworkin addressed this very point in his account of civil disobedience. Starting from the claim that it is 'much disputed, *of course*, what *particular* rights citizens have', Dworkin highlights that it is not necessarily the case that the government's view (on what is 'right' or 'wrong') is correct; otherwise it would follow 'that men and women have only such moral rights as Government chooses to grant, which means that they have no moral rights at all' (Dworkin 2013, 224). Furthermore, even where the constitutions protects citizens' basic rights, it may not be the case that it encompasses *all* moral rights; that is to say, there may be rights that are not (yet) protected by the Constitution. The Constitution can and does change (Dworkin mentions the case of constitutional amendments to 'remove' rights, like the right against self-incrimination). There can be no point in time where we could say that *all* fundamental rights have been established and are protected, because the very meaning and range of rights develops over time. On this point, Cohen and Arato write that

> because law is in a constant process of adaptation and revision, civil disobedience may be the pacesetter for long overdue corrections or innovation without which a vital republic could not maintain its citizens' belief in the continued legitimacy of laws inherited from the past. (Cohen and Arato 1992, 579)

From Dworkin's perspective, the role of political action goes beyond the mere defence of a settled conception of justice, and involves also questions about what principles and norms should be legislated into law. This perspective differs from the Rawlsian one, for it advances a dynamic understanding of the role of civil disobedience as a conduct aiming to create and revisit rights.

However, Dworkin's own account of justifiable civil disobedience, like the one from Rawls, seems exclusively concerned with *rights*, and in this way it appears to bear some counterintuitive results. Dworkin distinguishes three different forms of civil disobedience: *integrity* based, in which citizens object to a law they deem incompatible with the demands of their conscience – for example, pacifists vis-à-vis compulsory military conscription; *justice* based, in which the law's demands conflict with one's own *rights* – for example, an unwarranted limitation of free speech; and *policy* based, in which citizens object to a specific policy on grounds that it is unwise or will not bring about good consequences (Dworkin 1985, 107–9). In policy-based disobedience, citizens disobey a law not because they think it unjust, but because they see it as mistaken, dangerous or wrong in some other way. According to Dworkin, this kind of civil disobedience (as opposed to integrity- and justice-based ones) is not justifiable, for it amounts to a sort of 'civil blackmail' (112). Discussing the case of anti-nuclear protest, he claims that, if we were to analyse this policy-based disobedience closely,

> we would find that most – not all but most – did not believe that their government's decision to accept missiles was the act of a majority seeking its own interests in violation of the rights of a minority or of another nation. They thought, rather, that the majority had made a tragically wrong choice from the common standpoint, from the standpoint of its own interests as much as those of anyone else. (Dworkin 1985, 107)

Dworkin's view echoes Rawls's who, as we saw above, was sceptical of disobedience against anything short of an obvious violation of justice. Dworkin believes that resorting to illegal protest against the deployment of nuclear weapons amounts to a form of *coercion*; that is, a way to make it more costly, for the government, to pursue that policy, to the point the majority would have to yield to the protesters' objection. However (and this is where his conception of justifiable civil disobedience seems to overlap with Rawls's), Dworkin contends that it is

> not obvious, one way or the other, whether deployment of missiles in Europe is more likely to deter or provoke aggression, for example, or even what kind of an argument would be a good argument for either view. It is hard to see in these circumstances how discussion could be illuminated or debate strengthened by illegal acts. (ibid., 112)

Where rights are not at stake, Dworkin contends, illegal protest loses its persuasive nature and, therefore, cannot be deemed justifiable.[39] Yet as in the case of Rawls's approach, we can see how this excessive *formalism* imposes undue restrictions on the possibilities to engage in civil disobedience. It may be argued, for example, that those who protest against nuclear proliferation are indeed concerned with human rights; that is, with the impact nuclear weapons would have on people's lives, well-being and survival. This seems to be an accurate interpretation of the claim that a policy of nuclear deployment is 'dangerous'. Having said that, there may be room for an account of justifiable civil disobedience that goes beyond Rawls's and Dworkin's exclusive focus on *rights*.

As Peter Singer noticed, under the Rawlsian model we may have to accept animal cruelty as not breaching the 'basic principles' of a just society (1991). One could object to animal cruelty based on one's own morality; yet, as we saw above, this would not be a legitimate ground for civil disobedience under Rawls's or Dworkin's view, since both require a focus on a violation of rights. In fact, from the latter's standpoint, *environmental* civil disobedience may never by justified, due to its unclear focus on basic rights (at least under Rawls's restricted conception of them) or because of its targeting policies that are unwise and/or dangerous. Similarly, Eugene Schlossberger (1989) discusses the possibility of engaging in civil disobedience against a council's or a government's decision to raze historical buildings; although it does not target a violation of fundamental rights, this protest would strike as certainly legitimate. Thus, in addition to 'obvious violations' of basic rights, civil disobedience seems appropriate also to other cases, involving a concern with preserving natural habitats, historical artefacts and works of art; furthermore, civil disobedience may be justifiable as part of the attempt to redress power imbalances in the democratic arena, rather than to amend a specific law deemed unjust. That is to say, citizens may resort to this form of communicative, forward-looking breach of the law in order to draw attention to the process through which that law is arrived at. Civil disobedience may be justified as part of the attempt to promote the *democratic* procedure; that is, it may be justified on *procedural* rather than on *substantive* grounds. This will be the topic of the next chapter.

Chapter Three

Disagreement and Civility

We saw earlier that Rawls's theory of justice (and of civil disobedience) hinges on the existence of a 'shared conception of justice'; for Rawls, rational agents are able to identify a shared set of basic liberties by operating from behind 'a veil of ignorance' (Rawls 1999, 118–23). Through this thought experiment, according to Rawls, citizens would arrive at a conception of justice as fairness, built on the two principles he identifies. Notwithstanding the irreconcilable differences amongst their own 'comprehensive doctrines' – that is, their conceptions of the good life – citizens would be able, according to Rawls, to accept this conception of justice as defining 'the basic structure' of society: they could reach an agreement on 'the political' (Rawls 1993, 55).[1] Rawls famously believes that a political conception can be advanced as a freestanding view, one that is defended 'apart from, or without reference to' (12), any substantively wider background. Since the same political doctrine can be endorsed by different comprehensive views, it is possible to expect that individuals will reach some agreement about the political conception to be adopted. However, this will not be the case when it comes to comprehensive general views, which aim to be valid for everyone, seeking to encompass also non-political aspects of the life of the individual (13). Many religious views seek to be comprehensive in this sense: they are not political but rather advance complete moral theories, about which, according to Rawls, we cannot expect to achieve an overarching agreement. This does not endanger the possibility of peaceful and stable communal life, because 'a constitutional regime does not require an agreement on a comprehensive doctrine: the basis of its social unity lies elsewhere' (63).

Rawls is concerned with problems of *legitimacy*, a term directly related to the notion of autonomy. As we saw in the previous chapter, autonomy refers to the idea of self-legislation: an autonomous person has a right to give direction to her own life (by choosing values, ideals and projects) without undue interferences from others. Nonetheless, it is a fact of our political life that, as individuals, we have to defer to the collective will even when we disagree with the electoral outcome and have to restrain our choices in accordance with the directives of the law. Yet this exercise of power by others on our life must be justifiable to us; that is, it must be shown to be *legitimate.* As self-legislators, we have a right to demand a justification as to why we should not take these decisions as a mere imposition of others' will upon our own. The exercise of coercive power on an autonomous agent is legitimate only if it is morally permissible or morally justifiable (Mason 2012, 151).[2] Thus, the idea of legitimacy rests on *reason giving*: what makes a political authority moral or acceptable is its commitment to providing reasons for its decisions that are understood and recognised as sound by those who are to submit to that authority (Humphrey 2006).[3]

Thus, Rawls contends, 'Our exercise of political power is proper and hence justifiable only when it is exercised in accordance with a constitution the essentials of which all citizens may reasonably be expected to endorse in the light of principles and ideals acceptable to them as reasonable and rational' (1993, 137). This implies that we should defend our views, in the public arena, by appealing only to public reasons; that is, reasons that others could reasonably accept. Since, according to Rawls's view, people will not agree on 'comprehensive' views, it follows that disagreement in the public arena should be solved by focusing on 'political, not metaphysical' claims. Rawls states this is a '*duty* of civility'; that is, a *moral* duty for citizens to not justify their political decisions on fundamental issues by appeal to partisan values or controversial standards which cannot be publicly redeemed (Weinar 2017). This requirement hinges on the importance of respecting others as *equals*; that is, as autonomous agents able to choose and pursue their conception of the good. It would be *uncivil* to justify our view to others by appealing to our own, personal values (our 'comprehensive doctrine'): the liberal commitment to individual autonomy gives rise to a duty to respect individuals' different claims to the comprehensiveness of their views by framing our argument in *public* reasons, which for Rawls represent 'the right kind' of reasons to address a disagreement.[4] The implications of this view are visible, for example, in the account of Charles Larmore (1987):

> When two people disagree about some specific point, but wish to continue talking about the more general problem they wish to solve, each should prescind from the beliefs that the other rejects, (1) in order to construct an argument on the basis of his other beliefs that will convince the other of the truth of the disputed belief, or (2) in order to shift to another aspect of the problem, where the possibilities of agreement seem greater. In the face of disagreement, those who wish to continue the conversation *should retreat to neutral ground,*

> with the hope either of resolving the dispute or of bypassing it. (ibid., 53, added emphasis)

From this standpoint, citizens must be willing to avoid debating the issues upon which disagreement may be expected to persist; they should focus only on arguments others could reasonably accept. This is the behaviour that shows *respect* for fellow citizens as autonomous agents: given the incommensurability of conflicting comprehensive views, we *avoid* arguing over what cannot be agreed upon.

> A commitment to treating others with equal respect forms the ultimate reason why in the face of disagreement we should keep the conversation going, and to do that, of course, we must retreat to neutral ground. (67)[5]

In his deliberative account of civil disobedience, William Smith (2013) has interpreted Rawls's duty of civility more broadly than liberals like Larmore. For Smith, the duty of civility proscribes appealing to 'unreasonable' views, which he describes as those not resting 'on empirical premises that are not open to challenge or are clearly incompatible with reliable methods of inquiry' (20). For example, one should not defend one's own view in the public arena by appealing directly to the Bible, or to other religious texts. This is because those who do not adhere to that religion may not accept the premise on which the argument is based. Smith also describes racism as incompatible with his duty of civility – a point I also defend in chapter 5. In this sense, Smith's account of the duty of civility is less strong (and more plausible) than Rawls's, which forbids appeals to one's own comprehensive doctrines *tout court*, not on the ground that they are morally unreasonable (as with racism), but on the ground that they are (in Rawls's view) incommensurable.

This is not the place to provide an exhaustive analysis of Rawls's theory. Suffice to say that, as many have argued, the claim that our duty of civility – that is, our duty to *respect* others as autonomous agents, as self-legislators, requires 'avoiding the disagreement' altogether – generates odd results, as David Archard highlights in the following passage:

> I must prescind from what divides me from my opponent . . . I must appeal only to reasons that are within the domain of public reason. I must, as my opponent, be publicly reasonable. [However], this requires that we show mutual *disrespect* to one another. . . . The reasons that are mine for believing that abortion should be legalised, as with my opponent's for believing the contrary, are ones we have, respectively, conscientiously and openly come to embrace. They are ones we could honestly and sincerely affirm to each other. They are authentically ours. Yet we cannot display them to one another. (Archard 2001, 220)

A willingness to engage in a dialogue with others is always respectful. We tend to avoid discussing with people we disrespect, or dislike, or simply whom we think may not be able to engage properly with our views. Imagine a person who spends Christmas dinner with her racist relatives. Her choice to avoid talking politics with them would hardly display *respect* for their legitimate, though unacceptable, ideas; rather, it would stem from the belief that they would not be able to accept anything that goes against their media-fuelled racism. By the same token, our reluctance to talk about environmental issues to a convinced climate-change denier is not born out of respect for her different view, but rather out of frustration about her incapacity to engage with empirical evidence of global warming. The avoidance of substantive differences between the speaker and the hearer may signal that the former does not see the latter as fully rational: the speaker might deem the hearer unable to engage in a forward-looking conversation aiming for mutual persuasion.[6] In such 'restrained' exchange, the speaker may not see the hearer as an equal, as a 'subject' whose rational capacities enable her to enter a dialogue. Rather, the speaker treats the hearer as an 'object', adopting an 'objective' attitude towards her:

> We look with an objective eye on the compulsive behaviour of the neurotic or the tiresome behaviour of the very young child, thinking in terms of treatment or training. But we can sometimes look with something like the same eye on the behaviour of the normal and the mature. We have this resource and can sometimes use it: as a refuge, say, from the strains of involvement; or as an aid to policy; or simply out of intellectual curiosity. Being human, we cannot, in the normal case, do this for long, or altogether. (Strawson 2008, 10)

We treat those who are unable, or unwilling, to engage with our differing opinions, akin to how we treat children or mentally ill individuals. Far from acknowledging them as equals, we embrace the fact that, in a relevant sense, they are not like us: they cannot respond to reasons appropriately; for example, due to immaturity, illness, or even prejudices. If we are to treat them with respect, on the other hand, then we should strive to ensure they understand our reasons to hold an opinion that is different from their own, hoping they will engage with us in further discussion.[7] Respecting others in the democratic arena calls for sincerity and willingness to face the disagreement, rather than restraint and avoidance of conflict. This is something we owe them *as* autonomous agents. The next step involves considering in more detail how such respect should be displayed in the political arena.

3.1 THE DELIBERATIVE APPROACH OF DISCOURSE ETHICS

Let us return to the notion of an 'objective attitude'; that is, the disposition with which we approach people (like young children) we deem not fully able to engage with us as 'subjects'. An objective attitude questions the possibility of a successful interaction with the other party, and withdraws to a one-directional relation whereby the subject treats the other as an object; that is, as one with whom it is not possible to engage on an equal level. In his seminal work on the ethics of discourse, Jürgen Habermas has sought to emphasise, against this objective attitude, 'the intersubjective relation that speaking and acting subjects take up when they come to an understanding with one another about something' (Habermas 1987, 392). From these premises, Habermas's approach to the issue of agreement points in a different direction, claiming that

> coming to an understanding is not an empirical event that causes de facto agreement; it is a process of mutually convincing one another in which the actions of participants are coordinated on the basis of motivation by reason. 'Coming to an understanding' refers to communication aimed at achieving a valid agreement. (ibid.)

Habermas shares with Rawls the search for norms all participants could agree to in a rational discussion (McCarthy 1994, 45). However, he contends that the validity of a norm is not defined by the individual acting alone 'from behind a veil of ignorance'; rather, a valid norm has to undergo examination through a rational discourse involving all the moral subjects the norm could affect. Against the concept of an isolated moral consciousness, able to reach universally valid norms through solitary reflection (from behind 'a veil of ignorance'), Habermas defends the idea of a rational agreement amongst those who may be subject to the particular norm. It is on these premises that he formulates his Principle of Universalization,[8] from which he then derives the Principle of Discourse that grounds his discursive test: 'Every valid norm would meet with the approval of all concerned if they could take part in a practical discourse' (1990, 121).

It is true for Habermas, as it is for Rawls, that a norm is valid only if grounded on shared convictions; yet in Habermas's view, the shared convictions are arrived at collectively, through a process of mutual confrontation. Like Rawls, Habermas claims that for a norm to be valid, it has to be reasonably accepted by the subjects; yet the latter cannot be achieved without a process of reason giving between the various parties in the discourse. The practice of reason giving invokes the notion of a dialogue between the speaker and the audience in ways that are both fair and inclusive: from the deliberative account of democracy, this is taken as crucial to the legitimacy of political institutions. This notion of reason giving has been central to most accounts of deliberative democracy, who have sought to identify 'the conditions under which political decisions should be considered legitimate expressions of the collective will of the people' (Hauptmann 1999, 858). For example, Joshua Cohen contends that the principle of deliberative inclusion 'bridges the gap between "reasonable pluralism" and legitimate collective decisions' (ibid., 868). Goodin and Niemeyer (2003, 627) have stressed that deliberation is 'absolutely essential to democratic legitimation'. James Fishkin claims that deliberation aims 'to include everyone under conditions where they are effectively motivated to really think about the issues' (Fishkin 2009, 1). Gutmann and Thompson (1996) hold that deliberation has the capacity to render non-unanimous decisions legitimate. This deliberative approach to democracy is intrinsically interactive, and relies on the idea of a mutually persuasive exchange between the disagreeing parties.

The objective attitude ignores this dimension of human interaction, for it treats the other as an object to use or manipulate for a certain end, regardless of her own goals. Habermas, on the other hand, seeks to emphasise the interpersonal dimension of morality, and hence focuses on the role language plays in human interactions; to this end, he offers an analysis of the conditions for uncoerced and undistorted interaction amongst competent language users. Habermas's distinction between *strategic* and *communicative* action, and his claim that the latter is the original mode of language use, constitutes the core of his ethics of discourse (O'Neill 1997, 112). The terms *strategic* and *communicative* are meant to highlight two kinds of speaker's attitudes within a discussion; this distinction can help us address the problem of disagreement by appealing to the speaker's willingness to cooperate in the discourse.

In cases of strategic action, 'the agent seeks to *influence* the behaviour of the hearer by means of the threat of sanctions or the prospect of gratification in order to *cause* the interaction to continue as the first actor desires' (Habermas 1990, 58). In such situation, the agreement is merely a de facto one, for it is imposed upon, rather than accepted by, the hearer. In strategic action, the speaker aims to *use* the hearer to the achievement of her own goal: she may, for example, seek to convince a person to act in a certain way by appealing to that person's fears or desires: standard cases of coercion represent instances of strategic action. The speaker's objective attitude disregards the hearer's will: the hearer might 'cooperate' with the speaker – for example, by accepting the validity of the speaker's utterance – out of self-interest or of fear, rather than because she finds the speaker's goal inherently worthy. This form of action fails to fulfil a Kantian requirement to treat others 'as ends in themselves' which, as we will see in more detail in chapter 4, is at the core of the attitude of civility defended in this book.

In communicative action, on the other hand, agents relinquish the objective attitude in favour of a performative one, which involves a willingness to cooperate to achieve a goal (joint or individual) based on a shared acknowledgement that the goal is reasonable. While, in the strategic case, the agents succeed to the extent they achieve their individual goals, a successful communicative action is characterised by the actors' free and uncoerced agreement that their goal(s) are worthy of cooperation.[9] This approach avoids the objective attitude, which merely uses others as instruments to one's own ends, and rather aims for the other party's uncoerced endorsement. This is what an 'agreement' really looks like, in Habermas's view:

> An agreement cannot be imposed or brought about by manipulating one's partner in interaction, for something that *patently* owes its existence to *external* pressure cannot even be considered an agreement. (1990, 134)

The speakers approach each other with a performative attitude when they engage in what Habermas calls 'ideal role taking'.[10] In order to assume an impartial point of view for argumentation, any subject participating in the discourse is required to put herself in the position of all those who would be affected if a controversial norm were to be adopted.[11] For Habermas, ideal role taking is achieved during communicative action: by putting oneself in the position of the other person, one also can get a better grasp of her own view (Goodin 2000). The process of understanding is reciprocal, so that each participant approaches the deliberative arena with a willingness to identify with the claims of the interlocutors in the pursuit of a rational agreement.

Contrary to Rawlsian liberalism, the deliberative approach contends that disagreements should not be addressed from the perspective of a separated individual who has retreated to 'neutral grounds'; rather, the interaction required to address the disagreement involves and requires subjects to bring their own specific perspectives on the world into the deliberative arena.

> Communicative action can be understood as a circular process in which the actor is two things in one: an *initiator* who masters situations through actions for which he is accountable and a *product* of the traditions surrounding him, of groups whose cohesion is based on solidarity to which he belongs, and of processes of socialization in which he is reared. (ibid., 135)

Participants in communicative action are then 'supported from behind . . . by a lifeworld that not only forms the *context* for the process of reaching understanding but also furnishes *resources* for it' (ibid.). For communicative action to succeed, subjects enter the deliberative arena supported by a background of values, both cultural and linguistic, which reflect their own cognitive horizon. The Rawlsian liberal standpoint, on the other hand, asks citizens to leave their 'comprehensive doctrines' by the door before entering the deliberative arena: it requires a form of neutrality that rules out appeals to one's own substantive values. For Habermas, communicative action necessarily involves the interaction between what is *peculiar of each participant's own view*. This is not merely instrumentally valuable, in order to enhance the success of the communicative exchange: it is a way to show respect for others as autonomous agents. The deliberative approach suggests that we respect others as autonomous agents not by avoiding our differences, but by focusing on the possibility of persuading and being persuaded by others through a rational dialogue. It relies on the same forward-looking attitude that is central to civil disobedience.

3.2 LIBERAL VERSUS DEMOCRATIC DISOBEDIENCE

We saw in the previous chapter that, according to liberals like Rawls and Dworkin, civil disobedience is justifiable only in cases where a law or policy seriously infringes on basic rights. For example, a ban on certain religious practices, the arbitrary disenfranchisement of some citizens, or forms of race-based discrimination, would be legitimate targets of a campaign of civil disobedience, given their 'obvious' injustice; on the other hand, opposition to a government's decision deemed unwise, dangerous or wrong yet not necessarily unjust would not warrant the resort to civil disobedience. The latter cases would not focus on 'obvious' violations of citizens' rights. Given the emphasis on the protection of basic liberties, the Rawls/Dworkin approach is usually referred to as *the liberal view* on civil disobedience; it portrays the latter as a defensive practice against the risk of a government abusing its authority (Cohen and Arato 1992, 574). Citizens may resort to law-breaking protest in order to prevent a democratic government from crossing certain limits; when a law or policy threatens basic liberties, citizens may justifiably resist through illegal protest.

As already noticed, this approach is unduly restrictive. It rules out cases of civil disobedience that seem legitimate despite not focusing on violations of basic liberties. We already mentioned environmental protest, in which the rights of human beings may not be the main object of concern; similar considerations can be made in regards to illegal protest against nuclear proliferation (*pace* Dworkin), or to protect archaeological sites. The No-Globalization movement does not target any specific violation of human rights, nor calls for a particular legislative change; rather, it denounces structural injustices; for example, the fact that the richest countries' leaders meet behind closed doors to make crucial decisions about the world economy, without anyone else's input apart from members of their very exclusive club. This movement targets the exclusion, from the decision-making process, of people who have a stake in those very decisions: its aim is to expand the democratic process (by calling for the inclusion of other members) rather than to *limit* it (by preventing the majority from implementing a certain law).[12] To return to a distinction discussed above, civil disobedience may communicate a concern with *procedural* rather than *substantive* issues.

Daniel Markovits has provided the starting point for this kind of discussion, by advancing a 'democratic' conception of civil disobedience (Markovits 2005). He criticises the liberal account of democratic legitimacy, which identifies political authority in the application of the principle of liberal equality: for liberals like Rawls and Dworkin, a democratic decision must treat all members of the community with equal concern. In this way, however, the liberal approach can at best provide a *democracy-limiting* account of civil disobedience by identifying the limits of political authority; it can then justify disobedience only 'from without democracy'; that is, in response to abuses of democratic power by a government enacting a seriously unjust law. Markovits, on the other hand, advances an account of disobedience 'from within democracy', 'a theory of *democracy-enhancing* disobedience, or, more simply, *democratic* disobedience' (ibid., 1902). It aims to render plausible the counterintuitive claim that disobeying the laws of a democratic state can serve democracy' (ibid.).

This approach to disobedience involves two elements: first, an account of democratic authority that does not depend on notions of equality and justice, nor on the idea of 'public reason', which are central to the liberal account. Rather, for Markovits, democracy is a freestanding political value that arises from its own procedural aspects; what gives legitimacy to democracy's decisions is that they are the product of a democratic procedure that allows for freedom and self-governance. In this way, Markovits advances a republican view, centred on the idea that people are free only insofar as they are governed by laws that they have given themselves (Pettit 2012). Echoing elements from Rousseau's own philosophy, this view contends that citizens of a well-functioning democracy are free because they take authorship of the collective choices that the process generates. Although Markovits admits that Rousseau's account is 'famously obscure and unconvincing', he appears to endorse the latter's distinction between 'the will of all and "the general will"' (Rousseau 1968). This distinction relies on separating a mere majoritarian procedure, which aggregates the separate individual preferences, from an interactive process in which the individual preferences are not simply aggregated, but rather have to withstand scrutiny and reciprocal engagement. Only the latter procedure can give rise to a 'democratic sovereign'; namely, one in which each person 'uniting with all, nevertheless obeys only himself and remains as free as before'. Mere application of majority rule is not sufficient for a genuine democracy, because

> politics implicates, as it inevitably does, not just brute preferences, to which only the modality of satisfaction and frustration applies, but also beliefs and ideals, which may be answered, reasoned with, and so on. (Markovits 2005, 1915)

Markovits shares Habermas's idea of democracy as grounded on rational engagement, rather than on the mere aggregation of individual preferences. Like Habermas's, his view relies on a conception of citizens as subjects with whom to engage, rather than objects with whom it is not possible to reason. However, he is also aware of the necessary imperfections that may hamper democracy's 'engagement-enforcing mechanisms'; under some circumstances, Markovits argues, these mechanisms, designed to promote the democratic exchange, may 'misfire'. He labels those imperfections 'democratic deficits'.

> Democratic political authority . . . has built into the conditions of its possibility the inevitability of occasional democratic deficits, in which the political process no longer sustains individual authorship of the collective policies it produces. (ibid., 1903)

Markovits highlights the fact that democratic decisions sometimes depart from the general will, for the process leading to their creation may not allow for equal consideration of all members of the demos. The democratic deliberation may be hijacked by some members who aim to gain control of the discussion by keeping a certain issue off the deliberative agenda; influential groups within the demos may resort to bargaining and manipulation in order to constrain, rather than promote, engagement among the various political views. In many cases, the sheer need to arrive at a decision may hasten the deliberative process and afford limited space to some members' opinions.[13] As we will see in more detail in the next section, power imbalances within the public sphere may hamper some members' access to the public sphere. Although democracy emphasises the formal equality of citizens, the reality is that, in practice, citizens do not possess equal power to influence the deliberative agenda and discussion. It would be naïve to claim that citizens can equally influence the government: I may have the same voting power as members of the Australian Parliament, but I certainly do not have their same power to influence the government's agenda (through lobbying, bargaining, etc.).

We will return to the issue of power imbalances in the democratic arena later in this chapter. Let us now consider another way in which, according to Markovits, a community may experience democratic deficits affecting the 'authority' of a certain law or policy. Markovits's view centres on the notion of democratic *inertia*; namely, a sovereign's tendency to resist further engagement with a certain issue once a decision has been reached (ibid.,

1923–25). The problem with this inertia is that it can quickly turn into complacency, as Markovits explains via an analogy between the individual and the collective will. Consider the case of a person who is to choose whether to dine at home or at a restaurant (1924). Markovits claims that, upon forming an intention to do the latter, the individual 'excludes' countervailing reasons (in favour of staying at home), and focuses only on the reasons supporting her intention to eat out. Thus, while saving money continues to be a reason for her to choose to eat at home rather than at a restaurant, the intention she has now formed and the corresponding plan she has enacted set this reason aside: she no longer responds to it in the context at hand.[14] Should circumstances change, they may affect the weight of those countervailing reasons, to the point the individual may change her mind and abandon the earlier plan in favour of a new one. This may happen 'in an orderly way and according to cultivated habits or by being jolted out of (the early intention), as happens to us familiarly when we are shocked out of complacency – and come to attend to reasons that [we] had previously excluded' (1925).

While the parallel between the individual diner and the demos may require more effort than he thinks, Markovits highlights, by analogy, that some opinions are permanently left out of the deliberative discussion, due to the inertial mechanisms characterising the democratic process. A long-standing majority may settle on a certain set of policies and values, and regard them as the only elements to be factored into its decisions. However, if political circumstances were to change, other considerations may become more relevant; in this case, those citizens defending the previously marginalised views may manage to bring them back into the political arena by drawing attention to them 'in an orderly way' (ibid.); namely, through legal means aiming to redress imbalances in the deliberation. Should the legal means fail to elicit a reply, due to persistent inertia within the deliberative arena, those citizens might resort to illegal protest in the attempt to 'shock' the sovereign out of its complacency.

> The legally sanctioned means of protest that a political system incorporates are inevitably less able of correcting the full range of democratic deficits that arise in that system than the revisionary habit of persons are of correcting the defect in rationality that arise from time to time. The benefit to the democratic sovereign of the unanticipated and unwelcome shocks associated with disobedient protest tend, therefore, to exceed the benefit to the individual will of being shocked out of its complacency. (1935)

Markovits's view reflects a common argument in favour of civil disobedience, which sees the latter as justifiable in cases where the deliberative process fails to be inclusive. All members of the community should be allowed to contribute to the decision-making process: significant deviations from this ideal of communication may warrant the appeal to extra-legal means of protest, to redress the marginalisation of some participants' views.

However, William Smith has recently pointed out the problematic nature of Markovits's account of sovereignty, based on the 'ambitious, but fraught, republican aim of reconciling individual and collective autonomy' (Smith 2013, 62). We saw above that Markovits endorses the Rousseauian ideal according to which, in a democracy, each person remains *free* despite having to submit to the community's will; that is, the *general* will. The inclusion of every citizen's view into the decision-making process allows for this identification between 'individual' and 'collective' will. In this way, Rousseau can claim that the citizen is always (part of the) *sovereign*, even when the government fails to enact her preferred option. On the other hand, for Markovits this implies that in cases of democratic deficits, a citizen 'may reasonably conclude . . . that the policies in question do not reflect the will of any sovereign to which she belongs, in which case her individual sense of authorship of the collective decision will run out' (1927). That is to say: whenever the citizen is not fully included into the decision-making process, she is not part of the sovereign and, therefore, may claim to be unjustly coerced by her community. When decisions are not sufficiently inclusive, the government may lack legitimate authority over its subjects. Yet there are some obvious problems with this approach. The first concerns whether it is necessary that the individual view be marginalised, or it suffices that the individual feels that her view has been marginalised. As Smith notes,

> The danger is that disobedient citizens who cannot identify with collective decisions will reject outright the democratic credentials of the prevailing majority and claim, in an elitist fashion, an entitlement to speak and act in the name of what they believe to be an 'authentic' sovereign will. This orientation to protest may inspire a response of resentment rather than re-engagement on the part of those citizens who accept or support the prevailing law or policy. (2013, ibid.)

A person may be so convinced that her view deserves more attention from the sovereign that she might take anything short of outright acceptance as a sign of exclusion. As Smith further explains, it may be difficult to separate cases where the 'engaged preferences' of some citizens merely differ from those of the collective will from cases where their preferences depart to a point where these citizens cannot be deemed to also be 'authors' of the law. Even more puzzling is Markovits's view about the *aims* of democratic disobedience. Recall that his argument sought to provide an alternative to the liberal, 'democracy-limiting' account of civil disobedience, which defends the latter as justifiable in cases where a democratically elected government enacts laws that 'obviously' violate basic liberties. For Markovits, liberal disobedience 'seeks to impose a particular policy' or set of policies in line with basic principles of justice and equality; this form of disobedience aims to *constrict* the space of political options by ruling out those that are incompatible with the principles underlying the political community (2005, 1939). On the other hand, the account of democratic disobedience Markovits advances seeks to overcome not *a particular policy*, but *a democratic deficit*, which prevents the sovereign from taking up an issue by excluding 'essential' considerations from the legislative agenda (1940). Democratic disobedience seeks to expand the space of political options. However, Markovits appears to focus exclusively on the procedure, and to ignore outcomes, to the point he writes:

> it is natural (and perhaps preferable) for democratic disobedience to proceed without any positive agenda for replacing a protested policy, and unnatural (and perhaps mistaken) for democratic disobedience to insist on a specific policy outcome. (ibid., 1940)

Markovits seems concerned with cases such as the No-Global or Occupy Wall Street movements (1950–52), which are often accused of lacking a clear agenda and, therefore, a legitimate claim to justification (Pepitone 2011). When protesting against capitalism, it may not be possible to identify one specific law or policy to be changed; rather, the goal is to stress that everyone should benefit from a certain economic arrangement, and that people should not be exploited to the advantage of a restricted, privileged elite. Yet, on the other hand, there is a somewhat paradoxical implication in Markovits's argument: despite what some self-proclaimed champions of free speech may argue, certain views should not be allowed a space in the public arena, as they are not compatible with the underlying values of democracy. We will discuss this point in the next chapter, when considering the alleged right of racists and bigots to engage in civil disobedience to defend their 'ideals'. In fact, even the republican commitment to individual freedom is born of a concern with preserving equality; that is, of preventing some from dominating others' lives (Swan 2012). However, following Markovits, a group of neo-Nazis protesting against the exclusion of white supremacy from the legislative agenda may engage in democratic disobedience to ensure that their view is included in the sovereign will; their protest in favour of racism (and against equality) would *enhance* democracy. And the neo-Nazi may even complain that a process that excludes racism from the 'space of political options' may give rise to decisions lacking legitimate authority. As already mentioned, we will return to the issue of civil disobedience 'for the wrong reason' in the next chapter. Below, I will consider how other authors have tried to defend the idea of democratic disobedience; that is, of illegal protest that may enhance rather than hamper the democratic process. I will return to Habermas, whose account of 'legitimacy' differs from Markovits's. Then I will consider the works of Iris Marion Young and of Archon Fung, whose accounts of social protest rely heavily, though with important differences, on Habermas's view.

3.3 DELIBERATIVE ACCOUNTS OF CIVIL DISOBEDIENCE

Habermas devoted some attention to the topic of civil disobedience, most notably in an article (1985) in which he commented, like Dworkin had done the same year (Dworkin 1985), on anti-nuclear protests. In that article, Habermas defended a bold claim: 'Every constitutional democracy that is sure of itself considers civil disobedience as a normalised – because necessary – component of its political culture' (ibid., 99). We will see shortly what Habermas means by this. It is important to note, from the outset, that he appears to accept Rawls's account of civil disobedience discussed in the previous chapter, including the claim that civil disobedience is appropriate against laws or policies that are 'obviously' unjust.[15] Specifically, Habermas endorses Rawls's following claim:

> The problem of civil disobedience, as I understand it, arises *only for the citizens who recognize the constitution in a more or less just democratic state*. The problem consists in a conflict of duty. At which point is the duty no longer binding which demands conformity to laws mandated by a legislative majority (or to the acts of the executive power supported by it) in the face of the right to defend one's freedom and the duty to resist injustice? This question touches on the meaning and limits of majority rule. (Rawls 1999, 319)

Habermas takes this to imply that a 'mature' democrat cannot dismiss civil disobedience simply in virtue of its illegality: he takes specific aims at what he labels 'the dogma of the loyalists' (101); namely, of those law-and-order enthusiasts who believe that a democracy cannot afford its subjects the right to disobey the law for principled reasons. This 'dogma' claims that those who engage in civil disobedience endanger the tranquillity of the legal order, but doing so, for Habermas, is tantamount to 'taking an axe to democracy' (ibid.). Rather, 'mature' citizens take democracy as making a claim for *legitimacy*; that is, for the *moral* justification of its authority. In a significant overlap with Markovits's republican view just discussed, Habermas contends that democracy requires its citizens to 'recognise the rule of law not out of fear of punishment, but rather out of their own free will' (ibid.). This, in turn, sets some procedural constraints on how the law is to be crafted; that is, through deliberating, voting, and being approved by 'constitutionally sanctioned organs'. Like Markovits, Habermas contends that a democratic regime must be able to justify its authority not merely by reference to *legality* (namely, by claiming that citizens ought to X because X is a law); it can demand obedience from its citizens only insofar as it rests 'on principles worthy of recognition, in light of which that which is legal can be justified as *legitimate* – and, if necessary, can be rejected as illegitimate'. (102). Habermas, therefore, places himself in stark contrast with legal positivism, by claiming that a democratic state can only demand a 'qualified' (rather than unconditional) obedience from its subjects, for it does not derive legitimacy from 'sheer legality'. Like Rawls, Habermas focuses on a core of inviolable and inalienable human rights that enjoys 'supra-legal' validity; however, legality and legitimacy may often be in tension with each other, and the former may at times threaten the latter, as happened under Nazi Germany.

Habermas locates the role and justification of civil disobedience at the intersection of legality and legitimacy, as the product of

> a political culture that provides its citizens with the sensibility – with the measure of judgment and willingness to take risks – which is necessary in transitional and exceptional situations to recognise the legal offenses against legitimacy and, if need be, to act illegally out of moral insight. (103)

This highlights the demandingness of civil disobedience, for the choice to engage in a law-breaking protest cannot be taken lightly. The agent must scrutinise very carefully whether the circumstances in which she finds herself warrant the recourse to extra-legal measures, or rather whether she is falling prey to 'an elitist attitude or a narcissistic impulse' (105) by trying to impose her own view over that of the political community as a group. Note we have already considered this aspect in the previous chapter, when highlighting that *it is part of the citizens' civility* that she be able to assess whether the specific circumstances warrant the resort to illegal means of communication. At the same time, Habermas claims that the state is also under an obligation to see to it that the civil disobedients are not treated like common law breakers, *even in cases where they might be wrong about the presence of an injustice* (112). Habermas argues that the state should prosecute citizens who engage in civil disobedience; however, it should apply leniency when sentencing them. What is crucial is that the state 'let it be known that civil disobedience is not just another common crime', because a democratic constitutional order is not reducible to its legal order (106). As already noticed, for Habermas civil disobedience hinges on legitimacy rather than on legality, and for this reason it claims a 'dignity' that common crimes lack. The judges must respect this dignity lest they succumb to a form of 'authoritarian legalism', which identifies democracy with legality rather than with legitimacy.

Let us pause for a moment here, and assess Habermas's account in light of other authors discussed earlier. As already mentioned, Habermas's view overlaps with Markovits's insofar as they both believe that the individual must play an active role in the law-making process, lest the law lack legitimacy upon her. Markovits, however, appears to open the floodgate to *any* political cause, for he claims that a truly 'democratic' protest should not advance any particular agenda, and rather focus on removing the inevitable deficits that may affect the deliberative process. This is a troubling element of his view, for it leads to approaching neo-Nazi campaigners as 'true' democrats. Habermas, on the other hand, stresses that the appeal to morality from which civil disobedience stems must be 'reasonable for all':

> Only those moral principles are authoritative which are reasonable for all and upon which the modern constitutional state grounds the expectation of voluntary recognition by its citizens. (103)

Like Rawls, Habermas defends the existence of a core set of substantive values to which civil disobedience should appeal; however, Habermas does not endorse Rawls's static conception of rights and, like Dworkin, believes that the realisation of constitutional principles that can be deemed universally valid is part of a long process of trial and error. The constitution is not a 'finished product', but rather is the result of a legitimate legal order under constantly changing circumstances. The definition of such order is always *in fieri*; hence, imperfect and subject to changes. This is evidenced by the multitude of mechanisms for self-correction built into the constitutional order – for example, bicameralism and judicial review – that signal 'a high demand for revision' within a constitutional state (104).[16] It is against this background that Habermas portrays civil disobedience as 'guardian of legitimacy':

> That which is *prima facie* disobedience may soon prove to be the pace-setter for long overdue corrections and innovations because law and policy depending on principles are in constant process of adaptation and revision. In these cases, civil violations of rules are morally justified experiments without which a vital republic can retain neither its capacity for innovation nor its citizens' belief in its legitimacy. (ibid.)

This account seems very close to Markovits's idea of liberal disobedience; that is, of disobedience that seeks to limit democracy by opposing laws or policies that unduly infringe on basic liberties. But Habermas is also aware that many instances of justifiable protest do not concern violations of basic rights: as we saw earlier, the pre-emptive deployment of nuclear missiles may not easily be depicted as a breach of anyone's rights (e.g., the right to life). However, this does not preclude the possibility of engaging in a law-breaking protest against that decision. Habermas specifies that the fact a certain decision may have *irreversible* effects is problematic, from a democratic perspective, for it is part of democracy that a newly elected sovereign be able to change the direction of its predecessor if deemed appropriate.

Anti-nuclear and environmental protesters more generally base their opposition to certain policies exactly on the claim that, if implemented, the latter may lead to an irreversible damage; for example, the permanent pollution of the environment, the depletion of clear drinking water, not to mention loss of lives. In such cases, we may not accept the fact that 'the people have spoken' as conclusive reason for us to submit to that decision. This argument has been defended more recently by Matthew Humphrey, who has pointed out that when a certain policy's effects 'are irreversible, in the sense that they involve the loss of irreplaceable goods', we may not invoke 'one of the central arguments for accepting democratic outcomes – that the open democratic system ensures that any policy area can be revisited' (Humphrey 2006, 322). Once the policy is implemented, its effects will be permanent even under a new 'sovereign': this may warrant the use of extra-legal measures, such as civil disobedience, to draw further attention to the *irreversibility* of that political outcome.

Finally, we see the shift towards procedural concerns in the risk of 'errors in the process of the realisation of a legal order', which stems, in most cases, from imbalances of power within the public sphere:

> It is the downtrodden and oppressed who first experience injustice on their own persons. As a rule, those who feel injustice most immediately are not endowed with privileges or even with privileged opportunities for influence – whether concerning membership in parliaments, union or parties, access to the mass media, or the potential threat of those who can signal their intention to withhold investments during election campaigns. (104)

William Smith (2013, 64–68) has offered a clear summary of the role of civil disobedience within Habermas's conception of the 'public sphere'. The latter comprises all the public forums in which citizens debate issues of public concern, engaging in what Habermas calls a process of 'opinion-formation'. This involves the mutual exchange of different and often conflicting opinions, grounded on citizens' willingness to 'provide their pre-deliberative preferences about law and policy in light of what appear to be the most compelling reasons and arguments' (64). Thus, as Smith points out, for Habermas the public sphere plays a 'cognitive role' in a deliberative democracy, as the locus of an informed process of public debate in which participants can arrive at appropriate resolutions of social and political problems.

In his account of the public sphere, Habermas identifies both a 'centre' and a 'periphery'. The 'centre' of the public sphere refers to sites for reason giving in the legislature (e.g., in Parliament) and on the mass media (e.g., on the news). At the edges of this administrative core, Habermas locates the 'periphery' of the public sphere, constituted by various institutions 'equipped with rights of self-governance or with other kinds of oversight and lawmaking functions delegated by the state'; for example, universities, public insurance systems, and charitable organisations. This periphery also possesses an *outer* edge, identified with 'groups, associations and organisations that, before parliaments and through the courts, give voice to social problems, make broad demands, articulate public interests or needs, and thus attempt to influence the political process more from normative points of view than from the standpoint of particular interest' (ibid.). As opposed to the formal structure of the 'centre', the 'periphery' of the public sphere involves informal and highly differentiated channels of communication.

The public sphere as a whole approximates an ideal of a 'division of cognitive labour' (Smith 2013, 65), emphasising the collective effort of a citizenry towards rational agreement. We return here to the notion of 'sovereign', already discussed with reference to Markovits's account, which hinges on authorship; that is, on citizens' participation in the law-making process: the latter cannot simply be delegated to the legislative bodies, but requires that citizens themselves be authors of the laws and policies binding them. To be 'sovereign', citizens ought to do more than simply 'monitor' the exercise of political power by the state retrospectively, 'but more or less program it as well' (Habermas 2009, 300). Although, strictly speaking, only the political system can 'act' – that is, promulgate laws – the public opinion channelled through democratic procedures can contribute to directing the system's decisions. Hence, as already mentioned, it is often the case that a specific issue within the public sphere fails to gain attention from mainstream media and politicians. To reach the *centre* of the public sphere, such issue first arises at the 'periphery', within circles and associations where people draw attention to social problems that, though pressing, do not occupy a sufficiently relevant place within the deliberative agenda. Through deliberative discussion, these newly generated 'discourses' can progressively move from the periphery towards the centre of the public sphere, thus gaining more visibility and attention at the legislative level. Habermas talks about 'the sluices of democratic procedure' (2009, 327) to highlight the role of democratic deliberation to filter out those views that fail to penetrate the constitutionally organised political system. On the other hand, many important issues can only be detected at the periphery rather than at the centre of the public sphere and then, through discursive rationalisation, manage to gain attention of media and, eventually, of politicians. This is how Habermas summarises the process whereby the concern with the nuclear arms race, environmental issues, or world poverty has managed to gain visibility in the public sphere:

> Hardly any of these topics were initially brought up by exponents of the state apparatus, large organizations, or functional systems. Instead, they were broached by intellectuals, concerned citizens, radical professionals, self-proclaimed 'advocates', and the like. Moving in from this outermost periphery,

> such issues force their way into newspapers and interested associations, clubs, professional organizations, academies, and universities. They find forums, citizen initiatives, and other platforms before they catalyse the growth of social movements and new subcultures. (2009, 381)

However, some critics have highlighted the difficulties experienced by 'the downtrodden and oppressed' to move from the 'periphery' to the 'centre' of the public sphere. The ideal of 'rational deliberators, who approach each other aiming for mutual understanding, and of a communicative exchange "in which the only thing that counts is the compelling force of the better argument"' (2009, 103), seems ill fitted to the reality of social life, where powerful actors can steer the deliberation in their preferred direction. In the next section, I present the influential account of Iris Marion Young, who seeks to continue Habermas's analysis of the public sphere, from a *critical* perspective, by exposing the 'exclusions and constraints' that may undermine the *legitimacy* of the deliberative process as Habermas and his followers portray it.

3.4 IRIS MARION YOUNG AND ARCHON FUNG

Iris Marion Young has provided an important insight into the debate over the role of law breaking, disruptive forms of protest within a democratic system. In the tradition of critical theory, she sought to highlight the risk behind a too restrictive account of deliberation which might perpetuate, rather than overcome, social injustice (Young 1996, 2000, 2001). Her critical assessment of the deliberative model focusses on the idea of a rational, persuasive exchange between communicatively tuned actors, in which the final outcome builds on 'the better argument'. For Young, standard accounts of deliberative democracy tend to portray the democratic citizen as quiet, reflective, capable of expressing herself in an orderly fashion arguing from premises to conclusion. This has the unwelcome effect of penalising as 'undemocratic' forms of communication that rely on different codes; for example, it may end up privileging a male speaking style over a female one, the latter being more exploratory or conciliatory, the former being more assertive and confrontational. Similarly, people with a stronger educational background, which enables them to express their view in a clear and more effective way, may enjoy the advantage of being more *persuasive* than those who come from less socially privileged contexts. In addition to this, the idea of the rational deliberator seems to commend calm, self-control and absence of emotions: from this standpoint, feeding one's passions into the deliberative discourse, using more 'theatrical' means to give emphasis to one's view, or causing minor disruptions to other participants are considered, in a word, *uncivil*. Political activism, under this perspective, seems unsuited to the rules of deliberative democracy, and citizens who engage in disruptive forms of protest are often dismissed as 'irrational nihilists who bring a bad name to good causes' (Young 2001, 674).

In one of her often-cited articles on the topic, Young (2000) sets up an imaginary exchange between a deliberative democrat and an 'activist', a term she uses to encompass a variety of non-orthodox forms of political protest.[17] She starts from the premise that, according to the deliberative model, citizens must approach the democratic arena with a disposition to not only advance their own, self-interested view, but also to listen to the demands of others aiming for 'understanding' (i.e., a *performative* attitude). Rather than aiming to win over others' views by engaging in 'strategic action', truly democratic agents strive to reach an agreement with their fellow deliberators, seeking to bridge the gap between their differing views. This agreement, as already stated, is not achieved through force or coercion, but rather is based on rational argumentation; that is, on persuasion.

Deliberative democracy offers an *ideal* of rational discussion amongst equals. Under non-ideal circumstances, however, societies are unlikely to fit this account, for individual citizens are rarely equal in terms of the capacity to influence the deliberative agenda. As we already discussed in the previous chapter, it is against this background that we can grasp the positive role of civil disobedience within a deliberative democracy. Under non-ideal circumstances, the appeal to illegal protest can be shown to be compatible with a commitment to a deliberative procedure. The structural problems affecting the deliberation do not licence overthrowing the political system altogether, for there are alternatives citizens may pursue short of a revolution. It is from this perspective that Young seeks to defend political activism from the criticisms raised by supporters of deliberative democracy. According to her, the activist is concerned with some serious injustice within society, and yet finds the deliberative exhortation to sit at a table with politicians and decision makers, to discuss the matter in a rational way, 'laughable' (ibid., 673); even if those powerful agents were willing to sit down to talk, they would be able to steer the discussion in the direction they prefer. Young's main contention is that 'the deliberative democrat who thinks that power can be bracketed by the soft tones of the seminar room is naïve'(675).

However, it is important to note that this unwillingness to enter 'the seminar room' does not issue in a rejection of dialogue altogether. The disruptive nature of the protest may and should still be conceived as a communicative, forward-looking act, aiming to promote a fair exchange of information within society, and to persuade fellow citizens of the risk of a serious injustice requiring urgent action. Thus, in response to the deliberative democrat, who accuses activists to behave like a pressure group – that is, to force others to accept their own views – activists strive to promote a 'universalist rather than partisan cause' (675); seeking to redress injustice is different from seeking to win over others. Rather, it is those who perpetuate the unjust policies, in order to preserve their own advantage, who should be accused of resorting to coercive tactics. The activists' refusal to engage in orderly discussion – that is, to sit at the table and to articulate their views vis-à-vis those of others – does not turn them into extremists, for the use of alternative forms of communication, including slogans, humour, and disruption, does not necessarily signal an irrational appeal to emotions and instincts.

In fact, Young shifts the onus onto the deliberative democrats by raising objections against their over-idealised take on politics. Above all, the already mentioned power imbalances within the public sphere warrant scepticism about the possibility that the 'better' argument will win: public deliberations often contravene the requirement that all those affected by a decision should contribute to the discussion, as in the case of the G8 negotiations, where a few individuals make crucial economic decisions from behind closed doors. A further issue for deliberative democracy lies in the risk of 'systematically distorted deliberation', a term originally coined by Habermas himself, to highlight the case of *false* consensus; that is, of agreements conditioned by unjust power relations (Young 2001, 685). Focusing on the debate around climate change, Young draws attention to the fact that agents are only allowed to debate whether, and how far, fossil fuel consumption should be limited, yet no one is allowed to challenge the very assumption that fossil fuels should be used at all. The views of those who are against a fossil fuel–based economy are not allowed within the deliberation; the discussion takes place within a framework grounded on 'hegemonic discourse' – that is, a narrative participants are not able or allowed to challenge. Without addressing these structural problems, the plea for deliberation may be unrealistic.

However, the choice over whether to endorse deliberative ideals in the face of structural inequalities within the public sphere should not be framed in either/or terms; the fact that we live in less than ideal circumstances does not imply that we should not strive for the ideal of a democratic system where decisions are based not on power, but on persuasiveness. Thus, Cohen and Arato (1992, 592–93) have argued that real democrats must recognise that democracy 'can never be fully institutionalised', for we may never claim to have reached 'a perfect procedural institutionalisation of the principles of democratic legitimacy'. As it is impossible to claim, at any point in time, that the law protects *all* our moral rights, so it is to contend that a certain set of political arrangement has fully institutionalised the idea of democratic legitimacy:

> A fully democratic and just civil society is, of course, a utopia in the classical sense; it can never be fully realised or completed but operates as a regulative ideal that informs political projects. (ibid, 567)

Therefore, although the 'ideal' of a deliberative system may remain an ideal, we ought not to conclude that it is flawed or not worth our efforts.[18] We are not faced with an either/or choice between a deliberative democrat and a political activist, for many forms of activism seek to promote deliberative values. Hence, according to Archon Fung (2005), Young overstates the contrast between deliberative democracy and political activism.[19] Fung contends that a citizen can remain committed to the principles of deliberative democracy and act upon that commitment, even under conditions of structural injustice and power imbalances. He advances a view labelled 'deliberative activism', according to which 'widespread inequality and failures of reciprocity can justify non-persuasive, even coercive, methods for the sake of deliberative goals' (399). However, he warns about adopting a militant stance in the face of injustice, and he is wary of the claim that 'all bets are off before the revolution'. Even where circumstances are far from the deliberative ideal of rational dialogue, committed democrats should strive to improve the deliberative environment through 'incremental, non-revolutionary steps' by carefully choosing their strategy to deal with injustice:

> A hard-nosed deliberative democrat does not limit himself solely to persuasive methods of politics. Sometimes, forces more compelling than the better argument are necessary to establish fair and inclusive deliberation or the conditions that support deliberation. When circumstances justify the use of such force for deliberative democrats, they become deliberative activists. (402)

In the attempt to show how a committed deliberative democrat may, under some circumstances, forego the use of purely persuasive measures, Fung draws an analogy between deliberative activism and civil disobedience (401–4). This choice is puzzling, since from what Fung writes we can infer that civil disobedience *is* a form of deliberative activism, rather than its analogue – that is to say, a deliberative democrat may decide to resort to civil disobedience to further the deliberation; that is, as a form of deliberative activism. Nonetheless, Fung's argument shows why a civil disobedient, despite deliberately breaching the law, should not be accused of anti-democratic conduct. His goal is to analyse 'the middle ground of democracy'; that is, the significant range of alternative options for the committed democrat when circumstances are far from the deliberative ideal. Fung claims that a person does not cease to be a democrat merely by resorting to conduct that deviates, within limits, from the principles of deliberative democracy. The resort to deliberative activism hinges on a belief in the possibility of improving the deliberative system to better approximate the ideal of a rational discourse among equal, non-selfish agents. As long as the underlying injustice is not unreasonable, and as long as the powerful agents in society can be deemed capable of engaging in rational debate, the resort to deliberative activism may not betray the deliberative ideals. Fung grounds his argument on a principle of proportionality, according to which

> when others are simply unwilling to engage in the give-and-take of persuasive communication, the deliberative democrat can, and should, use an array of nonpersuasive means to change their attitudes. However, the choice of means should be scaled according to the extent to which political adversaries and opponents reject the procedural norms of deliberation and the substantive values that ground it. The greater their rejection, the more the deliberative activist is at liberty to conduct politics by non-communicative means. However, the object of these efforts is always to advance deliberation by ultimately persuading adversaries or by raising the costs of rejecting reason. (403)

This leaves open the question of *how far* the deliberative activist could go. There comes a point where the 'nonpersuasiveness' of the act would lose any semblance of a commitment to the ideals of deliberative democracy – for example, the use of force aiming to injure or terrorise others could not be justified as an expression of deliberative values. Nonetheless, Fung suggests the compatibility between the use of force, on the one hand, and a commitment to democracy, *under some circumstances*: the former may be necessary to overcome structural problems in the public sphere, and to bring the deliberation closer to the ideal of 'communicative action'. Importantly, this implies that we may not assess the democratic pedigree of a certain actor or action by focusing exclusively on its adherence (or lack thereof) to some specific constraints (e.g., nonviolence); we need to consider the *inner disposition* of the agent who performs said action. The fact that an act of protest, such as civil disobedience, involves a degree of force or violence may not undermine that act's abidance by the ideals of democracy. This claim, however, requires further analysis, especially in relation to the already discussed popular conception of civil disobedience as inherently *non-violent*. I focus on this task in the next chapter.

Chapter Four

Non-violence and Civility

Authors writing in the 1960s and 1970s had reached a broad consensus over the necessity of nonviolence in civil disobedience. Thus, Hugo Bedau (1961, 656) contended that 'only *nonviolent* acts' may qualify as civil disobedience.[1] For Marshall Cohen (1972, 298), 'There is a time for violence in human affairs, but when it arrives, civil disobedience is no longer an appropriate form of political activity'. John Rawls (1999), as we saw earlier, claimed that civil disobedience cannot employ acts likely to hurt or injure others; in fact, for Rawls *any* interference with others' liberties would 'obscure the civilly disobedient quality of one's act' (321).[2] Much of this emphasis on non-violence appears to be the product of historical, rather than theoretical, considerations: the influence of Gandhi and King's non-violent campaigns in the debate on civil disobedience in the 1960s is undeniable. At a time where political violence was becoming increasingly frequent as a means to express dissent, it was reasonable to look at nonviolent campaigns as an alternative to the extremely coercive and *uncivil* strategies of armed resistance. This may explain why theorists moved towards the 'other extreme'; that is, to a model of social protest which, while maintaining its principled commitment to justice, openly opposed the use of violence. For example, although Martin Luther King's *Letter from Birmingham Jail* features regularly in anthologies on civil disobedience, on closer analysis King's campaign may not fit the account of civil disobedience which concerns us here. First of all, as Candice Delmas has noted, the civil rights movement comprised much more than the campaign led by Martin Luther King and the Southern Christian Leadership Conference. This movement also comprised 'Black nationalism, the Black Panther Party, the Nation of Islam, pan-Africanism, Black workers' movements, prisoners' rights movements, Black feminism, third-worldism, and assorted Marxist liberation movements' (Del-

2018a, 30). We should not ignore the role of these more radical campaigns in promoting desegregation, and also in fostering (by contrast) the idea of King's 'civility'. Jennet Kirkpatrick raises a similar point, deeming it 'plausible that the civil rights movement might have turned to violence, especially if its protests were not successful and its demands were unmet' (Kirkpatrick 2008, 86). Second, Angelo Corlett claims that King's campaign should not be confused with civil disobedience, for the two represent 'rather different modes of political and social change' (1997, 245). Comparing King's own conception of nonviolent direct action to Rawls's account of civil disobedience, Corlett highlights that while the former was fundamentally a religious, not political, movement, Rawls's civil disobedience had no 'essentially spiritual overtones' (ibid.). Further, law breaking is a necessary element of Rawlsian civil disobedience, while nothing about the campaign advocated by King requires disobeying the law. Corlett concludes that King engaged in direct action, rather than civil disobedience.[3]

Habermas also noted that civil disobedience involves 'more than a merely tactical commitment to nonviolence' and rather hinges on the appeal 'to the capacity for reason and sense of justice of the majority' (1985, 99). Using force or violence to channel one's political view in the public arena seems incompatible with these persuasive aims, for violence may intimidate, threaten, *coerce* rather than persuade others. In Habermas's terms, violence may fit cases of strategic action, where speakers approach each other with that objective attitude that, as we saw in the previous chapter, disregards the other's status as autonomous; however, violence seems incompatible with the performative attitude characterising speakers engaged in communicative action. In this context, describing an act of disobedience as 'civil' means that it does not forcibly constrain or impel others into accepting the protesters' view, but rather seeks to lead them to further discuss the issue through argumentative means. Since violence is coercive, the argument goes, civil disobedience must be nonviolent.

The problem with this reasoning is that it conflates 'violence' with 'coercion' and, more importantly, 'nonviolence' with 'persuasion'. This seems incorrect, for there may be coercion in the presence of nonviolence (Aitchison 2018) and, as I will show below, persuasion in the presence of violence; separating persuasion from coercion may be no easy task (Smart 1978). In order to persuade others, we need to articulate our views in sufficiently clear terms to them; however, we often face obstacles in pursuing the goal of persuasion; for example, lack of access to the public arena or to media coverage. It is not possible to address others in persuasive ways, if the addressees are not paying attention: this may be due to a variety of reasons, some of which were discussed in the previous chapter; for example, power imbalances constraining some groups' capacity to channel their view in the public arena. In fact, even Gandhi and King, despite their commitment to non-violence, recognised that the inconvenience caused to the majority might have been a necessary means to focus their attention on a particular issue. As Bondurant highlights in her study of Gandhi,

> Despite the protestations of a few followers of Gandhi that satyagraha is always persuasive and never coercive, the method does contain a positive element of coercion. Noncooperation, boycott, strike – all of these tools which may be used in satyagraha involve an element of compulsion which may effect a change on the part of an opponent which was initially contrary to his will.[4]

Gandhi's satyagraha aimed at 'converting' the opponents, by facing them with the satyagrahi's willingness to suffer. Yet the fact that the satyagrahi would continue in their protest *until* the opponents were eventually converted signals a dubious commitment to persuasiveness, and rather reveals the attempt to force the others to eventually accept the satyagrahi's view. This is corroborated by King's statement that the goal of a non-violent campaign is to 'create such a crisis and establish such creative tension that a community that has constantly refused to negotiate is *forced* to confront the issue' (Bedau 1991, 71).[5] These points suggest that the absence of physical violence does not entail the absence of coercion. Consider the case of a boycott. Despite involving no physical force, boycotts can hardly be described as attempts to 'persuade' others; rather, their aim is to force others to change course of action. It is common to speak of customers 'threatening' a boycott of a certain product; for example, to protest against a company's unethical practices. This explains the efficacy of *divesting* campaigns, which have become one of the main strategies in the anti–climate change movement (Kormann 2018). Divesting (as opposed to *investing*) involves selling a company's assets (e.g., one's own share) as a means to apply economic, social or political pressure on that company. The latter is faced with the risk of becoming less competitive on the market – a risk which, in neoliberal societies, where profit is a company's raison d'être, is tantamount to the risk of death.[6] There are obvious differences between forcing a company to change its policies by withdrawing financial support, on the one hand, and forcing it by threatening to kill its employees, on the other; yet neither strategy is persuasive. One major difference is that the former involves a legitimate conduct, for one has the right to manage one's own finances as one prefers, including in strategic ways. In this sense, even the simple act of writing to an MP, threatening to vote for the opposition at the next election unless the MP keeps her promises, seems far from a 'persuasive' act of communication, despite the inherent absence of violence.

Sit-ins are usually listed among the non-violent forms of protest. But they can obviously expose others to the risk of harm; for example, the traffic disruption could prevent ambulances from reaching people in need of medical assistance. If we take Rawls's claim that 'any interference' with others' liberties may obscure the civility of the disobedience, then merely causing inconvenience to others (e.g., a small delay due to traffic disruption) may be deemed uncivil. Yet it seems implausible to treat 'inconveniences' as a form of coercion: many actions may cause inconvenience to others, yet this may not imply we should refrain from committing them. The sight of an injustice might certainly be 'inconveniencing', yet it is not the case that others act violently by facing us with the reality of an injustice.

> I was once involved in a campaign to end US financial aid to the contras in Nicaragua. . . . In one particular protest I was helping to organize, a leaflet was drafted that detailed some of the practices engaged in by the contras, for example cutting off women's breasts and throwing infants into the air and catching them on bayonets. Some of the other organizers argued that these leaflets were violent because of the abusive effect they would have on those bystanders who read them. While I did not share this opinion – in my view it was a characterization of violence rather than an act of it – the general point that the dividing line between calling attention to violence and engaging in psychological violence is elusive is worth bearing in mind. (May 2015, chap. 2)

Inconveniences are often unpleasant, and possibly troubling or disturbing, yet need not be treated as a form of *violence* or as the attempt to coerce others into yielding to the protesters' demands. On the other hand, some authors have suggested that civil disobedience may even employ *threats*. Angelo Corlett devises a scenario involving migrant farmers whose fundamental human rights are continually infringed by an unjust law (1997, 36). These farmers have exhausted all legal avenues for redress, and are faced with apathy from society concerning the importance of their claim. They then decide to steal a valuable artefact, refusing to return it unless political leaders accept to negotiate with them. Such act seeks to grant them a 'bargaining chip', which may increase the chances their plea for justice will be heard. Corlett contends that this act, while involving a threat, would fulfil the other requirements of Rawls's account (publicity, fair notice, acceptance of punishment), hence it should not be disqualified as an instance of civil disobedience.

As we saw in chapter 3, threats are problematic, for they appear to conflict with the principles of deliberative democracy, which Habermas identified with the notion of communicative action. However, the ideal of rational deliberation may be out of reach in non-ideal circumstances, where imbalances in the deliberative sphere prevent the fair exchange of opinions amongst participants. Thus, Fung argues that 'when others are simply unwilling to engage in the give-and-take of persuasive communication, the deliberative democrat can, and should, use an array of nonpersuasive means to change their attitudes' (2005, 403). After persuasive approaches, based simply on appeals to the sense of justice, have been exhausted, coercion may be proportionally 'scaled according to the extent to which political adversaries and opponents reject the procedural norms of deliberation and substantive values that ground it' (ibid.). The underlying assumption is that it is not possible to address others in purely persuasive ways when they are unwilling to listen to us; in similar cases, the use of coercive means to *force* them to engage with us might be compatible with a commitment to deliberative democracy, and with the display of a 'performative attitude'. Similarly, Daniel Markovits distinguishes coercion aimed at engaging others in a dialogue, with coercion aiming at forcing a certain outcome of that dialogue. According to his view, civil disobedience is compatible with force seeking to 'secure the fact of sovereign reengagement' (2005, 1941): once others have joined the communicative enterprise, however, the use of force may be unwarranted.

Some authors have taken a more radical approach to the issue of violence in civil disobedience, appealing to the notion of proportionality in cases where the 'democratic deficit', or the issue at stake, is particularly significant. Jennifer Welchmann (2011) has argued that what matters to civil disobedience is the attempt to frustrate, either directly or indirectly, laws or legally tolerated practices 'within the bounds of civility'. However, in a somewhat polemical response to what she takes to be 'the prejudices of the men (by and large) philosophically analysing civil disobedience', Welchmann concludes that we 'must recognise that violence, threats of violence, covert acts of sabotage, blackmail and even assault are all means by which laws and legal practices might be obstructed' (105).[7] In a similar vein, Michael Allen (2009) argues that Fung's 'deliberative activism' may allow even physical harm to others. Allen claims, for example, that 'tasering a public official responsible for a significant injustice', in order to trigger a deliberative response from the public could still fall within the boundaries of a persuasive form of address. However, he appears to assume rather than defend his conclusion, when he writes: 'Supposing that we are willing to grant the controversial assumption that such an action could be shown to be strategically sound as a means to promote deliberative ends, then the answer to this question surely has to be yes' (36). That assumption is indeed controversial, especially given the problematic role of the word *strategic* within the context of Habermas's ethics of discourse. There is one obvious reason why the case Allen presents may not be deemed an instance of democratic disobedience; namely, it treats the public official merely as a means to 'facilitate the desired deliberative end'. We will return to this problem in the last part of this chapter, where I will propose a different account in which the use of physical force may be compatible with a Kantian requirement to treat others also as ends in themselves.

Robin Celikates (2016) warns about the risk of identifying *civil* with *nonviolent* disobedience, a risk he links to a hegemonic strategy of dividing 'good' from 'bad' protesters. Only those whose conduct is non-disruptive are labelled 'civil', while those who seek to go beyond mere symbolic actions, and to have some impact on others through their protest, are censored as 'violent, uncivil and criminal' (3). The emphasis on non-violence, from this standpoint, may reveal the attempt to neutralise the political potential of illegal protest as an instrument for change. For Celikates, 'Describing an event, activity, person or group as "violent", far from being a neutral observation, is always also a politically charged speech act that can reproduce forms of marginalization and exclusion that are often racialized and gendered' (ibid.). In many cases, according to Celikates, civil disobedience can function as a symbolic protest 'only if it involves moments of real confrontation . . . which will sometimes be regarded as violent' (7). Similarly, Brownlee claims the role of nonviolence in civil disobedience should not be overstated. Like Celikates, she points out that focusing on the protesters' use of violence diverts public attention from the more relevant issues of harm, abuse and injustice, which often impact on people's interests in a more serious way, compared to moderately violent acts of protest (2012, 198). While there may be constraints on the amount of force civil disobedients may employ, it may sometimes be unavoidable for these protesters to use a degree of force or violence 'to get their issue on the table'. Thus, like Markovits, Brownlee acknowledges that violence may be necessary as an initial step to gain attention, after which the disobedients may aim 'meaningfully to persuade authorities and society of their view' (24).[8] Thus, we may not declare violence 'uncivil' without considering the specific political context in which the act takes place: where society is unwilling or unable, due to power imbalances within the public sphere, to join the communicative enterprise initiated by the civil disobedients, the use of some degree of force may not jeopardise the communicative goals of civil disobedience.[9] I will return to this important insight in the last part of this chapter.

However, even granting that civil disobedience may, in some cases, employ a degree of force or violence, we must remember its nature as a *constrained* act of communication; even when it uses violent means, civil disobedience respects certain boundaries. On the importance of 'constraints', the words of Joseph Raz (1979) still ring true. Raz is amongst those theorists who believe there is nothing specifically admirable in nonviolence, for nonviolent *legal* protest may be as harmful as (or even more harmful than) violent civil disobedience. For example, if ambulance drivers were to go on a strike, they may expose the community to a more serious risk of harm, compared to a group of environmental activists who temporarily block the runway of an airport (1979, 267). Thus, he argues, while we should indeed be reluctant to use violence in civil disobedience, we cannot categorically rule it out without looking at the specific circumstances (e.g., the severity of the harm the protest seeks to avert). Reluctance is warranted, according to Raz, for 'other things being equal, non-violent disobedience is much to be preferred to violent disobedience' (267). Raz offers three reasons in support of this claim: first, violence causes direct harm to others; using violence, even when justified in doing so, may encourage others to use violence when the latter is not warranted; finally, as already mentioned, the use of violence may be strategically unwise, as it may alienate support of potential allies while also increasing the hostility of opponents.

The above discussion warns against overstating the relationship between civil disobedience and nonviolence, and rather suggests focussing on a 'constrained' use of force, under some circumstances. In the next section, I provide some clarifications concerning the notion of violence. Then, I present a recent argument that allows for violence in civil disobedience, except physical violence directly aimed at other people. This argument is, however, unsatisfactory, due to its inability to account for the wrongness of *threats*.

4.1 VIOLENCE AS PHYSICAL HARM

In his insightful book on nonviolence, Todd May claims that the latter should not be interpreted as 'the absence of violence': rather, understanding nonviolence requires identifying 'the violence that nonviolence must reject' (2015, chap. 2). In the attempt to draw the line between violence that is, and violence that is not, compatible with civil disobedience, we should first identify what acts are 'violent'. Thus, let us begin by identifying some actions that most of us would consider violent; that is, those involving direct physical force. I follow Vittorio Bufacchi (2007) in labelling this account of violence 'minimalist'. Bufacchi notices that one of the earliest and most authoritative supporters of this account was John Dewey, who conceived of violence as 'force gone wrong' (Bufacchi 2007, 19). Dewey contended that 'energy becomes violence when it defeats or frustrates purposes instead of executing or realizing it' (1916, 361). As an example, Dewey mentioned dynamite that blows up human beings instead of rocks, which he described as force that 'destructs rather than constructs': in such cases, rather than 'energy', we have 'violence'. In and by itself, this seems to be an odd example of violence, for the latter further implies an *intention*: we would not claim that a hurricane 'acts violently', despite the destruction it brings about.[10] As Bufacchi notes (ibid.), in addition to being intentional or deliberate (by the perpetrator), an act of violence is unwanted by its victim(s): violence implies the absence of the victim's consent. Punching a wall differs from punching a person; although the two acts employ the same amount of force, only the latter is violent for, as opposed to the former, it has a 'victim'. Furthermore, we do not usually treat medical 'surgery' as a violent act, for those who undergo surgery have consented to it. Thus, under this basic, minimalist understanding, violence is the unwanted imposition of destructive physical force upon others. Bufacchi further discusses practices involving the acceptance of physical force, as in the case of contact sports, or cases of consensual yet extreme sex (e.g., bondage, domination). He warns against confusing the *definition* of violence with its *justification*, arguing that this kind of practice is still violent, although the fact participants have given their consent makes them ethically justifiable (20). For our purposes, we do not need to dwell on this latter question, for the kind of violence with which we are concerned is always non-consensual; that is, imposed upon unwilling citizens who would rather not face the various inconveniences caused by the protesters. Thus, our goal is to assess whether using force against unwilling agents may nonetheless qualify as a nonviolent act or, more specifically, as an act in which violence remains within the boundaries of civility.

Based on this minimalist conception of violence, Nathan Adams has recently claimed that civil disobedience may include various kinds of violence, *except* physical violence *directly targeted* at other persons (Adams 2018).[11] Adams adopts the basic or minimalist notion of violence just described, interpreting violence as excessive physical force on non-consensual individuals.[12] In his view, this minimalist conception has many advantages; for example, it avoids counterintuitive results such as treating violence as synonymous with rights violations and/or coercion. However, he also seeks to narrow the focus of the discussion upon one specific kind of violence, which he labels '*constitutive* violence'; namely, violence 'in the very act of law breaking' (483). For example, if violence occurs as a result of the protest, due to police repressing an otherwise peaceful protest, the latter would still be a nonviolent protest. Furthermore, and perhaps more confusingly, Adams separates constitutive from 'related' violence; that is, violence that does not stem directly from the act of lawbreaking 'but is still connected to it (e.g., responding to reprisals, resisting arrest, and so on)'. For example, if some neo-Nazis attacked a group of immigrants following a peaceful pro-immigration protest (and in response to it), the protest itself would not count as violent. However, this leads to some counterintuitive results. Suppose a group of protesters illegally occupied a public space to request some legislative change, at time t, threatening to blow up a building at $t+1$ unless their request is accepted: Would the violence occurring at time $t+1$ be merely 'related' to the protest? Could this protest meaningfully be described as nonviolent? Second, Adams understands violence only as force that is *other-directed*: it targets others' bodies, not one's own. Thus, he discusses 'self-immolation', with reference to the case of Mohamed Bouazizi, the Tunisian fruit vendor who set himself on fire in 2010, sparking the so-called Arab Spring (484). This is an odd example in this context, for Bouazizi's was not an act of *disobedience*. Also, in his exclusive focus on physical violence, Adams glosses too quickly, in my view, over the destruction of one's own property as part of the protest.

> Imagine that flag-burning is illegal. In order to protest this law, you buy a flag and then burn it in public. Again, whatever reasons we have for holding that civil disobedience is necessarily nonviolent, extending it to mean that burning your own personal flag to protest an anti-flag-burning law is excessive. This is an ideal case of civil disobedience in many ways: it is direct (it breaks the precise law it holds to be unjust); it is perfectly symbolic (it destroys the most prominent symbol of the political regime that imposes the contested law in addition to breaking that very law); it is self-contained (not risking harm or costs to anyone else); and it is public. Ruling out such an act on conceptual grounds is badly mistaken. (485)

This raises the same objection noted earlier, concerning the notion of *constitutive* violence. Adams seems untroubled by the symbolic message involved in flag burning: the latter may not only signal *disapproval* of the government, but also possibly channel hatred for the institutions and instigate (or even deliberately *incite*) other-directed violence. Claiming that such protest is 'self-contained' and therefore nonviolent misses the troubling nature of hate speech: the fact that the violence is 'related' rather than 'constitutive'; that is, that the harm may happen not as a direct result of the illegal act (as when A destroys B's property) does not suffice to establish that this violence is not troubling.

Having said that, Adams contends that civil disobedience cannot employ constitutive, other-directed violence, for this violates the 'commitment to the political' characteristic of this form of protest. This refers to a 'commitment to the idea of shared project of living together' (479); that is, the idea that the community's members 'are going to work together in the future' (481). In this sense, Adams appears to endorse Sabl's idea of 'forward-looking communication' which, as already discussed, aims to engage others in a cooperative exchange, rather than to coercively impose the protesters' view upon others. In line with this account, Adams also endorses the broad idea of civil disobedience as a persuasive form of communication, which rules out acts that 'would render future cooperation impossible' and would reveal 'a commitment to achieving your preferred outcomes no matter the means and regardless of others' position as members in the ongoing community' (ibid.).

However, Adams's commitment to persuasiveness is at odds with his views on permissible violence. With reference to the riots in Ferguson, USA, following Michael Brown's death at the hand of a police officer in 2014, Adams claims there was nothing wrong (uncivil?) with burning down police cars in protest, for the latter represented 'the very symbol of prowling oppression' (488). This would apply also to cases where the protesters deliberately target private property:

> Imagine a country of radical wealth inequality. Protesting against such inequality by seizing and destroying the gold-encrusted jet of a plutocrat is an eminently symbolic and striking form of protest. Given that the plutocrat himself is not threatened, I do not see why such an act would be conceptually inconsistent with a commitment to the political. It does not push the person outside of the bounds of the political community. (489)

One may legitimately ask how destroying the billionaire's plane reveals a commitment to cooperation. First of all, it is hard to accept that the plutocrat is 'not threatened' by this act: damage to one's own property does represent a threat to our private sphere, hence to our own safety. As already noticed, Adams is concerned only with direct physical harm, but it is unclear why only direct physical harm can push others 'outside of the bounds of the political community'. Could the protesters destroy one of the plutocrat's mansions instead of the plane? Could anti-government activists destroy the parliament, provided there is no one inside, given it symbolises the very corrupted policies the protesters are targeting? These actions would certainly render future cooperation, if not impossible, extremely unlikely. As an account of *uncivil disobedience* (as the title suggests), Adams's view may be successful; however, it seems unsuited to a persuasive and cooperative form of communication; that is, to *civil* disobedience.

There are significant issues with the idea that civil disobedience may use violence as long as it does not physically harm others. One main reason to be sceptical of this approach is that people also suffer non-physical harm: for coercion to occur, physical violence is not necessary. Threats are inherently violent, yet we cannot make sense of this fact if we stick to a minimalist conception of violence, which then leads to the counterintuitive results we just noticed. Thus, in the next section I look at accounts of violence that take a broader or, to use Bufacchi's label, 'comprehensive' perspective (2007, 24), one that goes beyond the mere idea of *physical* harm.

4.2 VIOLENCE AGAINST INTEGRITY

We saw earlier that, for Rawls, 'While it may warn and admonish, civil disobedience is not itself a threat'. Yet we cannot make sense of the notion of 'threat' by adopting a minimalist conception of violence, one that is concerned only with direct physical force. There are obvious ways in which one may be a victim of violence without suffering physical harm. When the local gang burns down a restaurant to 'punish' the owner's refusal to pay protection money, it commits an act of violence even if no one gets hurt in the fire. When No-Globalisation protesters smash the windows of McDonald's or Starbucks while there is no one inside, their conduct is still violent, though no one may be physically hurt. This is because we may expose others to harm even when not physically targeting them: the restaurant owner and her family will face extreme duress as a result of their restaurant being burned down, especially when the restaurant was their only source of income. While they may not suffer physical harm *in* the fire, they may certainly suffer it *as a result* of the fire. In fact, it is obvious that the local gang burned the restaurant with the intention to make the owner 'suffer' a significant loss. If we accept this analysis of the case of the restaurant owner, however, we may also have to grant that an employer who fires an employee, thus depriving her of her only source of subsistence, would commit an act of violence by exposing the employee to significant harm. This seems implausible, yet many authors contend that violence may also occur at the structural level; that is, when economic arrangements systemically expose some citizens to serious risk of harm. For example, Slavoj Žižek distinguishes between *subjective* and *systemic* violence (Žižek 2008).[13] The former is violence in the traditional sense; for example, beating or killing someone. The latter refers to 'the often catastrophic consequences of the smooth functioning of our economic and political systems' (1). From this standpoint, structural violence is treated as synonymous with social injustice. Yet as Tony Coady has pointed out, this may lead to some confusion, for while violence is sometimes justified (as in the case of violence in self-defence), social injustice never is. Treating social injustice as a form of violence thus leads to both a descriptive and a normative mistake, for it also fails to acknowledge that social injustice is always wrong (Coady 1986).[14]

Let us return to the case of violence against property, which involves no direct physical force against others. Damaging or destroying others' property does not only lead to economic losses for the property owner: the latter may also suffer *emotional* harm; for example, where the damaged property has a strong symbolic or sentimental value. The case of cultural genocide provides a telling example of how the destruction of monuments or icons may cause deep and lasting suffering on people, despite not targeting their body. There is an obvious sense in which this act violates the owner, without necessarily affecting her bodily integrity. As pointed out in the previous section, one problem with adopting the minimalist conception of violence is the seeming inability of the latter to make sense of *threats*. When the gunman orders 'Your money or your life', she is acting violently even if she does not pull the trigger. The violence lies in the fact that the victim is *forced to act against her will*, and to yield to the gunman's request. Note that offers may be as coercive as threats: a business owner offering a job to an unemployed mother in return for sexual attention may not be accused of acting 'violently' towards the latter. Yet the manipulative nature of his 'offer' seems undeniable, for he attempts to force the woman to act against her will.[15] In this case the violence employed is psychological, not physical. Words can be as harmful as deeds, and they may also incite physical violence, as in John Stuart Mill's 'angry mob' scenario:

> An opinion that corn-dealers are starvers of the poor, or that private property is robbery, ought to be unmolested when simply circulated through the press, but may justly incur punishment when delivered orally to an excited mob assembled before the house of a corn-dealer, or when handed about among the same mob in the form of a placard. (Mill 1975, 53)

Consider the case of racism. There is no question that someone who makes a racist remark is doing something wrong, yet not necessarily because that remark may incite physical violence against its target. A racist or sexist slur whispered in the victim's ear may still be extremely harmful to the victim, without causing any direct physical harm to her.[16] However, while yelling insults at others may not necessarily be physically violent, I would argue that it is always *uncivil.* It cannot and should not be part of a communicative, forward-looking breach of the law, which aims to engage the addressee in a rational exchange. This is an important point to stress: civility does not entail non-violence, for the absence of physical violence may still be uncivil; furthermore, as I will argue below, the presence of physical violence may not necessarily signal *incivility.* As Brownlee has pointed out, civility and violence are not mutually exclusive terms, for civility 'contrasts with *depravity*, *barbarity*, *disrespect* and *rudeness*, not with *violence*' (2012, 22). She offers the example of fencing, which she describes as 'a highly civil yet violent form of engagement governed by strict norms of fair play'.[17] Though perhaps this overstates the amount of force involved in fencing (given participants wear full-body protections designed to prevent any significant harm), her view seems to imply that even a 'duel' may also fit the description of 'civil yet violent', insofar as participants are expected to follow 'strict norms of fair-play' while aiming to fatally shoot each other. Without going to this extreme, we may consider other sports, such as rugby, martial arts or boxing as example of 'civil yet violent' practices, based on the same criterion of abidance by strict norms; in these cases, violence is deemed compatible with (and in fact implied by) the rules. We may even praise a well-performed tackle between rugby players, despite the physical violence it involves; at the same time, we disapprove of rugby players who commit a 'high tackle' or other unwarranted forms of physical contact during the match. The reason we take the former, yet not the latter, as 'civil' relates to the fact that, in the former yet not in the latter case, participants are respecting each other as fellow players by abiding by a shared set of rules. The rugby player knows that the game involves being violently tackled by the opposing team while attempting to score a try: she accepts that the game implies a serious degree of violence, which is nonetheless constrained by the game's rules. Thus,

Brownlee is right in stressing that civility and violence are compatible: as we saw earlier, the real contrast is between civility and coercion, where the latter refers to the imposition of a certain outcome (with or without physical violence) on an *unwilling* subject. Civil disobedience, in the account I defend, must stay within the constraints of a persuasive action: when force or violence become coercive (in the sense just mentioned), the act may not be deemed civil. This reveals that some forms of violence are incompatible with the idea of a forward-looking communicative action, and as such are incompatible with civil disobedience; other forms of violence may not involve a coercive element, and may be deemed compatible with civility.

We then need an account of violence that may capture the possibility of harming others regardless of the presence of physical force. In this sense, Bufacchi has proposed a broader conception of violence as 'violation of integrity', which occurs 'when the integrity or unity of a subject (person or animal) or object (property) is being intentionally or unintentionally violated, as a result of an act or omission. . . . A violation of integrity will usually result in the subject being harmed or injured, or the object being destroyed or damaged' (2007, 43–44). For Bufacchi, a failure to act (omission) can be deemed violent, as in a case where we may easily rescue someone from drowning yet fail to do so; furthermore, violence may occur unintentionally, as in a military operation that causes the foreseeable, yet unintended, death of innocent bystanders. This is an important point with reference to civil disobedience for, as we will see in more detail below, a peaceful protest may unintentionally cause harm to others; for example, in the case of a traffic disruption that prevents ambulances from reaching patients. Protesters may be morally blameworthy for overlooking the (foreseeable) risk of causing harm to others through their protest.[18]

For Bufacchi, the notion of 'integrity' refers to a person's 'wholeness or intactness'. He refers to an earlier account by Gerald McCallum, which relates not just to the wholeness of the body (physical integrity), but also to the *autonomy* of the person: violence, in this sense, harms 'the self-determination of what happens to one' (MacCallum 1993, 126). Todd May expands on Bufacchi's view, claiming that violence, in the broader sense that goes beyond 'physical' force, involves a failure to respect another's 'dignity', a failure 'to treat that other as having a life to lead, one that, while not immune to coercion, must at least be taken seriously as one goes about one's own actions'.[19] Violence, then, involves a failure 'to take into account the fact that others have their lives to lead and are not simply there to serve one's own ends' (May 2015, chap. 2).

We may have come closer to identifying 'the violence that nonviolence must reject'; that is, the kind of violence that is incompatible with civil disobedience. This has involved abandoning the idea of violence as mere imposition of physical force onto others, and moving towards Immanuel

Kant's Formula of Humanity, which prescribes acting so to 'use humanity, whether in your own person or that of another, always at the same time as an end, never merely as a means' (Wood 2008). From this different standpoint, what matters to civil disobedience is not the use of physical force, but rather the disrespect for the fact that 'others have their lives to lead'. That is to say, we may accept the idea that civil disobedience must be nonviolent, insofar as we interpret violence in this broader sense; that is, as targeting one's dignity. Civil disobedience must treat others with the respect due to their status as autonomous agents: it cannot coerce, only persuade. Physical violence does not deserve centre stage in this context, for, as I will argue in the next section, using physical force against others may not harm their dignity; that is, their autonomy.

4.3 RESPECTING AUTONOMY THROUGH THE USE OF FORCE

Let us take stock of the discussion so far. I have begun by highlighting a general tendency, amongst early scholars, to identify civil disobedience with nonviolent protest. I pointed out that there are both instrumental and non-instrumental reasons to stress the link between civility and nonviolence, although the instrumental ones fail to establish the necessity of nonviolence in civil disobedience (for, under some circumstances, using violence may be instrumentally preferable for the protest's success). Thus, in the above discussion I have focused on the non-instrumental view, according to which civil disobedience is persuasive; hence, it cannot resort to violent means: violence is unsuitable to a communicative, forward-looking illegal act that seeks to persuade others to engage in further deliberation concerning a certain law or policy. I first pointed out that the absence of violence does not entail persuasion, for nonviolent acts (à la Gandhi and King) may still be grounded in the attempt to coerce rather than persuade. I then considered Adams's view that only direct physical violence is incompatible with civil disobedience, while other forms of violence (e.g., against property) may be part of it. This approach is problematic, for it fails to capture the coercive potential of other forms of violence; for example, violence against property, or even of non-violent acts such as a boycott. Hence, I looked at a broader account of violence, centred on coercion rather than physical force, in the attempt to separate civil from uncivil violence. This account centres on people's dignity; that is, on people being in control of their own lives. I then employed Kant's Formula of Humanity to identify violence as a failure to 'treat others as ends in themselves', that is to say, to respect people as autonomous agents. In this way, I have come full circle with my account of civility, discussed in chapter 2: civility involves a disposition to respect others as autonomous agents, and violence may be compatible with civil disobedience insofar as it abides by this same disposition.

The next, and last, step in this discussion concerns explaining how acts of civil disobedience, despite using physical force on others, may fulfil the requirement to respect them as autonomous agents. Recall that, based on my account of autonomy discussed in chapter 2, autonomous agents are able to choose and pursue their own conception of the good, and to give directions to their lives according to those choices. I have claimed that autonomous agents have a right to autonomy, a claim to be respected as autonomous agents; this right generates both a negative duty not to interfere with a person's autonomous choices and a positive duty to assist others in exercising their autonomy. In what follows, I will argue that the use of a degree of force or violence in civil disobedience may comply with the negative duty just mentioned. I will return to this argument in chapter 6, to claim, further, that under some circumstances a degree of force or violence in civil disobedience *may be required* by the positive duty to assist others in exercising their autonomy.

In order to present my argument, I will refer to Gerald Dworkin's distinction between autonomy and *freedom*.[20] As Dworkin argues, the difference lies in the fact that the concept of freedom applies to a realm of human agency that is narrower than that pertaining to autonomy (Dworkin 1988, 13–20). While a person can be said to be 'free' at a specific moment in time, the assessment of her autonomy involves evaluating a substantial section of her life. This is because the role played by autonomy in one's life connects to an agent's identification with her own projects, values, goals and desires. There is a peculiar difference between, for example, the choice to have coffee rather than tea, and the choice to support a certain policy or political party: the latter mirrors, to some extent, the choice to be a particular kind of person, who endorses a certain conception of the good.[21] Autonomy implies self-identification: an autonomous person is able to see the projects and commitments in her life as her own, rather than as imposed on her by someone else. As Harry Frankfurt (1999) has further argued, one may have a certain desire while also resenting having it (as in the case of addiction): this would raise doubts as to her self-identification with that first desire. From this standpoint, an autonomous choice expresses the agent's self-identification not only with her own desires, but also *with the motivations behind those desires*. In addition to saying 'I want to X', an autonomous person is in the condition of saying 'I want to want to X' (Olick 2001, 86–90). Hence, if a person regrets having a certain motivation – that is, would like to be motivated by different influences – the motivation, though effective, might not be viewed as *her own*. For example, a drug addict may acknowledge as 'her own' the desire for heroin, while regretting being a person who has that kind of desires (i.e., a drug addict): from this standpoint, her choice to use drugs would not be fully autonomous. Dworkin labels autonomous choices 'authentic', for they involve a degree of *self*-identification of the agent with her higher-order desires (Dworkin 1988, 18–20). A choice that is not 'authentic' (as in the case of the drug addict) may not qualify as 'autonomous', for it would lack the agent's *endorsement*.[22] As a character ideal of persons who are *in control of their lives*, autonomy certainly requires *a degree* of freedom: however, while a degree of freedom is necessary in order to be autonomous, an autonomous life involves *more* than just being free (Young 2017, 8; Haworth 1986, 166–67). A drug addict may be free from interferences from others; yet as already mentioned, we would not describe her choices as autonomous: this is an important point to stress, for once we separate autonomy from freedom, we also pave the way for the possibility that infringing on a person's freedom may not imply infringing also on her autonomy. If this is correct, then using a degree of force of violence on others, as part of a form of address, may not be deemed coercive. In such cases, the use of force or violence may be deemed compatible with civil disobedience.

To grasp this point, recall that, when comparing coercion to persuasion earlier in the chapter, I pointed out we should not confuse 'forcing others to *face* the issue' with 'forcing others to accept our view on the issue'. Coercion occurs in the latter case, where one seeks to impose one's own view upon others; however, when A forces B to *listen* to A's opinion, to engage in a debate around a serious issue, and possibly to take a stand by *replying* (rather than yield) to A's demand, we may not talk of 'coercion' in the sense that concerns us here; namely, a failure to treat B with the respect due to her status as autonomous. For A to act coercively towards B, A would seek to impose her opinion on B through mere force. B's opinion would not matter, for A's only goal would be to subject B's conduct to A's will. In this sense, A would fail to treat B 'also as an end'.

The autonomy/freedom distinction allows us to have a better grasp of cases where, despite forcing B to *act* against B's will, A may not be said to *coerce* B; that is, to treat B merely as a means and not also as an end in herself. Acts of civil disobedience often involve forcing others to act against their will; for example, through the illegal occupation of public space. But this is not sufficient to classify these acts as coercive merely in virtue of this forceful imposition; that is to say, the protesters may not be accused of treating others 'merely as means', for despite using a degree of force they are not forcing them to accept their view. While they may infringe on people's *freedom* – for example, by temporarily obstructing public traffic – they may not be deemed to also threaten people's autonomy by forcing them to accept their views.[23] To appreciate this point, let us consider a concrete case of civil disobedience:

> In the early hours of the 8th of December 2008, fifty-seven activists cut through the security fences surrounding the runway at Stansted Airport, UK.

> They assembled fencing panels on the runway, and hooked themselves to the panels with chains and D-locks, while wearing high-visibility vests with the inscription 'Please Do Something' on the back. When police arrived, the activists did not try to resist arrest. Their act of protest *deliberately* caused the cancellation of several flights, and a serious disruption to passengers due to travel on that day. The protesters aimed at highlighting the environmental risks connected to the UK Government's plan to build a third runway at Stansted Airport. (Percival 2008)

Through this action, the activists intentionally forced other people to act against their own will. Passengers had to withdraw (at least provisionally) their travelling plans, facing a serious inconvenience.[24] This protest was intended to be an act of civil disobedience; that is, a way to address others in the public arena. However, notwithstanding the action's *communicative* aims (i.e., to offer an objection to a proposed policy), the activists used a degree of force: they sought to convey their message by imposing a choice (i.e., staying at the airport) on others, disregarding the latter's will. The presence of force seems to put the action at odds with the democratic commitment to autonomy, since it may reveal a failure to show the appropriate respect for the status of autonomous agents. Contrary to this view, I hold that the Stansted case illustrates a form of address that is compatible with the requirement to respect others as autonomous agents. With reference to the autonomy/freedom distinction, I claim that, although this was a forceful protest which infringed on people's *freedom*, it did not also infringe upon their *autonomy*: as an act of civil disobedience, the protest did not aim to coerce others into opposing the planned expansion of the airport. Rather, the protesters deliberately infringed upon others' freedom to draw their attention to the environmental risks of further air traffic expansion.

To clarify this point, let us return to the difference between 'freedom' and 'autonomy', as per Dworkin's account (1988, 12–14): while freedom applies at a local level – that is, it can be assessed at a specific point in time – autonomy applies at a global level – that is, it concerns more broadly the direction one gives to one's own life; for example, the values around which one chooses to inform one's own life. *Autonomy* involves *choosing one's own person*: an autonomous choice says something about the kind of person one wants to be. Some choices of ours do not say much about the kind of persons we are, although we are free to make them (e.g., boarding on a certain flight), while others do: choosing to support a certain policy or government says something about the kind of persons we are, what values we subscribe to, what conception of society we endorse (Möller 2009, 772). This is a choice for which we bear responsibility, since it shows our commitment to a certain idea of the good, and this is why interfering with this kind of choice, by forcing us to do otherwise, may seriously infringe on our status as autonomous agents.

What follows from this is that force employed against a person's freedom does not necessarily infringe also on her right of autonomy: by interfering with your choice to board a certain flight, I do impinge (temporarily) on your freedom of movement, though not necessarily also on your autonomy.[25] My claim is that, in the Stansted case, despite *forcing* others to act against their will, activists did not (try to) force them to choose to oppose the planned airport expansion: those who were stranded at the airport were still able to accept or reject the validity of the disobedients' claim. In this sense, the act remained *persuasive*.[26]

The idea that violence and coercion are compatible may be pushed even further. Consider a more extreme case, involving 'bossnapping'; that is, 'the kidnapping of the boss'.[27] This form of protest was popular in France, especially in the years following the global financial crisis: frustrated workers, faced with the prospect of lay-off with little or no compensation, resorted to taking their employers hostage in their own offices, to force them to enter a negotiation with the workers. While 'kidnapped', employers were treated with care, provided with water and food and allowed to make phone calls; nonetheless, they were literally kept prisoners for up to forty-eight hours (Parsons 2013). Bossnapping raises an interesting philosophical puzzle, for it lacks the threatening nature of standard cases of abduction, where the kidnappers are willing to kill the victim if their requests are not accepted: as mentioned above, bossnappers do not go to that extreme. However, few would be willing to treat bossnapping akin to civil disobedience, given the serious breach of the employer's freedom. And yet, from the autonomy/freedom distinction discussed above, I would argue that, at least conceptually, even bossnapping may represent a violent, yet *non-coercive*, form of address. The presence of a (very significant) amount of force does not entail that bossnapping is uncivil for, as we saw above, violence and civility are compatible. We may conceive of cases of bossnapping that lack the coercive elements of terrorism; that is, which treat the employer not only as a means but also as end in herself. For example, the workers could take measures to minimise the undeniable stress such situation would cause to her; they would not expose the employer to physical risk; for example, preventing her from taking her prescription medications, or ignoring other signs of ill health. They may (and should) express their regret, perhaps even apologising to their boss for having to resort to such an intrusive form of protest, under the specific circumstances, to draw attention to the seriousness of the situation. More importantly, the workers might act on the belief that cooperation is still possible; for example, that the employer may be open to reconsider the decision to lay-off the employees and to work with them in a 'forward-looking' manner. A similar case of bossnapping may fulfil the account of persuasion and of civility spelled out above because, despite the major infringement upon the employer's freedom, it might not also infringe on her autonomy; that is, her capacity to make uncoerced choices. As participant in a communicative enterprise, the kidnapped employer maintains her right to accept or reject the workers' proposition. The employer may come to realise that what she sees as a mere issue of economic efficiency has, on the other hand, momentous implications for the lives of the workers and their families. The workers might succeed in persuading their employer that there is room for compromise, that the impact these dismissals will have on the workers' lives would be disproportionate to the benefit for the company, that the dismissal is indeed unfair, and so on.[28] The employer may at least be willing to rediscuss the terms of the dismissal; in fact, we would expect this to happen, if workers and employers were to display a *performative attitude*. Furthermore, the bossnappers remain morally bound by a duty of care, requiring them to use the amount of force that is strictly necessary, under the circumstances, for the communicative exchange to start. In cases where the stakes are extremely high and there is no way for them to access the employer's office, the workers may devise other strategies to finally face her, keeping the focus on the employer's own well-being. Furthermore, as other civil disobedients, the workers should consider the impact their action would have on public opinion, since they would risk alienating support from other citizens if they were to employ a serious amount of force.

Finally, my argument does not imply that the employer has done something wrong, hence has forfeited her right against undue interferences. On the contrary, the employer preserves her right to be treated as an autonomous person in a deliberative exchange, regardless of whether the policies she is promoting are just. The discussion does not hinge on the merit of each party's claims, but rather on how parties should approach each other in the face of disagreement over crucial issues. *It may well be the case that the employer is right, and the workers are wrong*: still, if the latter thought their views had received insufficient attention in the decision-making process, and if they found no viable alternative, their resort to bossnapping may still be compatible with the requirements of civility.[29] Thus, I conclude, the use of force or violence to compel others to join the communicative enterprise, under some circumstances, may fulfil the duty to respect them as autonomous agents: a commitment to treating others with civility may require one to address others in ways that may infringe on their *freedom* (yet not also on their autonomy).

Chapter Five

The Moral Right to Civil Disobedience

Civil disobedience can play a positive role in a democracy, despite its illegal nature, and also, as I argued in the last chapter, despite the use of a degree of force or violence. Nonetheless, civil disobedients are usually required to accept the legal sanction following their law-breaking conduct; this may be puzzling if, as argued earlier, their action falls within the principles of democracy. Appealing to the fact that they have breached the law – that is, providing a *legal* justification for their punishment – is not sufficient within this context, since, as with the discussion of political obligation in chapter 1, we are looking for a *moral* justification for punishing civil disobedients. An obvious case where punishment is not justifiable is where the agent commits no wrong; if my breach of the law is justified by the circumstances, as we will see below, I may not be liable to the legal sanction. All things considered, I did the right thing. Another case where punishment may be unwarranted is where I do what I have the right to do: no one should be punished for acting according to one's own rights.

In this chapter, I consider the debate around these issues, with reference to the notion of a moral right to civil disobedience. As Joseph Raz (1979) has pointed out, having the *right* to do X does not mean that X is the right thing to do; it means, however, that others may not interfere with your X-ing, even if you should not X. Thus, if there is a right to civil disobedience, as many academics now believe, then others, including the state, should not interfere with a person who engages in this sort of conduct. If such right exists, then one may not be punished merely for engaging in civil disobedience, even if the latter implies breaking the law.

I begin by clarifying the notion of a moral right to civil disobedience, placing it within the broader framework of Hohfeld's influential theory of rights (Hohfeld 1919). I then consider Joseph Raz's argument against a right to civil disobedience, and its implications on how the law should respond to people who resort to this form of law-breaking protest. Even if they may have no right to civil disobedience, citizens may appeal to legal defences to show that their action, though illegal, should not be deemed wrong; hence, under those circumstances, punishment would be unwarranted.

I will then turn to arguments supporting the existence of a moral right to civil disobedience. In general, they interpret the choice to engage in a communicative, forward-looking breach of the law as the expression of a person's own conscience, of her status as an autonomous agent. I will focus on the recent contributions by David Lefkowitz, Kimberley Brownlee and William Smith, whose role in this debate cannot be understated. I will conclude by considering the implications of these claims for the alleged justifiability of punishing citizens who commit an act of civil disobedience.

5.1 MORAL RIGHTS AS CLAIMS AND LIBERTIES

Theoretical discussion of rights are usually framed along the lines of Hohfeld's seminal account, which describes rights as *claims*, *privileges* (or *liberties*), *powers* or *immunities* (1919). For our purposes, here I focus only on the first two; namely, *claim* rights and *liberty* rights.

The most straightforward way to understand the concept of rights refers to the idea of an individual's protected sphere of action. The right bearer is entitled to engage in a certain conduct, or to access a certain good, without suffering interferences from others. In this sense, having a right to X entails an entitlement to claim that others do *not* interfere with the right bearer's access to X (these are usually referred to as *negative* rights; that is, rights against interferences). Examples belonging to this category include the right to free speech, property rights and freedom of movement: these rights identify the right bearer's protected sphere of action. Note that interference need not be physical, as in the case where A locks B up to prevent B from moving freely; interferences may also take the form of coercion or manipulation; for example, where A *threatens* to visit some unpleasant consequences upon B if B moves freely. Any kind of pressure on A aiming at deterring her from exercising her right would constitute a violation (albeit justifiable) of A's *claim* against interferences.

Claim rights do not only imply protection from external interference. The right bearer may also justifiably *demand* that she be provided with the means and/or the conditions necessary for exercising her right; this, on the other hand, generates a duty on others to address those demands. In this case, we talk of *positive* claim rights. Thus, for example, my children have a positive right to demand that I provide for their food, clothing and education. Citizens, more generally, may demand that the state provide them with necessary services for a decent life; for example, clean air, education, health care, protection from crime. Importantly, while negative rights are usually treated as more stringent, positive claim rights tend to arise out of the special relationship between individuals or groups: I have a duty to provide for *my* children, not for my *neighbours'* children. I may have some duty also to help the latter – for example, if their parents were to neglect them – yet this would be based on charity, and on the fact that those who were supposed to assist them have failed to do so (it would not arise out of a special relation between me and my neighbours' children). On the other hand, the duty I owe my own children stems from the fact that *they are my kids.* This same reasoning can be applied to the political community. As we saw in chapter 1, an influential way to interpret the grounds of a citizen's duty to abide by the law centres on the special ties between members of the same body politic. This special relation generates reciprocal claim rights: our fellows have the right to demand from us that we comply with the shared rules of the joint enterprise.

While the idea of claim rights is meant to define a 'protected space' for human agency, *liberty* rights define the limits of this protected area. Claiming that A has a liberty right to X means that A has no countervailing duty not to X. Thus, we may demand that others not interfere with our exercise of free speech, but we may not demand that they not interfere with our assaulting an innocent person. This is because we do not have a right (we are not at *liberty*) to do what we ought not to do.[1] On the other hand, talking about liberty rights means that we are at liberty to exercise them: we can decide whether or not to speak up or to turn up at the polls and so on. Thus, when A has a right to X, A is at liberty to X; she has a claim that others not interfere with her X-ing, and she may as well have a claim that others assist her in X-ing. There are, nonetheless, some puzzling cases philosophers have been quick to identify; namely, where the right bearer may have a *claim* but no *liberty* to X: these are usually referred to as instances of a *right to do wrong* (Waldron 1993a, 63–87; Bolinger 2017). The puzzle arises because such right allows the agent to claim protection against interference from others while X-ing, despite the fact she should not X; that is, despite her having a duty not to X. Of course, this kind of right does not extend to inflicting physical harm or worse on others; if it exists, it is a right to do *some* wrong (Herstein 2012). Examples include being rude (within limits), spending one's own money in morally questionable activities (e.g., gambling), voting for a racist group (Waldron, ibid.). These are acts that we should not engage in, yet at the same time, others may not prevent us from engaging in these acts. The argument behind the notion of a right to do wrong concerns the alleged importance of protecting individual agency and the capacity to make morally significative choices, independently of the specific value of the option chosen. As Joseph Raz has discussed, we do not need a right to protect us when doing the right thing; rather, one needs a right to be entitled to do what one should not do. For Raz, this does not mean that rights exist to protect and encourage wrongdoing; rights exist to protect the agent's autonomy, to allow her to choose between right and wrong. Hence, they must also entitle the agent to do wrong (Raz 1979, 267).

I mention the right to do wrong here for, as we will see, recent theorists have not only argued for a moral right to civil disobedience, but have also claimed that it should be understood as a right to do wrong. This implies that citizens may resort to civil disobedience even in cases where they may be wrong about the need for legislative change.

5.2 THE MORAL RIGHT TO CIVIL DISOBEDIENCE

The brief outline in the previous section can help us make sense of the notion of a right to civil disobedience. The latter implies a claim against interference: if A has a right to civil disobedience, then others have a (defeasible) duty not to interfere with A's act of civil disobedience. Preventing a person from engaging in civil disobedience would be pro tanto wrong. The requirement against interference applies both *ex ante* and *post facto*: in addition to not being prevented from committing a communicative, forward-looking breach of the law, one who has a right to civil disobedience should not be punished for the mere breach of law this protest implies. Hence, if citizens possess a right to engage in civil disobedience, the state may not punish them for their illegal conduct. A large part of the discussion in this chapter will concern the debate around the state's (alleged) right to punish civil disobedients, vis-à-vis the latter's alleged right to civil disobedience. Furthermore, the right to civil disobedience may also imply a positive claim for the right holder: the state may have not only a duty not to interfere with the illegal protest, but also a positive duty to assist citizens in carrying out their civil disobedience. That is to say, the state may be required to ensure that citizens can exercise their right to civil disobedience; for example, by allowing free circulation of information in the media, and providing civic education programs in schools concerning this form of political, yet illegal, form of participation (Smith 2013).

Can the right to civil disobedience be interpreted also as a liberty right? Recall that one who has a liberty right to X has no countervailing moral duty not to X. However, civil disobedients are sometimes misguided about the cause they are protesting: their action may rest on a mistaken conception of justice, or on misunderstandings about the specific law or policy they are denouncing. They may have resorted to civil disobedience for a trivial reason, or paid insufficient attention to the availability of lawful avenues to channel their protest; or they may advance a morally repulsive cause; for example, white supremacy. If we interpret the right to civil disobedience also as a liberty right, then it may not apply to cases where citizens commit this kind of mistake (especially the last one). In similar circumstances, the right to civil disobedience would be conditional on the protest's *moral credentials*. Alternatively, we may think that the right to civil disobedience constitutes an example of a *right to do wrong* discussed above: even in cases where citizens may resort to the protest for the wrong reason, or may be mistaken about the issue at hand, it would be pro tanto wrong to prevent them from, or to punish them for, doing so (Lefkowitz 2007; Smith 2013; Brownlee 2012).

Raz contends that, if the right to civil disobedience exists, it should indeed be conceived as a right to do wrong; that is, it should protect citizens even when their resort to this form of illegal protest is misguided or unwise. While Raz believes that citizens are often justified in engaging in civil disobedience – that is, that they do *the right thing* – he rejects the existence of a right to civil disobedience under liberal, democratic regimes. According to his view, citizens may be entitled to this form of protest only in cases where the government does not sufficiently protect their right to political participation; that is, under an illiberal regime. Thus, Raz goes further than Rawls, who, as we saw in chapter 2, grants a role to civil disobedience in societies that are 'nearly just', however we want to interpret that label.[2] In doing so, Raz therefore rejects the idea of a right to civil disobedience; he claims that such an entitlement would arise only under unjust regimes, hence it cannot be considered a genuine right (which should apply to the agent regardless of the circumstances). Citizens have a right to political participation, which they exercise through the legal means provided by the institutional design of democratic governments; and the liberal state, in these circumstances, does not assess the legitimacy of political action based on the cause the latter seeks to support. However, Raz argues, the state does assess the legitimacy of citizens' political action when they resort to *illegal* protest, for citizens are not entitled to the latter. The right to political participation in liberal regimes does not include a right to break the law as part of a protest.

Furthermore, Raz points out the risk of self-contradiction in the very notion of a right to disobey. When one claims to have a right to political participation to engage in an illegal action, one is ipso facto criticising the law for outlawing this form of action; the contradiction lies in the fact that 'if one has a right to perform [this kind of illegal protest], its performance should not be civil disobedience but a lawful act' (Raz 1979). Since, under liberal regimes, this criticism is not possible, it follows there is no right to civil disobedience.

Let us pause for a moment on this claim. A crucial implication of Raz's denial of a right to civil disobedience is that the choice to engage in such conduct is pro tanto wrong, as a violation of a citizen's obligation to obey the law. As such, a person who resorts to civil disobedience is liable to being prosecuted and, if the judge or jury deem it appropriate, punished for the breach of the law. As we noticed in chapter 2, it is generally acknowledged that a civil disobedient must be willing to accept the punishment that may follow from her deliberate choice to break the law. Of course, the act of disobedience may be *all things considered* justifiable, for the circumstances that led to the breach of the law may provide a justification for the agent's choice. This is a common element of the criminal justice system: from the fact that a person is found responsible for the breach of the law, it does not necessarily follow that she is also liable to punishment. Where the prohibited action is justified by weightier considerations – for example, by the need to avert a more serious evil than the one the prohibited action causes – the agent's conduct may be all things considered the right thing to do under the circumstances. Declaring an action 'justified' signals approval of the agent who, while having a pro tanto duty to not X, has done the right thing by X-ing under the circumstances (Lefkowitz 2016).

Justifications are not the only means for a defendant to deflect the charge of wrongdoing, and the relative sanctions that may come with it. There may be cases where the conduct is wrong, and hence it does not warrant approval of the agent; nonetheless, the agent may not be liable to punishment. In such cases, the wrongdoing may be *excused*, rather than *justified*: 'insanity' is the main example of this latter case, in which the agent may have committed the wrongful act during a psychotic incident. While a justified action should be treated as right, an excused one represents a *wrong action done non-culpably*. In both cases, punishment may be unwarranted.

It goes without saying that a person who resorts to civil disobedience may not want to appeal to a legal excuse in order to avoid the legal consequences of her act. Pleading for an excuse is a means for agents to avert responsibility, by asserting they did not act as fully autonomous persons at the time of the breach of the law. It constitutes an admission that they *should not* have engaged in civil disobedience. However, people who resort to civil disobedience generally adopt the opposite view: they take full responsibility for their conduct, they act openly and do not deny the deliberate (and voluntary) nature of their breach of the law. Far from conceding that they acted wrongly, the civil disobedients are eager to claim that they did the right thing by breaching the law under the circumstances. For this reason, in what follows, I will focus on the possibility of civil disobedients claiming a legal justification for their illegal conduct, and will set aside the possibility of a legal excuse.

5.3 THE DEFENCE OF NECESSITY

Imagine you are walking in the street, when suddenly you hear someone calling for help from a nearby home. You peer through the window and see a person lying on the floor, holding her chest: it does not take long for you to realise that the person is having a heart attack. Suppose you are a trained paramedic and could perform CPR on her. Upon realising that there is no one else with her and that her life is in danger, you decide to break into the house, to give her assistance until the ambulance arrives. Under normal circumstance, you would have committed a breach of property (e.g., illegal entry), which would make you liable to legal sanctions, including going to prison. However, in this case it would be plausible for you to argue that your conduct was justified, as it was necessary to save the stranger's life. While the damage you caused to the woman's property is certainly regrettable, you were justified in committing what, under normal circumstances, would constitute a wrongful act. This is the rationale grounding the defence of necessity, which is usually available to a defendant in cases (like the one just mentioned) where the mere breach of the law does not suffice to establish the agent's wrongdoing.

The defence of necessity is often invoked in cases of civil disobedience, for the reasons just mentioned.[3] Protesters argue that their deliberate choice to break the law was necessary to avert a more serious harm and, therefore, should not warrant punishing them for acting illegally. As we will see in more detail below, they may do so not necessarily to avoid the punishment, but rather to show their fellow citizens that they should not be blamed for their conduct. In fact, even if the judge or jury refused the defence, the protesters would have at least achieved a widely publicised discussion of the issue they are protesting. It is, in fact, rare for a court to acquit civil disobedients based on necessity.[4] This is due to the fact that, for such defence to be granted, four elements must be jointly established; namely,

1. that the defendant was faced with a *choice of evils* and chose the lesser one
2. that she acted to prevent *imminent* harm
3. that she reasonably anticipated a *causal relation* between her conduct and the harm to be avoided
4. that there were *no legal alternatives* to breaching the law

If any one of these four requirements cannot be established, the court will refuse to grant a justification based on necessity. Historically, civil disobedients have been able to show (1) and (2) in court. Anti-war protesters, for example, have made the plausible claim that their breach of the law was less harmful than the death of innocent civilians in war zones, which was the target of their protest. Similar considerations address the *imminence* requirement, although the latter has been criticised for adding an undue restriction to the defence of necessity by assuming that the harm must be *proximate*. The problem with this further requirement is that it does not appear to add anything significant to requirement (1), and rather implies that the agent(s) must be in the proximity of the threat for the action to be deemed necessary. In some situations, by the time the harm is 'proximate', the window of opportunity to avert that harm may have already passed (Cavallaro 1993, 358).

The real problem for civil disobedients pleading necessity, however, concerns the causal relation. While the court may grant the gravity of the issue to which protesters are seeking to draw attention, it very rarely accepts that the act of disobedience was causally linked to the prevention of the harm; that is, that it was *necessary* to avert the harm. Environmental activists, for example, may find it very difficult to show that their protest against climate change was necessary to avert the harms caused by global warming. Similarly, draft protesters who burn their draft cards may hardly convince the court that their action was necessary to stop the war in Vietnam. Things are even more difficult with reference to the 'no-legal-alternatives' requirement. As we saw in chapter 2, there is a general assumption that civil disobedience should be used as a 'last resort', after legal avenues for publicity have been exhausted. However, strictly speaking, legal avenues are *never* exhausted, for we can always organise another lawful protest, write another letter to our MPs, hand a few more leaflets to the public and more. It is no coincidence, therefore, that most appeals for a justification of necessity, in cases of civil disobedience, fail to satisfy the 'no-legal-alternative' requirement.

Matthew Hall has proposed the introduction of a *guilty-but-civilly-disobedient* (GBCD) verdict to capture the specific nature of this form of principled law breaking, and to 'reconcile civil disobedience with the rule of law' (Hall 2007). In Hall's proposal, this may apply to cases where 'the jury finds that the defendant acted: conscientiously, openly and respectfully' (ibid, 2114). Though interesting, his account is extremely restrictive about the kind of disobedience it is intended to cover. By 'openly', Hall means that the defendant 'provided notice of the offence to a relevant enforcement authority in advance' and that she performed the act 'in the presence of a law enforcement authority'. Hall provides a long list of requirements the defendant must fulfil to show she acted 'respectfully', the following being the most striking: 'If the defendant committed the offense in a location or manner directed in significant part at a private party, the defendant did not act respectfully' (2115). Hall explains this in terms of coerciveness: by targeting a private rather than a public dwelling, the civil disobedients would presumably disrespect the dignity of those who own that space. This would be enough to turn them into 'uncivil' disobedients. One major problem with Hall's account is that it describes civil disobedience as a nuisance with which the legal order has to put up or, as he writes, an 'irresolvable problem' (2117). He claims his proposal would provide the disobedients with 'an incentive to view the legal system in a positive light' (ibid.), though it is not clear why the disobedients need such an incentive. Hall argues that one of the 'benefits' of the GBCD verdict is that 'the trial would not become a publicity theatre for dissidents'; however, he admits his proposal may have the unwelcome effect of rather providing people with an incentive to engage in civil disobedience, given the exculpatory label the GBCD verdict would carry.

The irony behind this last point should not escape us. If someone chooses to engage in civil disobedience, she may not be troubled by being labelled a 'civil' disobedient. Quite the contrary: she would certainly want to distinguish herself from the common law breaker. Hence, we may expect that a verdict of 'guilty, but' would be welcome by those who seek to prove the 'civil' nature of their illegal conduct. Hall sees this as a problem, rather than a strength, of his proposal: his underlying concern is with ensuring that citizens who resort to civil disobedience not escape the legal consequences that attend to the deliberate choice to break the law. In fact, some theorists contend that a civil disobedient *should not* try to avoid the punishment, for the attempt to do so may contradict the nature and goals of civil disobedience (Bauer and Eckerstrom 1987; McEwen 1991).

Another possible approach to the problem of justification focuses on the *communicative* nature of civil disobedience. As discussed at length in the previous chapters, the resort to this form of protest aims to communicate a serious and sincere concern about a certain law or policy. The breach of the law constitutes a 'form of address', or a 'speech-act', which sets it aside from standard law-breaking conduct. This is particularly relevant in the case of indirect civil disobedience, where the law disobeyed is not the one the protest targets: the breach of law X *is meant* to communicate criticisms of law Y. Since the law affords protection to the expression of free speech, it may be argued it should do the same to communicative acts of illegal protest; for example, to civil disobedience. A famous case, discussed by Barbara Katz, is *United States v. O'Brien*, in which the defendant had been convicted of a federal offence after burning his draft card (Katz 1985). The defendant claimed that burning the card constituted a political statement, through which the defendant was communicating his criticism of US military operations in Vietnam. As such, the defendant argued, the act was protected under the First Amendment. The Supreme Court rejected the claim that O'Brien's act was a form of 'symbolic speech', and argued that the First Amendment does not protect illegal conduct 'whenever the person engaging in the conduct intends thereby to express an idea' (ibid, 907). The underlying claim is correct: a political assassination may certainly *communicate* opposition to the assassinated leader, but could hardly be considered the legitimate exercise of free speech. Nonetheless, Katz defends the idea of allowing the defence of necessity to civil disobedients in cases where the illegal protest centres around 'a zone of moral flux'; namely, an issue on which consensus is lacking.

> Permitting the defense of necessity to be raised in cases of this nature would certainly encourage dialogue, both inside and outside the courtroom. It would facilitate the process by which one idea supplants another in our society, a process at the heart of the functioning of a democracy and one that the First Amendment itself protects. There is no reason to assume, moreover, that, simply because a court submitted the necessity defense to a jury, the jury would necessarily *accept* the defense. Civil disobedients would still need to convince the jury that the evil they opposed was sufficiently great to warrant their lawbreaking. (918)

The idea here is that necessity should be supplanted by the right to free speech, and by the contribution that an act of illegal protest would nonetheless provide to the discussion about the contentious issue.

5.3.1 Brownlee on the Necessity Defence

As we saw above, necessity defences are usually invoked in cases where the breach of the law is deemed 'necessary' to avoid a more serious harm. Kimberley Brownlee, whose view I will discuss in detail below, has argued for a version of the necessity defence for civil disobedience which does not apply exclusively to 'emergencies' (e.g., situations where someone's life is in danger), but also to cases where 'non-contingent basic needs and rights' are at stake (2012, 198).[5] Brownlee contends that where the civil disobedients aim to draw attention to government's neglect or abuse of non-contingent basic needs and rights, and where ordinary (i.e., legal) efforts to highlight this injustice would be ineffective, the disobedients could invoke the defence of necessity to show their breach of the law was justified. However, this defence is not available to *all* civil disobedients, as Brownlee further specifies that acts of disobedience that either disregard or oppose non-contingent basic needs and rights could not invoke the defence of necessity, for they would violate the 'principle of humanism'.[6] In this sense, Brownlee emphasises that the breach of law may be 'necessary' not only as an attempt to prevent someone from suffering physical harm or death, but also to prevent broader violations of a persons' basic needs and rights, such as recognition, inclusion and autonomy. This justification would also apply to civil disobedience in defence of animals and other animate beings, who may not be able to defend themselves. At the core of Brownlee's claim there is a concern with limiting the extent to which law can dictate citizens' conduct; she criticises the expectation that, when it comes to conflicts between law's commands, on the one hand, and the agent's own convictions, on the other, the law must always have the last word.[7] The legal system should acknowledge that such expectation places unreasonable burdens on the individual, who must always sacrifice her other moral commitments in deference to the law.[8] Brownlee claims that such a defence is particularly valuable in democratic regimes, for even liberal democracies may turn into tyrannies (194): a democratic government may indeed abuse the non-contingent rights of individuals (like the right of refugees to access the health system, or the right of prisoners to be treated humanely), and also neglect non-contingent basic *needs*. With reference to the latter, Brownlee defends as justifiable 'on ground of necessity' a campaign of civil disobedience targeting the government's decision to outlaw adultery, despite the fact that people should not commit adultery (195): this is because if the law were to legislate in that area, it would unduly infringe on a non-contingent basic need each individual has to exercise her autonomy. The latter, as we saw above, should also involve a moral right *to do wrong*. This raises the very interesting point that civil disobedience may be *necessary* to prevent the state from crossing the line of its legitimate authority, a point that was central to the Rawlsian account of civil disobedience as an instrument to protect citizens from the government.

5.4 DAVID LEFKOWITZ: PENALISING, NOT PUNISHING, CIVIL DISOBEDIENCE

The previous discussion hinged on the assumption that civil disobedience, as a breach of the law, is pro tanto wrong, and therefore may deserve punishment, unless it can be established that the illegal act was justified. But there is another way to look at this issue; namely, to challenge the assumption that civil disobedience is pro tanto wrong. As mentioned at the beginning of this chapter, the illegal act may be considered a legitimate exercise of the agent's rights, despite involving a breach of the law. While the defence of necessity, discussed in the previous section, focuses on the consequences the illegal act intends to achieve (e.g., avoidance of a serious harm or injustice), the idea of a right to civil disobedience shifts the focus towards a non-consequentialist, non-instrumental account of this form of illegal protest. From this different standpoint, if there is a right to engage in civil disobedience, a protester may not need a justification for her choice to breach the law.

However, this approach gives rise to an obvious conflict between the notion of a duty to obey the law, discussed in chapter 1, and the alleged right to (civilly) disobey it. Academic interest around this problem has led to a wealth of important contributions, over the past fifteen years, from political and legal philosophers, who have debated the existence of a moral right to civil disobedience. This debate was sparked by a paper by David Lefkowitz (2007), which provided the first systematic analysis, after Raz's sceptical view, of the possibility of such a right under liberal democratic regimes. Contrary to Raz, however, Lefkowitz provides a compelling case *in favour* of such right. As we saw above, Raz contended that if one claims to have a right to engage in an illegal action, then one is ipso facto criticising the law for outlawing this form of action: the right bearer has a (defeasible) claim on others that they not interfere with her conduct, hence the law should not interfere either. For Lefkowitz, however, the moral right to civil disobedience protects the right bearer from some, but not all, kinds of interference; specifically, Lefkowitz claims that the state may impose *penalties*, but not *punishment*, on the civil disobedients (despite the latter having a moral right to engage in civil disobedience). To understand Lefkowitz's argument, we first need to identify what grounds his account of the right to civil disobedience. Lefkowitz takes issue with Raz's claim that it would be inconsistent to talk of such right under liberal regimes, where citizens have access to legal avenues to express their political views and partake in the political life of their community. For Raz, a right to engage in illegal protest can exist only under illiberal regimes – those that unduly limit, or prevent, citizens' political participation. Lefkowitz argues, on the other hand, that even under liberal regimes citizens may differ in the capacities to access the public arena, and thus to partake in the life of the body politic. Echoing an argument I considered in the previous chapter (concerning power imbalances in the public sphere), Lefkowitz points out that, when a decision is finally reached at the end of the deliberative process, some citizens 'may justifiably complain that, had there been further time for debate and deliberation, or had they enjoyed greater resources for the dissemination of their arguments, their own (reasonable) views might have won majority support' (2007, 213). Lefkowitz contends that the right to political participation should not only be understood as a right to partake in the political decision-making process – for example, by casting a vote during elections – but also a right to keep contesting the decision reached by such a process through a variety of means, including through civil disobedience.

Note that Lefkowitz's argument implies that *some* citizens – namely, members of a marginalised or disempowered minority – have a right to engage in civil disobedience.[9] Those who, on the other hand, have not been penalised by power imbalances do not have such right. In this sense, his argument goes further than Raz's, which denies that there is a right to civil disobedience under democratic regimes; Lefkowitz, in fact, points out that even under democratic regimes citizens may not have equal access to legal avenues for political participation. Those who are excluded, due to 'bad luck', should be able to resort to illegal means of protest, including civil disobedience, to bridge the power imbalance in the deliberative arena.[10] However, at best this implies that whether or not a citizen has a right to civil disobedience *depends on the circumstances*.[11] Lefkowitz makes this clear when he writes that

> the best understanding of the moral right to political participation is one that reduces as much as possible the degree to which it is a matter of luck whether

> one attracts majority support for one's reasonable views regarding what justice requires. (215)

An agent's moral right to political participation should then include not only access to legal means, such as the right to vote, but also to illegal means, such as to civil disobedience. However, an agent's ability to exercise her right to vote does not depend on the circumstances: one either is or is not included in the franchise.[12] It is not clear, then, why Lefkowitz would claim that the same does not apply to the right to civil disobedience. The peculiar element of Lefkowitz's account concerns the alleged impermissibility of interfering with the right bearer's conduct. I already mentioned that, for Lefkowitz, the right to civil disobedience implies a (defeasible) claim against *some* interferences. More specifically, Lefkowitz claims that the state cannot punish citizens for resorting to civil disobedience; however, the state maintains the right to penalise them for doing so.

Lefkowitz invokes a familiar distinction in the philosophy of the criminal law between a 'punishment' and a 'penalty' (Feinberg 1965). The difference between the two lies in their *expressive* function: the imposition of a 'punishment' expresses blame, resentment and moral censure of the wrongdoer, and signals public condemnation for her conduct; penalties, on the other hand, are said to lack this condemnatory element. Sentencing someone to prison conveys a different message about that person's conduct and character, compared to sentencing her to pay a fine. The latter, based on the punishment/penalty distinction, does not express moral condemnation of the agent's conduct. Thus, although both a civil disobedient and a tax dodger might be sanctioned for the same action (failure to pay taxes), only the latter would be 'punished', while the former would be 'penalised'. The civil disobedient, according to Lefkowitz, acts within her right (despite breaching the law), and the state ought to acknowledge this fact by 'penalising', rather than 'punishing', her. In fact, punishing a person for engaging in civil disobedience would be 'equivalent to punishing a person for exercising the right to vote or the right to free speech' (219).

However, the state does neither punish nor penalise people for exercising their right to vote or to free speech. Why, then, may the state penalise people for exercising their right to civil disobedience? Lefkowitz claims that the state is justified in imposing costs on those who resort to civil disobedience, apparently because this will preserve political stability and deter people from engaging in this sort of protest unless 'the injustice of existing laws and policies is believed to be significant' (220).[13] The imposition of penalties on the civil disobedients 'simply serves as an institutionalized incentive to such agents to consider the potential cost to justice of their engaging in such acts' (ibid.). Lefkowitz adds that these penalties may be interpreted as ex post facto licences for committing an illegal protest, akin to the permits that citizens acquire to run legal protests. However, following Lefkowitz's argument, the state does not merely have the right to impose penalties on the civil disobedients: it can also send them to prison. This comes as a surprise, as Lefkowitz had previously invoked the 'expressive' difference between fining and imprisoning an offender, where the latter but not the former conveys resentment and blame. Yet Lefkowitz now explains that incarcerating civil disobedients can still be considered a 'penalty' rather than a 'punishment'; for example, the state may detain individuals carrying contagious disease in quarantine, yet it does not seek to convey any specific condemnation for those who are so incarcerated. It is a necessary evil to avoid a worse outcome. The same should apply to the incarceration of a civil disobedient: while she has done nothing wrong to deserve being blamed, she may be justifiably detained in order to prevent risks to political stability.[14] Thus, while both a civil and an uncivil disobedient may end up in prison, the former would be merely penalised, while the latter would be properly 'punished'.

Despite its clever approach to the issue, this argument faces significant objections. Kimberley Brownlee has highlighted some of the most pressing problems with the idea of a right against being punished but not against being penalised. First of all, Feinberg's distinction (despite the attention it has rightly received in philosophy of law) may be considered mainly semantic, for if 'a judge imposes a burden weighty enough [on the civil disobedients], . . . then, to all involved, that burden will look and feel like punishment' (2018, 295). This is particularly true in light of the fact that, as we saw above, Lefkowitz treats imprisonment as an appropriate form of 'penalty' for committing civil disobedience: if both the civil and the uncivil disobedient are sent to prison, it may be difficult to pinpoint the difference between the two cases of illegal conduct. Furthermore, as Brownlee points out (ibid.), the civil and the uncivil person may engage in exactly the same conduct (e.g., damage to property): Would the civil disobedient then deserve a harsher sentence since, as opposed to the uncivil one, she has breached the law *and* engaged in civil disobedience?

These practicalities notwithstanding, there are also notable theoretical worries with Lefkowitz's account of the right to civil disobedience. These concern the very idea of penalising someone for exercising their rights. It is one thing to say that I have a claim right against interference, when engaging in civil disobedience, which the state may justifiably override when preventing widespread disobedience; it is another to say that I do not have a right against interference. In the former case, I have the right to complain if the state punishes *or penalises* me merely for engaging in civil disobedience; the state may have a justification for interfering with my right, and I would be entitled to an explanation and, if appropriate, even an apology for the burdens imposed upon me. In the latter case, the state would act legitimately, and owe me no explanation (or apology) for the sanctions it imposes upon me. Lefkowitz's argument for penalising civil disobedience rests on considerations of deterrence; namely, 'on an instrumental calculation of the effect that penalising, or not penalising, a public disobedient will have on the stability and effectiveness of the legal order' (2007, fn. 41); yet deterrence is traditionally ill suited as a justification of punishment (or penalty) vis-à-vis the normative force of individuals' rights (Brownlee 2012, 245–46).[15] One main problem is that it disrespects individual autonomy, for it may justify *using* people as means rather than ends in themselves; an innocent person may be justifiably punished if that successfully deterred others from committing crime. Furthermore, the state may justifiably punish civil disobedience in a disproportionately harsh way, if that was to keep society 'stable'. These considerations sit oddly against Lefkowitz's claim that 'respect for agents' moral right to political participation requires that potential barriers to their effective exercise of this right be diminished as much as possible' (215). Lefkowitz is concerned with reducing the effects of luck on citizens' effective capacity to influence the law-making process: those who are unfairly *penalised* (pun intended) by bad luck should be provided with additional avenues for redress *as a matter of justice*. For this reason, it is not obvious how further penalising them for engaging in civil disobedience could fulfil Lefkowitz's goal.

5.5 BROWNLEE ON A MORAL RIGHT TO CONSCIENTIOUS ACTION

Brownlee's book *Conscience and Conviction: The Case for Civil Disobedience* is amongst the most notable contributions, to date, to the literature on civil disobedience.[16] Brownlee provides much more than a discussion of this form of protest in the attempt to single out its distinctive features vis-à-vis other forms of political participation, for she offers a fully fledged account of conscientious conduct, moral convictions and practical reason. It is not possible to do justice to the breadth and complexity of her project, and in what follows I focus on her own argument in defence of a right to civil disobedience. This argument hinges on the distinction between civil disobedience and what Brownlee labels 'personal disobedience' (27–29), already mentioned in chapter 2 above. The latter refers to an individual's refusal to obey the law on grounds of moral conviction; for example, a doctor may refuse to conduct an abortion due to her deeply held belief about the sanctity of human life. This form of non-compliance lacks the communicative aims that characterise acts of civil disobedience: the key concern of someone engaging in personal disobedience is 'to keep her hands clean'. Brownlee points out that liberal societies tend to be more tolerant of this form of disobedience, to which the law accords some leeway through the provision of exemptions. Thus, the law recognises that individuals have a right to object to some laws, when the latter make demands that are too costly vis-à-vis the agent's strongest moral convictions. Legal provisions supporting a right to *conscientious objection* are meant to guarantee a protected sphere of action to citizens by granting exemption from legal directives that may be too onerous (from the perspective of one's own convictions) for the individual agent.

Yet Brownlee points out this does not happen in the case of civil disobedience, which is not allowed protection in law, despite also being grounded on a sincere and serious conviction about the wrongness of a certain law or policy. As we saw in chapter 2, civil disobedients go further than conscientious objectors by demanding not a personal exemption from an alleged wrongdoing, but rather that the law be changed. As Brownlee writes, some see this as a form of arrogance; that is, a citizen's attempt to place herself above the law and/or to impose her views on others, compared to the more modest goals of the conscientious objector, who simply asks to be exempted from existing legal provisions. In fact, the idea underlying Brownlee's book is that civil disobedience is *more conscientious* than personal disobedience, and as such has a stronger claim to the kind of right-based protection that is appropriate to conscientious action. Societies should be more accommodating, and more appreciative, of 'civil' than of 'personal' disobedience: the former is more praiseworthy, for (as opposed to personal disobedience) it fulfils four requirements of conscientious action. These are (a) *consistency* between the agent's action, beliefs and attitudes towards herself and others; (b) *universality*, in that the agent's judgement applies universally to all relevantly similar agents in relevantly similar circumstances; (c) *non-evasion*, for the civil disobedient does not seek to escape the consequences of defending her convictions (e.g., legal punishment); (d) *dialogue*, in that civil (as opposed to *personal*) disobedience implies a willingness to *communicate* one's own conviction to others, with the aim of engaging them in reasoned deliberation about law's merits or demerits (29–30). Such dialogic effort, in Brownlee's view, further epitomises the conscientiousness of the agent's conviction; that is, its sincerity and seriousness.

Based on these premises, Brownlee argues for a *moral right to conscientious action* (140–52); that is, a right to act upon one's own conscientious convictions. This right delineates a sphere of conduct with which others are not meant to interfere, not even the state: contrary to Lefkowitz's view discussed above, she claims the state should *neither punish nor penalise* citizens simply for engaging in conscientious actions such as civil disobedience. The right to conscientious action stems from the need to respect our agency and dignity as persons. It is grounded on what Brownlee labels 'principle of humanism', which requires

> appreciating that our deepest commitments come with non-evasive, dialogic efforts. Society and the law place undue pressure on us when they require us always to privilege the law before our deeply held moral convictions. And they place undue pressure on us when they tolerate only our non-communicative, private disobedience in support of our convictions. . . . [Our] society has a duty to honour the fact that we are reasoning and feeling beings capable of forming deep moral commitments. (7)

The principle of humanism contains an important statement about our political obligations. It points out that our role as 'citizens' is one amongst many that we occupy, and its requirements do not trump those of other roles under all circumstances. We do have other commitments in life, writes Brownlee, in addition to the political ones to adhere to the law, and it is disrespectful of our status as autonomous agents to demand that we always sacrifice the former to the demands of the latter. Under some circumstances, we should be able to act on those other commitments even if, in doing so, we might engage in law-breaking conduct. William Scheuerman has criticised Brownlee for the 'anti-legalism' that underpins this argument; that is, for interpreting civil disobedience as grounded on moral convictions at the expense of the demands of the law. For Scheuerman, we should not lose sight of 'the legal prong' of civil disobedience; that is, of its being an act of 'fidelity to the law', as per Rawls's account. By abandoning the legal understanding of civil disobedience, we may 'undermine its conceptual foundations and rob protestors of a vital line of defence' (Scheuerman 2018, 150).[17]

While the focus on the principle of humanism relies on non-instrumental considerations, Brownlee also highlights some benefits to societies granting a moral right to civil disobedience. She refers to a 'double harmony' between, on the one hand, civil disobedients' interests in having this right to conscientious action protected and, on the other, society's interest in 'the deliberation-enhancing effects of this kind of constrained breach of the law' (146). That is to say, a moral right to conscientious action would serve not only the interest of the citizen but also those of society at large. Echoing John Stuart Mill, she claims that the civil disobedients' communicative efforts may enhance the quality of the deliberation by providing alternatives to the views presented by mainstream media, calling the state to account for its conduct and further engaging fellow citizens in communicative exchanges. More importantly, the act of civil disobedience may play this role even when protesters are mistaken about either facts or principles.

The claim against interference is not absolute, for Brownlee acknowledges that there may be cases where the state would be justified in sanctioning the civil disobedients for their breach of the law. This may be required by the specific circumstances; for example, if not sanctioning them may lead to further social unrest due to a volatile political environment. In similar cases, the state may be justified in infringing on citizens' right to civil disobedience – for example, imposing fines or even a prison sentence upon the protesters. Nevertheless, writes Brownlee, this should be accompanied by an apology; namely, an acknowledgement by the state that punishment is, under the circumstances, a necessary evil: the state should express its regret for having to impose a sanction on the civil disobedients; that is, for disrespecting their agency and dignity as persons (251). One of the most striking features of this account is that it does not discriminate based on the protesters' specific cause: being grounded on the idea of humanity, the moral right to civil disobedience applies to all agents equally. This means, therefore, that anti-war, environmentalist, social justice *and neo-Nazi* protesters all have a right to engage in constrained, communicative breaches of the law in defence of their cause (7). More importantly, this means that the state should apologise to all these protesters, including the neo-Nazi, for having to punish them for their illegal protest.

This, however, seems counterintuitive, as noted by William Smith, who highlights the oddness of claiming that a judge, who punishes unlawful neo-Nazi protesters on reasonable grounds, has some kind of moral duty to express regret for having to do so (Smith 2016). The judge, according to Brownlee, should convey her appreciation for the societal value of the protest, and offer an apology to the neo-Nazi for the need to punish them. Yet Smith points out, given the nature of the convictions expressed by those protesters, it is far from obvious that expressions of regret are necessary or appropriate. Our intuition about the inappropriateness of expressing regret for punishing a 'white supremacist' should be taken as a sign that, in such case, 'there is no rights-based consideration that needs to be, in some sense, overridden by countervailing considerations' (702). Smith concludes, contra Brownlee, that there is no moral right to civil disobedience in defence of odious causes.

This is a fair comment to Brownlee's proposal, involving a key issue in the debate on pluralism; namely, whether and how to tolerate the intolerant. Brownlee touches upon this objection in her reply to Smith (Brownlee 2016), explaining the judge should make it clear what she is apologising for. The judge does not express regret for punishing someone who promotes racist views; rather, the apology is 'for not being able in this case, for whatever reason, to make some space for the person's suitably constrained, civilly disobedient expression of his conviction' (ibid., 731). Yet this reply is underwhelming, and evokes Brownlee's own objection to Lefkowitz's punishment/penalty distinction; namely, that 'judges, politicians, society, and civil disobedients may well find this distinction merely semantic' (2018, 295). As I argue in chapter 6, I share Smith's (and Lefkowitz's) intuition that civil disobedience in defence of 'odious causes' should not enjoy the same protection afforded to other instances of communicative law breaking. Furthermore, as already mentioned, Brownlee talks of a *double harmony* between the interest of the agent in being able to act on her convictions and, on the other hand, the interest of the political community in having a vigorous and engaged deliberation. This double harmony is served, in her view, even when people advance, for example, racist ideas, for by doing so they force society to respond by reaffirming its commitment to the notion of equal respect. Once again, to a large extent this echoes John Stuart Mill's claim that any opinion, if left unchallenged, becomes prejudice; hence, allowing racists the freedom to challenge the idea of equality may strengthen that very idea by demanding that society reaffirm it even more strongly. But there is reason to resist Brownlee's optimism about this alleged 'double harmony', especially at the present time, where racist views seem to receive a significant amount of attention on mainstream media. While the occasional racist comment may be a 'healthy' reminder of what is wrong with racism, claiming that citizens have the right to make racist claims risks *normalising* what, instead, should be condemned as incompatible with the values of democracy. Far from harmonising with society's interest in an enhanced democratic debate, an unconditional right to conscientious action may jeopardise the values underlying democracy.

Brownlee acknowledges this point, as she claims that those who resort to civil disobedience for morally odious causes may be allowed a legal *excuse*, not a justification. As we saw above, only the latter signals approval for the agent's conduct: when the state finds a person justified in her decision to break the law, the state determines she committed no wrong, despite breaking the law. Her acquittal signals she made no mistake in terms of practical reasoning – she did what she had most reason to do. An *excuse*, on the other hand, lacks this positive endorsement of the agent's conduct: it signals the agent's failure to take the legal prohibition as an undefeated reason for action. The agent should have known that, under those circumstances, her decision to break the law was wrong; nonetheless, she is acquitted in recognition of the fact that she had an undefeated reason for thinking that she was justified in breaking the law. She made a mistake in practical reasoning, but the mistake was excused by the specific circumstances. Hence, in the case of the racist civil disobedient, Brownlee claims that the decision to breach the law is born of 'psychological costliness and *akrasia*' (167). As with those who engage in civil disobedience for less detestable ideas, we cannot disregard how demanding it is, for the individual, to always have to give priority to literal adherence to the law over her own convictions:

> [The legal excuse] recognises the psychological risks of self-alienation, incongruity and akrasia that dog absolute expectations that we adhere to formal norms. In valuing autonomy, it is necessary to value also the conditions for autonomy, one of which is an integrated mind and the capacity for practical reasoning. (2012, 168)

This echoes the previous discussion concerning the *right to do wrong*, which implies a claim right to do what we have a duty not to do. As we saw above, supporters of this idea argue that a right to do wrong is important to protect the agent's autonomy: the possibility of making mistakes is a constitutive element of our agency, part of 'the conditions' for being an autonomous agent. The law should be sensitive to this fact about our nature by acknowledging that some mistakes should not be sanctioned, when they occur in a situation in which adherence to the law, rather than to our own convictions, would be overly costly for us.[18] It is nonetheless troubling that, for Brownlee, the law should provide room for mistakes falling below a minimum threshold of reasonableness: there is something uncomfortable in the claim that the racist is unjustly burdened when asked to conform to the law rather than being allowed to engage in civil disobedience supporting white supremacy (Hindkjaer Madsen 2018). It is hard to take the avoidance of racism as a 'cost', and if it is a cost, it is one we should be willing to bear. The commitment to respecting individual autonomy need not lead to granting rights to racists. First, autonomy is not valuable per se, since an 'autonomous' murderer is morally worse than one who murders while hallucinating. By the same token, a person who deeply believes that non-white people are inferior is more blameworthy than one who had been brainwashed into thinking so. Second, there is the paradox, already mentioned above, of defending autonomy by protecting views that deny that very idea: as Jeremy Waldron (1993, 223) points out, 'The speeches that [the racists] claim the right to make are calculated to bring an end to the form of life in relation to which the idea of free speech is conceived'. As I discuss in detail in chapter 6, *the cause* advanced by the protesters impinges on the civility of the action: communicative breaches of the law that signal disrespect for individual autonomy should not be considered acts of *civil* disobedience, and hence should not enjoy the same treatment vis-à-vis the law as the latter.

5.6 WILLIAM SMITH ON A POSITIVE RIGHT TO CIVIL DISOBEDIENCE

In another book-length analysis of civil disobedience, published shortly after Brownlee's one, William Smith has provided further insight into the notion of a moral right to civil disobedience (Smith 2013). Like its predecessor, Smith's book offers more than a simple account of civil disobedience, as it also articulates a theory of deliberative democracy able to accommodate this form of illegal behaviour. For the present purposes, my discussion will focus on his argument for the moral right to civil disobedience.

Smith defends this right mainly on instrumental grounds; that is, by focusing on the benefits it brings to the individual citizens and the community at large. He claims that a moral right to civil disobedience may act as a safety valve, by allowing those whose view has been defeated, after the democratic deliberation, to release some of their resentment in ways that do not escalate to outright violence (86). A right to civil disobedience allows minorities to avoid the feeling of being ignored, marginalised, or even condemned for their own defeated view. It thus plays an important role in maintaining a stable society and preserving 'civic friendship', for it supports the idea that 'all must be regarded as equal citizens with a right to articulate and advance their interests and opinions within the democratic process' (16).

Citing Rawls, Smith further explains that a moral right to civil disobedience enhances citizens' moral responsibility. If society requires citizens to always defer to the majority, even when they sincerely and reasonably believe that society is implicated in a serious injustice, citizens may end up divesting themselves of their responsibility and transferring the blame onto others. Thus, 'in order to cultivate our ability and willingness to assume responsibility for our society's apparent failings, citizens should enjoy access to a suitably constrained form of unlawful political participation' (87). Smith further links the right to civil disobedience to Thomas Christiano's notion of a right 'to be at home on the world' (Christiano 2008), which outlines the importance of providing 'the condition in which one has a sense of fit, connection and meaning in the world one lives in' (Smith, ibid.). I understand this as involving the importance of self-respect, and of creating social arrangements that ensure citizens are treated as equals. This view, which has its roots in Rawls, contends that only when citizens are provided with a social environment that fosters self-respect they may develop and exercise their moral powers and pursue their goals in life. Smith continues his analysis by pointing out that, when citizens are outvoted in a democratic decision, they may nonetheless maintain a strong opposition to the prevailing view: if the opposition is particularly intense, these citizens may feel compelled to publicise their discontent through political protest. Despite the alienation they experience at being relegated to the minority, these citizens would benefit from the possibility to resort to suitably constrained acts of civil disobedience: 'The public recognition of our right to express our dissent through unconventional channels might help us, gradually and with difficulty, to regain our sense of place in our common world' (88).

Smith endorses the notion of a claim right against interference which, as we saw above, is central to both Lefkowitz and Brownlee's accounts. In fact, to a large extent, his view overlaps with Lefkowitz's, including the problematic idea that the state may penalise citizens who engage in civil disobedience. In response to Brownlee's objection that a claim right should forbid *any* interference, not only those that are meant as punishments, Smith argues (again echoing Lefkowitz) that the state is justified in imposing moderate costs upon the disobedients for the choice to engage in the illegal protest.

Like Lefkowitz, however, Smith places under the umbrella of 'moderate penalties' sanctions such as 'fines, community service, suspended custodial sentences or *even brief periods of incarceration*' (2013, 95. Added emphasis). Yet in his response to Brownlee's objection, he focuses on fines, the justifiability of which he defends by analogy with a fee for obtaining a permit for a legal protest. In some jurisdiction, Smith points out, citizens have to pay a fee as part of their application for a permit to hold a rally: 'The legal obligation to secure a licence or permit is defensible on the grounds that political demonstrators should contribute to the efforts of authorities to secure the safety of third parties and sufficient levels of public order' (ibid.).[19] Hence, it is only fair to demand that also those who engage in illegal protest face similar costs. Let me consider this claim in more detail.

First, law enforcement agencies may refuse to issue a permit (for a variety of reasons, including pressure from powerful agents whom the protest may target), despite the protesters having paid the application fee. In this case, agents may decide to use *illegal* forms of protest, since appeals to legal means have failed. It would be odd to contend that these protesters should face penalties, in the form of fines, for the reasons Smith advances, for they have already faced that cost. Second, in many jurisdictions (e.g., Australia) permits for public protests do not require the payment of a fee; hence, in such jurisdictions, Smith's argument also may not apply. Third, Smith is (rightly) concerned with ensuring 'the safety of third parties and sufficient levels of public order'; yet not all forms of civil disobedience create such risk. Rosa Park's famous refusal to surrender her bus seat to a white passenger did not threaten public order, nor third parties (unless we adopt the perverse idea that white Americans were unjustly made to feel 'unsafe' by her act of defiance). Fourth, if citizens have a moral right to engage in civil disobedience, then the state should shoulder the (admittedly very modest) costs of allowing citizens to resort to it. People do not have to pay a fee to be able to vote, although elections are significantly more expensive, for the state, compared to managing the average public protest. Finally, the amount of a fine falls within a predetermined range, as do fees for permits: a person already knows how much she will have to 'pay' for engaging in a certain conduct. The same may then be said of civil disobedients: protesters may know *before the fact* that they will be sentenced to pay the standard fine for holding an illegal public protest. Thus, there would be no need for a trial, as protesters could be fined on the spot for their 'unpermitted' protest. This poses a further problem for Smith, as he also claims that the state owes it to the civil disobedients to penalise them in order to show that it takes their protest seriously. Referring to an argument made by William Edmundson (1998), Smith (rightly) points out that where the state fails to sanction citizens for engaging in illegal protest, it 'deflates' the protesters' communicative act by refusing to take note of their disobedience; a refusal to punish . . . may amount to a form of 'repressive tolerance'. [20] And yet, if we institutionalise a system of fines akin to the one Smith proposes (i.e., as analogous to licence fees for legal permits), we risk 'normalising' civil disobedience and de facto neutralising its communicative potential. This may hamper, rather than protect, the moral right to civil disobedience.

Smith contends there is also a symbolic reason to accept penalties for civil disobedience. The reference, once again, is to Lefkowitz's claim that, by accepting fines for civil disobedience, the protesters 'symbolically recognize the costs they impose on others by doing so and, perhaps more important, . . . symbolically affirm the citizens' collective authority to settle reasonable disagreements over the design of morally necessary collective-action schemes' (Lefkowitz 2007, 220). Similarly, Smith argues that 'the acceptance of fines is an important means through which civilly disobedient citizens can maintain or repair ties of civic friendship' (2013, 97). In reply, we should reiterate that not all disobedience imposes costs on others (e.g., Rosa Parks). And when it does, we ought not to confuse 'compensating' third parties for the costs imposed on them with 'paying penalties for engaging in civil disobedience'. I may have a duty to pay compensation to a private citizen whose property I seriously damaged during my protest, but this does not show that civil disobedience per se is liable to fines. If I do not damage anyone's property during my act of civil disobedience (i.e., I impose no significant costs on others), I have no penalty to pay. Brownlee has also raised scepticism about the alleged symbolic function of penalising civil disobedience. She highlights that penalties are not accepted voluntarily; once we are faced with them, we have no choice but to comply, lest we get criminally prosecuted. 'Penalties are not offered, but inflicted upon people. . . . We do not offer a person a meaningful way to symbolically affirm anything when we impose a penalty [upon her]' (Brownlee 2018, 294). And even if, Brownlee continues, many civil disobedients may be willing to take on these costs *in order to* acknowledge 'citizens' collective authority to settle reasonable disagreements', others may not: we cannot take the acceptance of a penalty as a de facto sign of the agent's acceptance of wrongdoing (ibid.). Hence, Smith falls prey to the same objections that mar Lefkowitz's account. It seems to be self-defeating to defend a moral right to civil disobedience while, at the same time, arguing that one may be sanctioned for exercising it. In fact, one cannot help finding the punishment/penalty distinction underwhelming, given that both Lefkowitz and Smith consider short prison sentences a perfectly justifiable 'penalty'. Yet prison seems to be the last place where a person should be sent, however briefly, for doing what she has a right to do. The moral right to civil disobedience, if it exists, must imply the agent's claim against *any* interference.

Smith's support for penalising civil disobedience sits oddly with other aspects of his important contribution to this debate; namely, his emphasis on the positive side of the moral right to civil disobedience. This is an element to which neither Lefkowitz nor Brownlee devote significant attention, and hence it deserves further discussion. Smith explains that the right to civil disobedience does not only give rise to a negative claim on others not to interfere with the illegal protest, it also generates a positive claim on the state to provide assistance to citizens in exercising this right (93–94). This is an intriguing claim: the state may wrong citizens not only when *punishing* them for engaging in civil disobedience, but also when failing to assist them in committing a communicative breach of the law. For example, if citizens were to give advanced notice of their intention to commit an act of civil disobedience, or even if authorities were to discover this intention before its official declaration, the state should explore available avenues for accommodating citizens in their attempts to conduct an act of civil disobedience (94). Smith also claims the state should take steps to educate citizens about their moral right to civil disobedience. This should aim for 'the inculcation of knowledge, skills and qualities that enable citizens to make informed judgments about whether and when to engage in civil disobedience' (ibid.); that is, ensuring that citizens can discern to which acts of civil disobedience they have a right. Furthermore, Smith contends that the state has a special duty to educate the police force about the moral right to civil disobedience. This is to ensure that police officers do not take the illegal nature of civil disobedience as conclusive reason to shut down the protest and treat the disobedients as common law breakers. Rather, police officers must acknowledge *and accommodate* the legitimate claim of citizens to engage in suitably constrained illegal acts of protest. This generates a requirement for the police to engage protesters in what Smith calls 'negotiated accommodation', a policing approach that he contrasts with 'prevention' and 'management' (110–23). 'Prevention' seeks to avoid the illegal conduct altogether by incapacitating the protesters; for example, through 'kettling', whereby the police cordons the protesters off and forces them to leave the area. 'Management', on the other hand, acknowledges the role of a dialogue with the protester, but its goal is to minimise the protesters' visibility and impact (e.g., by setting too strict limitations on the protest's route).

Smith's 'negotiated accommodation' highlights the need for *under-policing* the protest, to acknowledge the fact that protesters are exercising their moral right to engage in civil disobedience. The police should facilitate, rather than obstruct, the protest, even if the latter involves law defiance. This does not mean that the police should refrain from arresting the civil disobedients, as the arrest may as well be in order at a certain point during the protest. This would be based on the good of restoring public order and, argues Smith, on the interest of third parties; however, as we already noticed above, Smith contends that arrest can often be a means to assist the civil disobedients by providing publicity to their cause and thus enhancing the communicative aims of their protest. To facilitate this process, Smith argues that protesters and police may agree on pre-negotiated arrests, whereby the two parties meet to discuss, before the event, with the police providing pre-arrest forms and requesting estimates of how many arrestees there will be, and whether they will actively or passively resist arrest (114). Smith contends that, in this way, the civil disobedients may enjoy the best of both worlds: the 'appearance of transgression' implied by arrest, yet without the risks of violent confrontation or extended periods of incarceration, which are often the result of police action in standard circumstances.

Chapter Six

Moving Forward

In this book, I have offered an overview of the philosophical debate surrounding the concept of civil disobedience. In this conclusive chapter, I seek to offer my own argument to solve some of the issues discussed earlier; specifically, I will focus on three problems on which the academic debate, as I showed above, may have reached deadlock. These are (a) the question whether disobedience of the law is *pro tanto* wrong; that is, of whether citizens have a pro tanto duty to obey the law; (b) the relationship between civil disobedience and nonviolence; (c) the question whether a civil disobedient must accept the punishment for her law-breaking conduct. I begin by offering an account of political obligation, to address point (a) above. My account hinges on the notion of *respect for*, rather than *obedience to*, the law. This shift has important implications for our understanding of disobedience as an act through which a citizen may discharge her political duties, under some circumstances. From this different standpoint, I then return to the issue of violence (point b) above, to advance the claim that, under some circumstances, employing a degree of force or violence in the protest may be required by the duty to respect fellow citizens as autonomous agents. After that, I argue, with reference to point (c), that a civil disobedient is under a moral obligation to answer to her fellows for her law-breaking conduct (e.g., by appearing at the trial, if summoned); however, she may have no pro tanto duty to accept the punishment.

6.1 A DUTY TO DISOBEY?

Civil disobedience poses an interesting philosophical problem only if we assume that disobedience is wrong and, therefore, that it requires a justification. However, as we saw earlier, the major arguments supporting a duty to obey the law fail to establish the pro tanto wrongness of disobedience; in some cases, citizens may comply with the theories' underlying values (e.g., natural duty of justice) through an illegal act such as civil disobedience. In those cases, the breach of law would not constitute a justifiable violation of the agent's political obligation – that is, of her duty qua citizen. Rather, it would fulfil that duty. Candice Delmas has recently argued for a political duty to disobey the law (2018a). She claims that the major accounts of political obligation (fair play, Samaritanism, associative duties) imply that, where the regime is unjust, citizens have a moral duty to resist the injustice by disobeying the law. As we saw in chapter 1, the moral obligation to obey the law arises, if at all, only under conditions of basic justice, and in relation to not outrageously unjust laws. Citizens in Nazi Germany had no moral duty to obey the law of the Third Reich; in fact, it may be argued they had a moral duty to disobey that law and overthrow that regime. This implies that, where basic justice is not achieved, there is no political obligation; that is, no specific duty to obey the law. Delmas claims, on the other hand, that under such circumstances, political obligation still arises, yet it involves a duty to disobey (through civil or uncivil disobedience). According to her view, "Resistance to injustice is our *political* duty" (ibid., 5).

Delmas correctly points out that, under the seriously unjust regimes she discusses, agents may indeed have a duty to disobey the law and fight the unjust regime. However, I would argue that this is not a political duty; that is, a duty that originates from their status as members of the political community. It is a moral duty that applies to them qua human beings. A successful account of political obligation must fulfil a *particularity requirement*; that is, it must capture the special relationship between a citizen and her political community. *Political* duties (as opposed to other moral duties) are owed to one's own fellow citizens. Even philosophical anarchists claim we have a moral duty to, for example, comply with traffic regulations, but this is grounded in an independent moral duty not to expose others to undue risks rather than in a political duty to obey the law. By the same token, when Delmas claims that we have a duty to fight injustice, this duty is not political; it is an independent *moral* duty that applies to us qua human beings, not qua members of the political community. Thus John Simmons, a strenuous denier of political obligations, holds that 'we have a duty to support and further our government . . . (as well as a duty to fight injustice), even if we have no political obligations' (Simmons 1979, 193). My duty to rescue or assist people in Third World countries is a moral duty I owe everyone, not a political duty I owe to my fellow citizens. In some cases, the former may override the latter; in those cases, I have an all-things-considered moral duty to disobey. However, in such cases, my duty qua moral being overrides my duty qua citizen.

Thus, while agreeing that political obligation cannot be reduced to mere obedience to the law, I also believe we need a different approach to identify the specific duties of citizens. This approach should mirror the one I employed in my analysis of civil disobedience, which focussed on the citizen's *disposition*. We saw earlier that the problem with Rawls's account is that it sought to establish the 'civility' of one's conduct by simply focusing on its external features; yet a person may still act coercively and noncooperatively – that is, uncivilly – despite engaging in a nonviolent act and being willing to accept the punishment. Similarly, the fact that the citizen complies with the directives of the law may not suffice to establish that she has fulfilled her duty qua citizen; as I argue below, there may be nothing praiseworthy in a citizen who merely obeys the law 'because it is the law'. In this sense, I propose an important shift in the approach to the problem of political obligation, a shift from 'conduct' to 'disposition'. I argue for a duty to *respect*, rather than merely *obey*, the law; by 'respect for the law', I mean respect for the values grounding the legal system, which I identify with a commitment to individual autonomy. The duty to respect the law, according to my view, arises out of the natural duty to respect others as autonomous agents, which I discuss in chapter 2. I contend that, in order to assess whether a citizen fulfils her political duty to respect the law, we need to consider the specific circumstances under which the act is performed; in some cases, citizens may show respect for the law by engaging in civil *disobedience*.

In what follows, I first outline an account of political obligation that builds 'from the inside out' rather than 'from the outside in'; that is, an account that centres on citizens' disposition rather than on their compliance with the law.[1] After that, I present a natural duty–based account of political obligation, grounded, as already mentioned, in the duty to respect others as autonomous agents. In order to address the particularity requirement, I then further employ the principle of fair play, which provides the citizen with a pro tanto reason to prioritise her own fellows over other human beings. The upshot of my argument is that, in some cases, citizens may fulfil their political duty through a law-breaking act. I then consider the implications of this account for the analysis of civil disobedience; chief amongst them is the fact that citizens may have not merely a right but also a duty to resort to civil disobedience. I argue that, in some cases, civil disobedience may be necessary to fulfil a positive duty to promote others' capacity to self-legislate. Finally, I consider the consequences of my argument for the claim that a civil disobedient should accept the punishment for her law-breaking conduct. I argue that civil disobedients have a duty to answer *to their fellows* for their choice to deliberately break the law, if called to appear at the criminal trial; they do not, however, have a pro tanto duty to accept the punishment merely for engaging in civil disobedience.

Before I start, I should stress two important differences between my own account and the one by Delmas I have just mentioned. First, my account does not require the kind of serious injustices Delmas discusses. I argue that civil disobedience, despite its illegal nature, may fulfil an agent's political duty even where the society is reasonably just, and – more importantly – even when targeting a *just* law. This is necessary to make sense of acts of *indirect* civil disobedience, where the law being disobeyed is not the one being targeted (as in the case of Occupy Wall Street, where protesters violated laws about public space in order to denounce structural injustices in society). The protesters may comply with their political duties despite disobeying a legitimate law of a nearly just state, for their aim is to start a communicative enterprise about the necessity of reconsidering a certain law or policy. This leads to the second difference between my account and Delmas's; in my view, those who engage in civil disobedience are not necessarily right. Their beliefs must be *sincere, yet not necessarily correct*: they may fear a serious injustice where, in reality, there may not be one. It may turn out, upon further examination, that the law or policy they are protesting should *not* be changed.[2] As discussed in chapter 4, civil disobedients may *force* others to engage in the communicative exchange, if circumstances warrant doing so, but they cannot impose their opinion upon others. Doing so would turn their conduct into a coercive act, which would undermine the 'civil' nature of their protest. This point was discussed in the previous chapter, where I described how supporters of a moral right to civil disobedience hold (in different ways) that it should apply also to cases where the protesters make reasonable (Lefkowitz and Smith) or even unreasonable (Brownlee) mistakes in advancing their case.

6.2 POLITICAL OBLIGATION: 'INSIDE OUT' VERSUS 'OUTSIDE IN'

In emphasising the dispositions of citizens towards the law and their fellows, I approach the problem of political obligation from the standpoint of 'citizenship theory'. This outlook stems from a dissatisfaction with some forms of liberalism instantiated by Rawls's theory of justice, according to which the object of political philosophy lies in 'the way in which the major social institutions distribute fundamental rights and duties and determine the division of advantages from social cooperation' (1999, 6). Critics have pointed out the risk of over-emphasising the 'basic structure of the society' while neglecting the motivations of the individuals to whom they are meant to apply (Dagger 1997, Sandel 1998, Barber 2003, MacIntyre 2007). In fact, for the structure of society to maintain its stability, citizens must also possess certain dispositions towards each other; as we saw in chapter 3, Rawls, for example, argued for a 'duty of civility' to address inevitable conflicts amongst different conceptions of the good within the public sphere (hence, his appeal for a 'retreat to neutral grounds').[3] This suggests that, for a liberal state to maintain its stability, the 'basic structure' needs to be sustained by citizens' commitment to the democratic values: 'The institutions of constitutional freedom are only worth as much as a population makes of them' (Habermas, 7).[4] Hence, Kymlicka and Norman (1994) stress that the principles of justice cannot guarantee, by themselves, the subsistence of the overall structure of the community. Even when institutions 'work', the lack of civic engagement can lead to a progressive decline in citizens' ability to bond and interact with each other in the interest of the common good. We can grasp this point with reference to Robert Putnam's oft-cited idea of 'social capital':

> Whereas physical capital refers to physical objects and human capital refers to properties of individuals, social capital refers to connections among individuals – social networks and the norms of reciprocity and trustworthiness that arise from them. In that sense, social capital is closer to what some have called 'civic virtue'. (Putnam 2000, 19)[5]

Putnam highlights the importance of mutual trust, of networks that improve a society's stability, by enhancing coordinated action. This, in turn, requires a degree of citizens' participation in the life of their political community: membership to the polity, or 'citizenship', requires more than an uncritical disposition to follow state's directives. For a society to maintain its stability, citizens must display a 'civic' character, involving dispositions such as loyalty, reasonableness, willingness to cooperate with each other and dedication to the promotion of the public interest (Macedo 1990, Galston 1991, Dagger 1997).

This analysis shifts the emphasis from citizens' compliance with *external* constraints – that is, the law – to their *inner* dispositions as members of the political community. Political philosophers should certainly investigate what kind of institutions are necessary to achieve justice in society; however, they should also consider what kind of individuals are necessary to maintain these institutions in place and ensure they deliver the expected results. Thus, we should analyse political membership as one of the roles individuals have (Hardimon 1994), but when we start doing that, we may struggle to identify the specific acts of citizens, in the same way we may not identify the specific acts of friends. This is due to the fact that the circumstances play a crucial role in determining how one should act towards a friend, and towards one's polity. Like Benjamin Barber points out (2003, 123), being a citizen is 'something that we do, not something (such as a power, for example) that we possess or use or watch or think about'. A study of the source and nature of political obligation – that is, of the duties of citizens – should abandon the exclusive focus on citizenship as a set of rights that are bestowed upon the individual qua member of the political community. While these rights play a central role in our understanding of liberal regimes,

> there is another, more active and demanding dimension to liberal citizenship, vital though perhaps subordinate. By exploring the active, public side of liberalism . . . we can distil liberal conceptions of virtue and community that constitute positive rejoinders to republican and communitarian criticisms; we can, as well, better understand what the liberal polity requires of its citizens to flourish or even survive. (Macedo 1990, 38–39)

To this end, I aim to connect the liberal emphasis on autonomy to the republican focus on 'civic virtues', thus endorsing a form of 'liberal republicanism' (Kymlicka 1995, Duff 2001, 48–56). My aim is to show that once we analyse the concept of political membership from this richer viewpoint, we may understand civil disobedience as grounded in the agent's commitment to 'action' (Arendt 1958). This implies that, under some circumstances, individuals who disobey the law should be praised for being 'good citizens'.

By choosing to emphasise the moral disposition of the agent, I endorse a virtue ethical approach to the problem of political obligation.[6] The main assumption of an ethics of virtue is that the rightness of an action depends ultimately on whether the agent who performs it displays a certain kind of moral disposition. For the action to be morally right, it is not enough that it achieves what is 'good': it is necessary that the act be done 'at the right time, for the right motive, in the right way' (Aristotle 2004, II, 1109a27). This moral approach gives central importance to the context in which agents act, and their capacity for situational appreciation; hence, it focuses on their *inner* disposition in responding to the features of the specific context in which they act (Crisp 1996, Swanton 2003). For the purposes of this discussion, I do not engage with the metaethical issues surrounding virtue ethics, concerning, for example, whether it should be conceived as an independent moral theory or rather as a complement to consequentialism or deontology (O'Neill 1983, Driver 2002, Louden 2011).[7] Also, my account remains neutral between 'agent-centred' and 'agent-focussed' approaches to virtue ethics (Slote 2001). Finally, as Rosalind Hursthouse (2001, 3–4) notes, although virtue ethics is grounded on Aristotelian premises, I do not regard myself 'as committed to any of the lamentable, parochial details of Aristotle's moral philosophy, any more than many deontologists inspired by Kant think they are committed to his views on, for example, animals'.

In proposing an account of political obligation developing 'from the inside out' rather than 'from the outside in', I follow William Edmundson's defence of a 'virtue of law-abidance' (2006).[8] Edmundson acknowledges that the debate on political obligation is now defined by the 'deadlocked positions' of apologists and deniers of the duty to obey, 'which, between themselves, have tacitly assumed to occupy all the spaces on the board' (ibid., 2). In the attempt to break this deadlock, Edmundson proposes a shift from the notion of 'law-obedience' to that of 'law-abidance'. The latter aims to capture a broader disposition in the agent qua political actor; namely,

> a disposition to regard the bare unlawfulness of an action as a nontrivial and normally adequate though not necessarily conclusive reason against performing it. The virtue [of law-abidance] does not, however, comprise a disposition to obey the law *qua* law, regardless of its moral merits; although it does include a disposition to conform to the not-patently-unjust conventional moral norms of the actor's society – especially where those norms constitute customary law. (ibid.)

Edmundson highlights the positive connotation of the label 'law-abiding' in everyday language, as we tend to praise those who are 'law-abiding citizens'. However, abidance must involve more than 'a settled disposition to obey the law because it is the law', for there may be nothing particularly admirable in one who complies with law's directives without assessing the qualities of the law. Thus, Edmundson claims, a law-abiding citizen may engage in acts of disobedience where the balance of reasons available to her sufficiently favours doing so: for a law-abiding citizen, the law is 'invariably a reason for action', yet she is not generally disposed to obey regardless of her own assessments of the moral and rational merits of the law (3). The claim that there is nothing *admirable* in 'obedience' as such is convincing, as we do not 'admire' Nazi officials for 'obeying' the orders coming from the Reich. Rather, as the Nuremberg trial showed, these officials were rightly blamed for having *obeyed* such directives.[9]

Edmundson also considers the case of civil disobedience, a 'faded subject' which, after Simmons's dismissal of political obligation (1979), was 'destined never again to be topical' (7). He credits Rawls, however, for having rescued civil disobedience from this dark fate; Rawls advanced what Edmundson labels 'the petition view'; namely, a conception of civil disobedience as a form of address demanding that a serious injustice be redressed (as we saw in chapter 2). Edmundson claims that we may make better sense of this form of illegal conduct from the perspective of law *abidance* rather than of law *obedience*. His argument hinges on a distinction between what he calls a state's 'wholesale' and 'retail' operations. The former refers to the setting of general rules – for example, 'legislative enactment, administrative rule making, adjudicatory precedent' (2); the latter consist in the 'specific interferences with the ongoing stream of conduct by specific measures focused on individuals – such as issuing a subpoena or a summons, revoking a license, making a traffic stop or an arrest or a judicial sale' (ibid.). Thus, a citizen faced with traffic regulations (e.g., a certain speed limit) would be dealing with law's *wholesale* operations; on the other hand, a citizen faced with an officer's demand to 'pull over' or to pay a fine would be dealing with law's *retail* operations. Edmundson understands the virtue of 'law abidance' as a disposition to 'generally' comply with the state's wholesale operations:

> The law-abiding acknowledge that the existence of a legal rule directing one to φ is always a nontrivial reason to φ. But that is as far as they need go. . . . What is disallowed is the idea that the existence of a legal norm is 'neither here nor there' for purposes of practical reasoning, or that the law may lightly be disobeyed. (9)

However, Edmundson contends that the state's 'retail' operations pose a 'much more stringent constraint' on the law abiding. It is for this reason that, in his view, a 'law-abiding' citizen may engage in civil disobedience (by defying a certain law), yet 'will not slip away from arrest, even if she might do so safely' (ibid.). Edmundson appears to endorse Rawls in treating the willingness to accept the punishment as central to an act of civil disobedience; however, he adds that a law-abiding civil disobedient 'will either comply with or openly defy an official seeking personally to enforce a judicial order', which seems to leave open the possibility of an open refusal to comply with the arrest.[10] What is important for our present purposes is that Edmundson's virtue-based approach highlights, once again, the unattractiveness of a fully non-voluntarist account of political obligation: it is not plausible to claim that a citizen ought to obey the law regardless of her own assessment, for such claim would conflict with the very conception of autonomous agents discussed throughout this book; that is, of individuals able to give directions to their own lives.[11] As I will argue in the next section, the notion of autonomy sits at the foundations of a successful account of political obligation that builds 'from the inside out'; I will employ Edmundson's virtue-ethical framework to argue that the *disposition* of a law-abiding citizen involves an attitude of respect for fellow citizens as autonomous agents. In doing so, I propose a multi-principled account of political obligation: in my view, the best way to make sense of the specific obligations that arise from membership to a political community involves (a) a virtue-ethical standpoint, focused on dispositions rather than on mere obedience to the law; (b) a natural duty of autonomy and (c) the principle of fair play, to capture the special relationship between the members of a political community. Having outlined (a) above, I now turn to presenting a natural duty–based account of political obligation. After that, I will consider the third element; namely, the role of fair play.

6.3 A MULTI-PRINCIPLED ACCOUNT OF POLITICAL OBLIGATION

6.3.1 A Natural Duty to Respect the Law

The notion of individual autonomy has played a central role throughout this book. In chapter 2, I argued that what matters to civil disobedience is the agent's commitment to treating fellow citizens with the respect due to their status as autonomous agents. In chapter 3, I claimed that an act of civil disobedience, despite its law-breaking nature, may be compatible with a democratic procedure that respects the equal status of citizens as 'self-legislators'. In chapter 4, I argued that some forms of violence may be compatible with the agent's duty to respect others as autonomous agents; hence, they may be part of an act of civil disobedience (I will return to this point below). In chapter 5, I showed that arguments supporting a moral right to civil disobedience also rely, in different ways, on the notion of autonomy. Furthermore, in chapter 1, I pointed out that life under the rule of law is the only way for agents to collectively exercise their rights and lead a meaningful and rewarding existence. The rule of law does indeed constitute a necessary institution for the fulfilment of the right to autonomy.[12] The state plays a key coordinating function by enforcing rules (i.e., laws) preventing agents from unduly infringing on each other's choices in the pursuit of their own ends in life. Furthermore, the state defines the content of other rights necessary for the fulfilment of the right to autonomy (Stilz 2009, 27–56, Renzo 2011, 588) by settling reasonable disagreements concerning the interpretation and scope of many rights (e.g., Does the right to sell one's own property extend to one's own body?). Raz has argued (1986, 400–30) that the state promotes its subjects' autonomy by (amongst other things) providing them with valuable options from which to choose. But if the state is necessary for the agents' exercise of their right of autonomy, then agents must support the state in order to fulfil their duty to respect each other as autonomous agents. That is to say: the duty to respect others as autonomous agents gives rise to a duty to support the state in its autonomy-protecting function. Where the law is structured so to preserve its subjects' equal right to autonomy, citizens face an obligation to abide by its directives; they ought to respect the law because they ought to respect each other (Stilz 2009, 87–88, Higgins 2004, 66). The agent's obligation is, first and foremost, to her fellows (as bearers of the right to autonomy); the obligation to the law is secondary, and only derives from the former (Zwiebach 1975, 75–76; Walzer 1970, 22).

However, the duty to *respect* the law does not entail a duty to *obey* it. There are two reasons, in my view, that support shifting from the notion of 'obedience' to that of 'respect'. First, as already mentioned with reference to Edmundson's argument, there may be nothing per se admirable in mere obedience to the law, nor anything per se reprehensible in mere disobedience (Edmundson 2006, Klosko 2011). 'Respect' indicates a disposition; hence, it may not be captured by the same act under all circumstances. An act of obedience to the law, in and by itself, may not display respect for others as autonomous agents (in the same way in which, as discussed earlier, a willingness to accept the punishment may not show respect for the law). Even reasonably well-functioning democracies issue defective laws that may unduly target some citizens' basic rights (Lyons 1998); obedience to these laws (and perhaps, in some extreme circumstances, even mere cooperation with the state implementing them) might conflict with the citizen's requirement to respect others' right to autonomy. A lot depends, of course, on what is at stake; that is, how serious the violation of the right to autonomy is, what overall implications the act of disobedience might have under the circumstances, and more; however, the focus on individual autonomy may suggest that disobedience of a legal directive might even be *praiseworthy*; that is, it might display admirable traits of character in the disobeying agent.

It could be objected that I misread the natural-duty account of political obligation, which prescribes obedience to the not-unreasonably-unjust laws of an overall just state. Where the law is structured so to protect the autonomy of its subjects, the latter have a general obligation to obey all its directives, not only those they deem correct; the fact that a specific law may disrespect some citizen's autonomy does not imply it can be disobeyed (Stilz 2009, 78, Wellman & Simmons 2005, 45). It is by submitting to a common juridical order, including its less desirable directives, that citizens respect each other as autonomous agents (Lefkowitz 2005). Based on this objection, my claim that the right to autonomy may accommodate disobedience, in the way described, appears to be incorrect. To address this point, I refer to a second reason we should focus on respect rather than mere obedience to the law: the emphasis on the latter has led to an enduring misconception about the nature of civil disobedience, one I mentioned earlier in this chapter. Claiming that a citizen has a political duty to obey the law ignores the fact that civil disobedience is also a political act, one performed with the aim to contribute to the life of the political community (Parekh 1993). Obedience-based accounts of political obligation fail to make sense of this aspect of civil disobedience, for they deem the latter either (a) unjustified, as the agent's failure to comply with her own political duties (e.g., disobedience of a just law); (b) justifiable, all things considered, when moral obligations override political ones (e.g., disobedience of a law to resist a serious injustice); or (c) permissible, when political duties do not apply (e.g., disobedience of invalid or unreasonably unjust laws). In all these cases, civil disobedience is treated as falling outside the realm of political obligation and, at best, as an exception to the agent's political duty 'to obey'.[13]

Yet in some cases civil disobedience should not be interpreted as a justified exception to the agent's political duty: rather, it often constitutes its fulfilment. There certainly are cases where the choice to engage in civil disobedience may be justified as the result of a conflict between 'law' and 'morality', where the person's duties as moral agent may override her duties as a member of the political community. However, in my view this approach may overlook the *political* nature of civil disobedience: agents engage in this kind of conduct as citizens; that is, to fulfil their role as members of their political community.[14] The fact that they defy the letter of the law does not suffice to establish their failure to act on their political duties.

We may look at the case of Edward Snowden, discussed in chapter 2, from this standpoint. Snowden sought to draw attention to the risk of an undue breach of individual autonomy, of which privacy constitutes a key element (Solove 2008). His action was in breach of the law, but it showed a commitment to the value of individual autonomy: Snowden's disobedience was an act of *respect* for the law, in its attempt to draw attention to a serious, and unwarranted, violation of citizens' status as autonomous agents. Snowden displayed the disposition of a 'law-abiding' citizen; that is, his commitment to the underlying values of society. He sought to protect individual autonomy from the risk of unwarranted interferences. As citizen, he fulfilled his political duty to 'contribute to the law, and to try to improve the alignment between the law and the central values of a liberal polity' (Brownlee 2012, 225). The mere illegality of an action may not suffice to establish the agent's wrongdoing in relation to her duties qua citizen; as Feinberg claimed, there is a 'statistical presumption' that an illegal action may be wrong; however, illegality 'may be a more or less reliable index or clue to the presence of wrongness, nor its ground or basis' (1974, 173).

6.3.2 The Principle of Fair Play

The third feature of my account involves the notion of fairness. As noted in chapter 1, natural duty–based views are ill equipped to address the particularity requirement, for they cannot establish that an individual owes something specifically to her political community. The same could be said of the autonomy-based account I just sketched: from the fact that we ought to respect others as autonomous agents, it does not follow that we ought to obey the law of *our* government. I may refuse to pay taxes to my country, and send that money to support a government abroad, insofar as that contributes to the protection and promotion of the autonomy of *its* subjects. However, we do have reasons to prioritise our fellows' interests over and above those of foreigners: these reasons are grounded in considerations of fairness; that is, in the fact that an individual can enjoy the benefits of the state because of her fellows' cooperation. This can be understood in relation to the social dimension of autonomy, which I discussed in chapter 2. Autonomy as 'condition' requires a web of relationships with others; we need other people in order to exercise our right to autonomy (Dagger 1997), for we apply standards that are not entirely determined by ourselves, but are partly the product of the context we have grown into (Anderson and Honneth 2005). Autonomy requires a degree of proximity to others, for the kind of choices it involves cannot be made without a background of shared values against which the individual can make autonomous choices (Mendus 1989, 96–97). The independence that characterises the autonomous agent can be realised only from within a life shared with others. As Richard Dagger points out,

> All of those who can exercise autonomy do so only because they can count on the efforts of others. This is not to say that these 'others' do what they do *in order to* enable the autonomous person to exercise his or her autonomy: in a great many cases, 'the others' will not even know the person or persons whom they help to act autonomously. Yet this is just what these 'others' do when they pass, enforce or observe traffic laws. . . . When 'others' observe traffic laws or wait their turns in line, they expand our opportunities, even if this is not what they specifically intend to do. By expanding our opportunities in these and numerous other ways, they enhance our capacities to choose – that is, they make it possible for us to do, and therefore to *choose* to do, far more than we could without their help. (1997, 67).

While we have a natural duty to respect everyone as autonomous agents, we have one reason to prioritise the autonomy of our co-nationals. It is through their 'law-abidance' that we enjoy the opportunity for a 'rewarding and meaningful' life under the rule of law: then, we owe it to them, as our fellow citizens, to display our 'law abidance' within the context of our specific community.

6.4 MORAL OBLIGATION AND CIVIL DISOBEDIENCE

We can now consider the place of civil disobedience within the account of political obligation I have just sketched. I have argued above that citizens are under a moral obligation to respect their fellows as autonomous agents. In chapter 2, I have described civil disobedience as an act that, despite its law-breaking nature, shows respect for others as autonomous agents. What follows from my discussion, therefore, is that, under some circumstances, citizens may be under a moral obligation to engage in civil disobedience: the duty to respect others may require the citizen to resort to this form of protest. There may be circumstances that are so unjust that citizens may have to do more than engage in civil disobedience; for example, resort to a revolution against a despotic regime in order to live up to their commitments to the value of individual autonomy. Nevertheless, where circumstances are not outrageously unjust, I argue that a citizen may have to resort to civil disobedience in order to treat her fellows with the respect due to them as autonomous agents.[15]

To understand this point, let us return to the problem of violence in civil disobedience, which I discussed in chapter 4. I concluded that chapter by claiming that forcing others to listen to the disobedients' message may still fall within the boundaries of a persuasive form of address. In that sense, a degree of force or violence in civil disobedience may comply with a negative duty to avoid undue interferences with an agent's choices; however, the right to autonomy implies also a positive claim. We saw above (chapter 2) that respecting others' autonomy also requires taking positive action to support them in the exercise of their capacity to make choices. Our duty to respect others as autonomous agents generates a requirement to promote their capacity to make choices in life; for example, by ensuring they are free from coercion, but also by ensuring that they have a set of morally valuable options from which to choose. It is in this sense that one may have a duty to resort to civil disobedience in the attempt to make others aware of issues concerning a certain law or policy.

I mentioned above that autonomy has a social dimension: we cannot exercise our autonomy without a background of relations and institutions enabling us to make autonomous choices. One way in which our social environment supports the exercise of our autonomy is by providing us with options: we cannot choose what kind of person to be, what kind of life to have, what kind of values to subscribe to, if we do not have alternatives available. The provision of valuable options, therefore, is among the requirements stemming from a positive duty to promote others' autonomy (Raz 1986, 375, 408). Thomas Hurka has compared two scenarios, one in which an agent chooses one option out of two alternatives, and in which she makes the same choice, yet out of ten alternatives (Hurka 1993, 149–50). In the second case, the choice bestows a higher degree of responsibility on the agent, since it results from a reflection over a much larger range of possibilities. By choosing option A in the second case, the agent also chooses not-B, not-C, . . . , not-J; in this sense, she determines 'what she does not do as well as what she does', and this enhances her responsibility, and accountability, for her choice (ibid., 150). Her choosing A out of ten options says more about what kind of person she is than her choosing A out of two options only: it reveals a richer identification with her own desires, goals and values. To every 'choosing to' there correspond a number of 'choosing *not* to', so that 'rather than deciding to create oneself, one is choosing to reject some of what one is in the light of other commitments or values' (Gaus 1999, 130). Note here the emphasis is on *quality* rather than *quantity*: providing a number of very similar options does not enhance the agent's responsibility for choosing one over the other. By the same token, a choice between various morally repugnant actions does not enhance one's autonomous condition: to promote one's autonomy, we must provide morally valuable options.[16]

We can grasp this point with reference to the 2008 protest at Stansted Airport, in the UK, which I discussed in chapter 4 (Percival 2008). That protest was troubling, for the protesters deliberately forced people to (temporarily) abandon their travelling plans and face significant disruptions. I argued earlier that, notwithstanding the imposition on others' freedom, the act did not involve also a violation of their autonomy; hence, it may not be deemed coercive. I now contend, furthermore, that the use of force in that protest was part of the disobedients' attempt to provide fellow citizens with valuable options from which to choose. By highlighting the environmental risks caused by airplane traffic, the protesters sought to promote their fellows' autonomy by enhancing the latter's capacity to identify with their own beliefs. Their message raised a question not only about what policy the non-disobeying citizens would support, but also about what kind of persons they would want to be. The protesters appealed to the status of agents that see their desires and motivations as authentically their own. As I already explained, those who were forced to remain at the airport were not being coerced, for they were still able to choose whether or not to join the disobedients' plea. However, after acknowledging the protesters' message, their choice would have had a richer meaning: it would now be a choice made against a set of options that contains 'caring for the environment'. The non-disobeying citizens would assess their own values according to a ranking that also comprises environmental ideals. After facing the disobedients' message, their choice will say *more* about what kind of persons they have chosen to be – that is, what values they endorse – they might support economic advantage (if any) over environmental concerns by rejecting the disobedients' plea, or vice versa, by deciding to oppose the government's plan for airport expansion. Either way, they will be held accountable, *to a higher degree*, for the choice they have made – and treated accordingly (i.e., blamed or praised). In both cases, their self-identification may not be diminished, but may rather be promoted by the act of protest (Moraro 2014). Despite forcing others to act against their will (by forcing them to listen to their message), the civil disobedients may enhance their fellows' power to 'define their nature, give meaning and coherence to their lives, and take responsibility for the kind of person they are' (Dworkin 1988, 20). It is in this sense that, I argue, acts of civil disobedience may fulfil both negative and positive obligations towards others' autonomy.

My claim has a further implication, one I have already mentioned above. In arguing that, under some circumstances, one may have a duty to resort to civil disobedience, I am making a stronger claim than the one discussed in the previous chapter, concerning the existence of a *right* to civil disobedience. My suggestion is that, under some circumstances, our duty to respect others as autonomous agents may *require* us to resort to illegal forms of communication, and to force our fellows to engage in a communicative exchange with us concerning the necessity of a legislative change. This implies that a failure to engage in civil disobedience, under some circumstances, may fall short of the duty to respect others as autonomous agents; that is, to address them in ways fulfiling both our negative and positive autonomy-based duties. Where there is a significant issue at stake, there are avenues for future cooperation with the authorities of the state, and yet there are structural problems preventing the circulation of opinions within the democratic sphere, citizens may have a duty to engage in civil disobedience (as opposed to continue obeying the law or, on the other hand, resort to non-persuasive forms of protest) to address others with the respect due to their status as autonomous agents.[17] A citizen may flout her political obligation by failing to engage in civil disobedience, and may be blameworthy for such failure.[18]

But if the civil disobedient acts according to her duty, how is the law to treat her? Would she still be required to accept the punishment (or the penalty)? More importantly, on what grounds could the state punish a citizen that *fulfils* her duties qua member of the political community? I turn to this question in the last section.

6.5 ANSWERING FOR CIVIL DISOBEDIENCE

Civil disobedience, despite its communicative nature, is an illegal act. For this reason, as we saw earlier, many believe it is not exempt from legal punishment. The civil disobedient is indeed responsible for the breach of the law; as such, she is also liable to face the consequences of law breaking; that is, to accept the punishment a judge or jury may deem appropriate. From this standpoint, responsibility implies liability; one who is responsible for disobeying the law is also liable to being punished for that. However, we may adopt a different conception of 'responsibility', one which does not entail liability.[19] There is an important moment, in the relationship between a citizen and the law, which occurs after the act of disobedience yet before the imposition of punishment: it involves the process of reason giving through which the citizen is called to answer for her conduct to the community (Duff 2007). In this sense, agents are not only responsible *for* their conduct but also *to* other individuals; when applied to the political context, this conception of responsibility implies that a citizen is responsible *to* a specific audience *for* her law-breaking conduct (Fischer and Ravizza 1998; Watson 2004, 260–88; Darwall 2006; Duff 2007; Fischer and Tognazzini 2011; Renzo 2013). This kind of responsibility, as we will see shortly, *does not* imply liability: a citizen may not be liable to punishment, despite being responsible for breaking the law.

For the purposes of this discussion, I follow Antony Duff's conception of responsibility as answerability, according to which an agent X is responsible for her conduct S to an individual or group Y, who has the standing to call her to account for S (Duff 2007). The special relation between X and Y means that Y has the right to call X to answer for S (ibid., 23). Others may not have that same right: hence, X may be answerable to Y, but not to W, if X's conduct was not W's business. For example, a football player is responsible for her football performance to her own team members; the latter have the right to demand that she answer to them for the way she played (e.g., 'Why did you not pass the ball'?). She could dismiss that demand if it came from a passing stranger by arguing that the way she plays is not the stranger's business, but she could not ignore that same request from her team mates, given the special relation she has to them. As a team member, she owes *them* an explanation for her conduct on the football field. Equally, one parent cannot dismiss the other's demand for an explanation concerning their child's education (e.g., 'Why did you let her watch so much TV'?). Under normal circumstances, parents do not owe this kind of explanations to strangers, for the way they raise their own kids is not the strangers' business. The latter are free to express their disapproval of the parents' educational style; however, strangers have no right to demand that the parents answer to them for their child-rearing conduct. Parents owe such explanations to each other, though, because their child's education is each other's business.

The important feature of this conception of responsibility is that the agent owes an explanation of her conduct to the members of the relevant group. The football player may indeed have failed to pass the ball yet may have done so to avoid an off-side, or because she was being obstructed; the parent may have indeed allowed the child an extra half hour of TV, but did so to let the child watch a long documentary. These are explanations that are owed to the relevant parties (team members, partner) but which, once provided, may warrant a different attitude towards the agent. They show that although the latter is indeed responsible (i.e., answerable) for a certain conduct to those who have the right to call her to account, she may not be liable to blame or punishment, given the specific circumstances under which her conduct occurred. Upon answering for her conduct to the relevant party, she may not be deemed guilty or blameworthy. She may argue she deserves no blame, for she has not failed to act according to reasons that apply to her; that is, according to her duties qua member of the group. Several philosophers have argued that criminal responsibility should be understood along these same lines; that is, as based on an offender's duty to answer to the community for the breach of the law (Renzo 2013). Citizens are, in this sense, answerable to each other for their conduct vis-à-vis the law. The state, acting on behalf of the community, has the right to call a law breaker to answer, at the criminal trial, for her conduct, because a breach of the law is the business of all citizens. However, during the trial, the defendant may also be able to 'block the transition from responsibility to liability' by providing an explanation for her conduct (Duff 2007, 22). In those cases, her action, while against the letter of the law, may not defy the values on which the civic enterprise depends; rather, as I have argued above, it may enhance the connection between these values and the legal system.

As a form of law breaking, civil disobedience should be analysed through this same perspective. The fact that a civil disobedient is responsible *for* her law-breaking actions imply that she is answerable *to* her fellow citizens; yet it does not imply that she ought to submit to the punishment. The civil disobedient should answer for her law-breaking conduct to her community if summoned by the state at the criminal trial; she should provide an explanation for her decision to disobey the letter of the law. As a citizen, she owes that explanation to her fellows; but this does not imply submission to the punishment. A civil disobedient may contest the charges and plead not guilty; she may argue that while she is responsible for disobeying the letter of the law, she should not be deemed liable to punishment. She may not have to accept the punishment merely because she has breached the law as part of her communicative act.

It may be pointed out that the choice whether or not to punish the civil disobedient is up to the judge or the jury, not to the defendant: even granting that a civil disobedient has a duty to answer for her act of disobedience, the judge or jury may still issue a guilty verdict after listening to her explanation. I do not deny that the disobedient may have all-things-considered reasons to submit to the sanction, having fulfiled her duty to answer for her conduct to the community. For example, her refusal to accept the punishment might incite unlawful behaviour by individuals with less noble motivations; it might cause resentment in the population at large, and possibly encourage civil unrest (e.g., at the hands of citizens who do not share the protesters' political agenda); or, as discussed earlier, it might hinder the communicative process, alienating support from citizens and hampering the prospect of legislative change. Under such circumstances, the civil disobedient would indeed have reasons to accept the punishment, but these would refer to the specific circumstances rather than to a supposed ex ante right of the state to punish her simply for engaging in civil disobedience. It could be replied that, if the citizen accepts to be answerable in a court (on the assumption that the court represents a legitimate constitutional state or community), she is also subject to its judgement by the very fact that she recognises the authority of the court in answering to its procedures. However, the court is *not* at liberty to punish innocent people (i.e., it does not have the moral authority to punish people who commit no wrong). That is why, as Brownlee has argued (2012, 250–51), a court may have to apologise to the civil disobedient for having to punish her.[20]

A related problem concerns the case of civil disobedience for unreasonable causes. Could racists use this argument to escape punishment after an act of civil disobedience supporting white supremacy? Could they be said to have fulfiled their political duties if, during the trial, they were to argue that their illegal action was based on a sincere concern with the danger multiculturalism poses to individual autonomy? The response is that racist protesters would not be able to appeal to the autonomy-based account of political obligation I defend: their racist views would be incompatible with the natural duty to respect others as autonomous agents. In fact, any view that challenges the equal dignity of human beings would be incompatible with my account of political obligation, and of civility. In this sense, a racist protester would have not fulfiled her political duty to respect the law: the state, in that case, may have the right to sanction her for her law-breaking conduct, even if the latter was part of a communicative (though uncivil) act. I will return to the case of civil disobedience in support of a racist cause at the end of this chapter.

A third objection to my argument involves the idea that punishment is something owed to the civil disobedient; that is, protesters have a right to be punished as part of their communicative exchange with the state. William Edmundson has argued that a state that fails to punish protesters for breaching the law also fails to recognise their political message (Edmundson 1998, 58). By publicly sanctioning the illegal act of protest, the state shows that it takes the protesters and their message seriously; by letting them go unpunished, on the other hand, it might engage in what Herbert Marcuse called 'repressive tolerance' (Marcuse 1965). According to this view, punishment plays an important symbolic role in the communicative enterprise between the civil disobedient and the state, for it expresses the state's appreciation of his opposition to a certain law or policy (Smith 2013, 98). From this perspective, an unwillingness to be punished may impair the communicative aims of civil disobedience.

This objection stresses the relevance of acknowledging the civil disobedient as a member in the communicative enterprise. While this is certainly correct, it does not lead to endorsing punishing a civil disobedient; rather, it may offer further support to the answerability-based view I have presented. Taking the civil disobedient seriously implies acknowledging her status as a responsible agent; that is, as a subject who can offer reasons to explain her own conduct. But in simply punishing her for the illegal action, the state treats the civil disobedient with the 'objective attitude' discussed in chapter 3; that is, as someone with whom it is not possible to engage in a rational exchange (Strawson 2008). It is by calling the civil disobedient to answer for her conduct that the state acknowledges her status in the communicative enterprise, and her political message; it is the failure to do this, rather than the failure to punish her, which may make the state guilty of repression. By the same token, it is the agent's unwillingness to answer to the state for her conduct, rather than her unwillingness to be punished, which may impair the communicative aims of civil disobedience.

6.5.1 Why a Racist Cannot Be Civil

Finally, I want to return to an issue discussed in this and in the previous chapter, with reference to the right to engage in civil disobedience in support of racism. Lefkowitz, as we saw in the previous chapter, defends a conception of the right to civil disobedience as a right to do wrong; that is, as applying also to cases where the protesters commit 'reasonable mistakes' about the necessity for legislative change (2007, 232). Brownlee, on the other hand, acknowledges that the right to civil disobedience may also protect unreasonable mistakes; her account is grounded on a principle of humanism, and hence it applies also to 'bigots and xenophobes', who may resort to civil disobedience to defend their morally despicable ideals (2012, 10, 148). It should be clear, from what I argued above, that I side with Lefkowitz on this issue; in my view, racists would not be able to appeal to the account of political obligation I have presented in this book. Their racist views would be incompatible with the idea of respecting the right to autonomy, which grounds my argument. Their protest, even if communicative, non-coercive, and possibly even forward looking, may not qualify as an act of civil disobedience; there cannot be civil disobedience in support of a racist cause, because racism is incompatible with the account of civility defended in this book. One who promotes a racist agenda denies the very notion of equality that grounds the concept of individual autonomy; hence, the idea of civil disobedience in defence of racism is self-contradictory. A citizen cannot consistently claim to be committed to the value of autonomy, as the principle underlying the legal system, when supporting racist policies (Quong 2004). Therefore, my argument does not condone every illegal communicative act of protest; the action cannot contradict the very principle upon which it claims to be grounded – namely, the equal right of each person to be respected as an autonomous agent. Citizens who are not committed to this equal right cannot be said to satisfy the account of political obligation discussed above. My argument may protect reasonable mistakes, as when protesters wrongly believe that a certain policy would unduly undermine the equal status of autonomous agents, but it does not allow acts that attack the very idea of equal dignity underpinning the right to autonomy.

Notes

1. WHAT'S WRONG WITH DISOBEDIENCE?

1. I prefer to use *pro tanto* in lieu of Kramer's prima facie duty. As Julia Driver explains, 'A pro tanto obligation still has weight, even when it is overridden in specific circumstances', while a prima facie obligation 'can be overridden and eliminated, so that it has no more force in the circumstances' (Driver 2011, 183). On 'content independence', see Raz (1999) and Klosko (2011).

2. Political philosophers tend to separate moral duties from moral obligations (Simmons 1979, 11–16). However, in this book I will not be concerned with this distinction and will use the two terms interchangeably.

3. An excellent book-length discussion is provided by John Horton (2010).

4. John Horton dismisses these kinds of scenarios as 'trivial and unimportant', and too far-fetched to satisfy any reasonable account of political obligation (Horton 2010, 10).

5. Some political philosophers have sought to separate the problem of state legitimacy from that of political obligation. The two concepts are usually considered 'correlative': *if* the state has a legal authority (i.e., a right) to rule over its subjects, the latter are under a pro tanto duty to obey its directives (Simmons 1979, 14–15). However, some theorists have sought to separate the two concepts, claiming the state may have a legitimate right to coerce its subjects, though the latter may have no pro tanto duty to obey (Applbaum 2010, Wellman 1996).

6. I use the terms *utilitarian/utilitarianism* and *consequentialist/consequentialism* interchangeably.

7. Furthermore, my view overlaps with act-consequentialism, insofar as I will hold that an act of disobedience can be morally right. Of course, this overlap should be seen as coincidental, rather than as the result of shared theoretical assumptions.

8. The locus for the discussion of *indirect consequentialism* is Sidgwick (1874). See also Railton (1984).

9. But see Beran's attempt (1987) to respond to this problem by advocating the creation of a dissenters' territory; namely, a place where those who do not consent to any state may live. As Fabien Wendt points out (2018), this does not solve the problem of what justifies coercing dissenters to move to this territory.

10. I use the terms *fair play* and *fairness* interchangeably.

11. Hart further points out that a utilitarian account would be unable to capture the peculiar wrongness of free riding, an issue I already mentioned earlier.

12. The claim that the state makes us safer will probably match the experience of many citizens; however, the reality of social inequality also reveals that such claim should not be

overstated or romanticised. A cursory look at the prison population in Western democracies reveals that white, wealthy males are much more likely to enjoy the protection of the state, compared to their less privileged fellows (Shelby 2016).

13. The locus of this view is to be found in Immanuel Kant's *Metaphysics of Morals*: 'Even if we imagine men to be ever so good natured and righteous before a public lawful state of society is established, individual men, nations, and states can never be certain that they are secure against violence from one another, because each will have his own right to do what seems just and good to him, entirely independent of the opinion of the others'. Cited in Waldron (1993b, 14).

14. Candice Delmas has claimed, on the other hand, that the fair-play principle still applies under conditions of serious injustice, yet prescribes *disobedience* rather than obedience. Thus, White people living in the American South from 1880s to 1970s had a fair-play duty to overthrow the racially segregated system based on Jim Crow laws, despite the benefits that, as white people, they received from it (Delmas 2018a, 110–35). Delmas's point is that disobedience may not necessarily flout the agent's commitment to the principle of fairness.

15. For a rejection of Waldron's account, see Pukas (2007).

16. For discussions of this principle, see Feinberg (1984), Murphy (2001) and Fabre (2002).

17. Added emphasis.

18. Dudley Knowles responds that fairness and Samaritanism offer separate pro tanto reasons for actions, hence it makes perfect sense to prioritise one over the other, when they conflict (Knowles 2012).

19. For an excellent and up-to-date defence of this account, see Vossen (2011a, 2011b).

20. The first formulation of this argument is to be found in Platos's *Crito*, where it was used to support an argument based on *gratitude*. For a contemporary version of the gratitude-based account of political obligation, see Walker (1988).

21. Note that, under this reading, I might still owe an apology – for example, to my Mafia group – for *not* killing, *not* kidnapping and so on.

22. A true community, for Dworkin, must fulfil four conditions. 'First, [the members] must regard the group's obligations as special, holding distinctly within the group, rather than as general duties its members owe equally to persons outside it. Second, they must accept that these responsibilities are personal: that they run directly from each member to each other member, not just to the group as a whole in some collective sense. . . . Third, members must see these responsibilities as following from a more general responsibility each has of concern for the well-being of others in the group . . . Fourth, members must suppose that the group's practices show not only concern but an equal concern for all members (Dworkin 1986, 204).

23. Horton rejects the charge that this 'subjective' requirement reintroduces voluntariness 'through the back door' (186), arguing that the *acknowledgement* of one's own obligation is not the *source* of that obligation.

24. On this point, see Parekh (1993).

25. Delmas (2016a, 686) contends it is surprising that 'philosophers have not realized that the very same grounds they use to defend political obligation can also support, under defective socio-political conditions, duties to resist injustice and disobey the law, civilly and non-civilly'. I will argue this may apply also to societies that are sufficiently or nearly just.

2. THE CONCEPT OF CIVILITY

1. To be clear, I do not argue against constraints in civil disobedience. In fact, as I claim immediately below, I understand civil disobedience as a *constrained* act of communication. However, such constraints should not be understood as strictly external ones (i.e., concerning the features of the act) but also as internal (i.e., concerning the agent's disposition to respect fellow citizens as autonomous agents).

2. This section follows my discussion in Moraro (2018a).

3. The same conception of civility underlies Delmas's discussion of civility as 'decorum', which stresses a requirement for civil disobedients to 'treat their audience respectfully, as people they seek to persuade' (2018a, 43).

4. 'He who lets the world, or his own portion of it, choose his plan of life for him, has no need of any other faculty than the ape-like one of imitation. He who chooses his plan for himself, employs all his faculties' (Mill 1975, 58).

5. My account of autonomy has strong affinities with Charles Taylor's notion of 'strong evaluation' (Taylor 1989). For discussions of this notion in the context of civil disobedience, see Cooke (2016).

6. 'One who is able to decide the direction of her life has to be respected for this ability. It is prima facie impermissible to interfere with an individual's right of autonomy where the individual is respectful of that right in others. Someone who is self-governing faces minimal interference in the formation and execution of her actions and choices, and it is proper that interferences be kept to a minimum' (Oshana 2006, vii).

7. Ibid. See also Strawson (2008). This claim will be central to my discussion of civil disobedience in deliberative democracy (chapter 3) and of a conception of responsibility as *answerability* (chapter 6).

8. See Stephen Darwall's distinction between 'appraisal' and 'recognition' respect (2006, 122–30).

9. For criticisms of this notion of respect, see Leslie Green (2010).

10. See Dagger (1997, 15).

11. This is not to deny that others can also impair our ability to make autonomous choices: conformism and fear of social stigma may lead to choices we would not endorse in the absence of social pressure.

12. An old-fashioned approach, championed by Abe Fortas, contends that this form of indirect civil disobedience is *never* justifiable (Fortas 1968).

13. As already mentioned in the introduction, we may not assess whether an illegal *act* constitutes an instance of civil disobedience without also focussing on *the agent*'s motivation.

14. A similar point is made by Celikates (2016), whose account I consider later in this chapter.

15. Of course, most of these acts are aimed at drawing public attention to the perceived wrongs, and to engage public opinion with the need to work towards legislative change. But the communicative aim is not the *defining* goal of these acts.

16. William Edmundson refers to this understanding of civil disobedience as 'the petition view' (2006).

17. Recent accounts of civil disobedience have also broadened the concept to civil disobedience to include a transnational dimension; that is, by opening up to the possibility of addressing also citizens in other countries. See O'Sullivan, McCausland and Brenton (2017), Smith (2017).

18. Candice Delmas has criticised Rawls for ignoring that the civil rights movement included much more than King's non-violent campaigns (2018b, 30).

19. However, David Lyons had earlier argued that such view 'can reasonably be characterised as a derivative but socially important form of racism' (Lyons 1996, 49), for it assumes that a regime that treats black people as sub-humans is still worthy of allegiance.

20. But see Alan Carter's (somewhat obscure) claim that 'civil disobedience is, in effect, a *conditional* denial of political obligation' (Carter 1998, 31). Added emphasis.

21. Of course, uncivil disobedience may be all-things-considered justified: the concern with respecting others as autonomous agents may be overridden by other considerations; for example, the need to save innocent people from imminent death.

22. In fairness to Rawls, he also wrote the following: 'Of course, the conditions enumerated should be taken as presumptions; no doubt there will be situations when they do not hold, and other arguments could be given for civil disobedience' (1999, 326).

23. Tony Milligan (2017) has argued that some form of covert disobedience may still qualify as 'civil', although the example he discusses (the Animal Liberation Front) seems rather a case of direct action.

24. Rawls compared the 'civil' to the 'militant' disobedient, pointing out the latter's unwillingness to accept the punishment as one of the defining characteristics of her 'militancy' (1999, 323).

25. 'The only course open to you, the Judge and the assessors, is either to resign your post and thus disassociate yourselves from evil, if you feel that the law you are called upon to administer is an evil, and that in reality I am innocent, or to inflict on me the severest penalty, if you believe that the system and the law you are assisting to administer are good for the people of this country, and that my activity is, therefore, injurious to the common weal'. Cited in Kamath (2007, 185).

26. For Alexander Livingston (2017), Gandhi's willing acceptance of the punishment exemplifies civil disobedience as a 'fearless practice of fidelity to truth profoundly at odds with liberal conceptions of disobedience as fidelity to law'.

27. Sabl also points out, nonetheless, that 'against a Hitler or a Stalin, civil disobedience amounts simply to suicide' (ibid., 310).

28. For recent criticisms of Rawls's account of civil disobedience, see Cervera-Marzal (2013).

29. In chapter 4, I argue Gandhi's campaign did not fulfil the requirements of civil disobedience, for it was coercive rather than persuasive (despite its non-violence).

30. However, we must be wary of assessing the conscientious objector harshly. The demand to be exempted from a certain legal requirement is meant also to bear witness to the fact the law is unjust, and should be changed. Furthermore, as Harel (2002) pointed out, many anti-war activists choose *both* conscientious refusal (to avoid conscription) and civil disobedience (to denounce the injustice of a particular war) to express their convictions. Nevertheless, conscientious objection does not *require* the agents' intention to enter the public arena to bring about a change in legislation, and this separates it from civil disobedience.

31. See also Santoro and Kumar (2018).

32. For a critical assessment of the Espionage Act, see Edgar (1973).

33. In this sense, his conduct differs from that of other whistleblowers, like Chelsea Manning and Julian Assange, who dumped a large amount of classified documents online indiscriminately. See Boot (2017).

34. Delmas contends that Snowden's conduct was not *civil disobedience*, for the latter 'does not risk harming social security'.

35. 'All I wanted was for the public to be able to have a say in how they are governed' (Gellman 2013).

36. On this same point, Michael Walzer (1970, 30) wrote that 'there is nothing evasive about civil disobedience'.

37. "Edward Snowden Is No Hero', *New Yorker*, 10 June 2013.

38. As already noted, Rawls's comments are in tension with his further claim that civil disobedience is appropriate only in 'nearly just' societies, for a society that allows for this kind of abuse would hardly be deemed 'nearly' just.

39. Dworkin seems to imply that coercive protest may still be deemed civil disobedience, though an unjustifiable instance of it. Based on my own account, however, coercion is incompatible with civil disobedience.

3. DISAGREEMENT AND CIVILITY

1. In Rawls's view, a 'general' doctrine applies to a wide group of individuals or even to all subjects universally. A 'comprehensive' doctrine is one that includes conceptions of what is of value in human life, ideals of personal character, as well as ideals of friendship and of familial and associational relationships.

2. I sidestep here the discussion (Simmons 2001) as to whether the problem of 'justification' and that of 'legitimacy' should be addressed separately.

3. For a recent criticism of this idea of legitimacy, see Horton (2012).

4. Rawls later reframed this 'requirement' as a 'proviso', which 'allows us to introduce into political discussion at any time our comprehensive doctrine, religious or nonreligious, provided that, in due course, we give properly public reasons to support the principles and policies our comprehensive doctrine is said to support' (Rawls 1997, 776).

5. A similar claim is defended by Bruce Ackerman, who argues that we should 'simply say *nothing at all* about this disagreement, and put the moral ideas that divide us off the conversational agenda of the liberal state' (Ackerman 1989, 16).

6. We will see below that the capacity to engage in a mutually persuasive dialogue is crucial to my understanding of civility and of civil disobedience.

7. Mouffe (2005, 20) contends that, in the democratic arena, citizens should see each other not as 'enemies' but as 'adversaries': 'While in conflict, they see themselves as belonging to the same political association, as sharing a common symbolic space within which the conflict takes place'.

8. 'Every valid norm has to fulfil the following condition: (U) *All* affected can accept the consequences and the side effects its *general* observance can be anticipated to have for the satisfaction of *everyone's* interests (and these consequences are preferred to those of known alternative possibilities for regulation)' Habermas (1990, 65).

9. Habermas (1990, 111) claims that communicative action constitutes the original form of language use, prior to strategic action. In order to use language to succeed in a strategic way, subjects must already have developed the rule consciousness necessary for strategic action, and this implies a previous action oriented at reaching understanding. We can approach the hearer with an objective attitude, aiming to exploit him as an object for our goals, only if we are already competent language users: however, we develop that kind of competence via communicative action, through which we then also understand a means-end approach.

10. Habermas refers to a procedure first outlined by G. H. Mead. Habermas (1990, 182).

11. This is what grounds Habermas's Principle of Discourse, stated above (ibid., 121).

12. Similar considerations may apply to Occupy Wall Street or Black Lives Matter.

13. David Lefkowitz (2007) has appealed to similar issues in the democratic process to defend the existence of a moral right to civil disobedience.

14. Markovits draws on ideas from Michael Bratman (1987) (concerning the normative authority of intentions) and Joseph Raz (1986) (on the concept of 'exclusionary reasons' for action). I am not sure to what extent these ideas can be applied to the context of democratic sovereignty, and Markovits himself acknowledges that 'Raz would likely not endorse' his characterisation (fn. 64).

15. However, Habermas also grants that it may be unclear to what extent his account overlaps with Rawls's (101).

16. Lasse Thomassen (2007, 205) has argued that 'it is not clear [in Habermas's view] whether constitutional democracy is imperfect in the present because of empirical obstacles to its realization, or whether it is inherently imperfectible'.

17. For a critical response to Young's article, see Talisse (2005).

18. This is one of the central contentions of Robert Dahl's seminal account of democracy (Dahl 1989).

19. However, we should not overlook Young's admission that her deliberative/activist opposition is 'artificial', and aimed to highlight that 'both are important for democratic theory and practice' (2001, 688).

4. NON-VIOLENCE AND CIVILITY

1. Bedau (ibid.) also lists as examples of uncivil conduct 'deliberately destroying property, endangering life and limb, inciting to riot (e.g., sabotage, assassination, street fighting)'.

2. See also Cohen (1972, 24).

3. Furthermore, as we will consider in more detail below, both Gandhi and King's campaigns saw nonviolence as a *strategic* tool, aiming to enhance the protest's publicity, rather

than as expressing their 'civility'. While non-violent, these campaigns were far from 'non-coercive'.

4. Cited in May (2015, chap. 3).

5. Added emphasis. Note the reference to forcing the community 'to face the issue', a notion to which I will return later, when offering my own argument for permissible violence in civil disobedience.

6. Joel Bakan (2004) famously compares the behaviour of corporations to that of psychopaths, who have no concern with morality, empathy, altruism, and whose only goals (in the corporation's case) are profit accumulation.

7. Welchmann does not explain how these practices are compatible with acting 'within the bounds of civility'.

8. William Smith also claims that limited force in civil disobedience, to provide publicity to one's own view, may be compatible with 'deliberative respect' (2013, 33).

9. Recall that, as per my account of the communicative nature of civil disobedience (chapter 2), 'joining the communicative enterprise' does not mean *accepting* the opponent's argument. The main goal of a communicative enterprise is to elicit a response, whether positive or negative, from the addressee.

10. Kent Greenawalt also understands violence in this narrow way, as 'acts of force against persons that cause deaths, substantial physical pain, or impairment of physical faculties or that restrain physical liberty for a significant period of time' (1987, 245).

11. Note that Adams somewhat muddies the waters by describing his goal as showing that '*violent civil disobedience*, or *uncivil disobedience*, is a coherent concept' (477). If the latter, then he has not showed that violence and *civility* are compatible.

12. It is along these lines that Brian Smart (1978) described violence as 'a *considerable or destroying* use of force against persons or their property, a use of force which violates their human rights'.

13. Žižek further posits a third kind of violence, which he calls 'symbolic'; namely, violence performed in the very act of using language. I agree with Todd May that this third conception of violence casts the net a bit widely, and thus I focus on the other two (2015, chap. 2).

14. See May (2015), chapter 2, for further analysis of this term.

15. Hillel Steiner discusses what he calls 'throffers'; that is, 'Kill this man and you'll receive $100 – fail to kill him and I'll kill you'. In this case, Steiner writes, 'The compliance-consequence represents a situation which is (let us suppose) preferred to the norm, while the non-compliance-consequence represents a situation which is less preferred than the norm'. See Steiner (1974, 39).

16. One may make a series of racist comments over time that do not incite 'physical' hatred, yet may have a lasting impact on the addressees of those comments, eventually leading him or her to commit suicide. See Coady (ibid., 16).

17. Brownlee claims that even throwing teddy bears at the police, during a protest, would constitute a violent act, involving some risk of harm to others and also some intention to cause harm (21).

18. The risk should be foreseeable only, of course, as it is always possible that *any* action, even the most innocuous one, could cause harm to third parties. An utterance might always be interpreted in ways that cause psychological harm in others, and it seems plausible to argue that one is responsible only for avoiding harm that could be reasonably expected or foreseen (otherwise, very few acts could ever be deemed completely 'harmless').

19. May follows the account of dignity discussed by Rosen (2012). He is concerned that Bufacchi's integrity-based account may be overly inclusive, hence his proposal for a different (though admittedly very similar) notion.

20. In this section, I refer to the argument I have presented in Moraro (2014).

21. See Brennan and Lomasky (1993, 186): 'To cast a Klan ballot is to *identify oneself* in a morally significant way with the racist policies that the organization espouses'.

22. 'What makes a preference autonomous is that it has survived a certain process' (Rostbøll 2005, 377).

23. On this very point, see Habermas (1985, 99), who writes that 'nonviolence does not necessarily exclude . . . impairments of the freedom of movement of third parties'.

24. Of course, the protest did not inconvenience only passengers, but also airport staff, neighbour businesses, and more.
25. On this point, see Robert Nozick (1997, 15): 'If I lure you into an escape-proof room in New York and leave you imprisoned there, I do not coerce you into not going to Chicago though I make you unfree to do so'.
26. Habermas discusses the notion of 'communicative freedom'; that is, the freedom to say 'no' to a certain validity claim. This freedom is not infringed by violent *civil* disobedience, such as the Stansted case discussed here. See Gunther (1998, 237).
27. Here I refer to an argument I have presented in Moraro (2018a).
28. A similar scenario occurs in Hans Weingartner's movie *The Edukators* (2006), in which three young anti-capitalist protesters kidnap a millionaire to protest about social inequality. During the imprisonment, the millionaire begins to empathise (though only temporarily) with the motives behind their act.
29. It may even occur that, by resorting to bossnapping, the workers get to finally accept that the changes imposed upon them, though onerous, may be justifiable.

5. THE MORAL RIGHT TO CIVIL DISOBEDIENCE

1. There are some exceptions to this claim, which I discuss immediately below.
2. Rawls appears to conflate the conditions for justifiable civil disobedience, on the one hand, with the possibility of a right to civil disobedience, on the other – that is to say, he discusses the conditions under which civil disobedience may be *right*, not whether there is a right to civil disobedience.
3. Here I follow the discussion presented by Cavallaro (1993).
4. Brownlee contends that 'in common law jurisdictions, the lack of success that civil disobedients have had in advancing a defence of necessity may be due less to anything special about civil disobedience than to an apparent rejection by common law judges of a general principle of necessity' (2012, 181).
5. A non-contingent need represents a necessary condition for the non-contingent ends a person cannot but have; for example, the need for clean drinking water.
6. I discuss this principle, together with Brownlee's further argument for a legal *excuse* (which she labels 'demands-of-conviction defence') for civil disobedience, later in this chapter.
7. Loesch (1991, 1106) makes a similar comment about the 'conflicting moral obligations' faced by civil disobedients, and argues for the availability to protesters of a 'motive-based' legal defence.
8. Brownlee refers to this as 'the *modesty of law* thesis' (192).
9. Brownlee (2018, 291) writes that 'despite Lefkowitz's claims to the contrary, the political-participation ground that he offers does not yield a general moral right to civil disobedience for all members of a polity regardless of their political status. It yields a right only for people who are sufficiently politically disadvantaged'.
10. Emanuela Ceva (2015) has recently advanced a similar argument in support of a right to civil disobedience for members of some minority groups.
11. Note that this need not be particularly controversial. Daniel Weinstock, in his critical commentary on Brownlee's account (which I describe in the next section), argues that the right to civil disobedience may be interpreted only as a 'remedial' right; that is, a right that 'should only be granted to groups who find themselves subjects of gross injustice at the hands of majorities' (2016, 709). Brownlee, however, interprets the right to civil disobedience as a 'primary right': for this reason, according to Weinstock, her account warrants 'the suspicion that those who engage in civil disobedience in the context of tolerably well-functioning liberal democracies are acting undemocratically' (708).
12. The fact that one *might* lose the right to vote (e.g., due to a change in citizenship status) does not defy the objection; namely, that when one has the right to vote one can use it under any circumstances.

13. In the sentence immediately after this one, however, Lefkowitz specifies that 'of course' citizens of a legitimate state may have a right to engage in civil disobedience 'no matter how small the injustice' (ibid.), and that this makes his account more capacious than Rawls's, which, as we saw in chapter 2, allows for civil disobedience only against 'blatant violations' of the principles of justice.

14. Lefkowitz never articulates the nature of such danger, but it can be inferred from his argument that he is concerned with the possibility of widespread disobedience, which may weaken the state's ability to coordinate collective action.

15. Lefkowitz has offered a reply to Brownlee's objections in (2018).

16. In his critical note on Brownlee's book, Daniel Weinstock begins by introducing it as 'the most systematic philosophical account we possess of the place of civil disobedience in liberal democratic theory' (Weinstock 2016, 707).

17. Brownlee does indeed draw a clear line between law and morality by describing the former as 'the *most blunt* manifestation of the social rules' of a reasonably good society (2012, 23). In this sense, her view differs from the one I will defend in the next chapter, in which law and morality are strongly intertwined.

18. The idea that a moral right to civil disobedience should apply only to cases of 'reasonable mistakes' is defended, among others, by Raz (1979), Haksar (2003) and Lefkowitz (2007).

19. A similar argument is advanced by Andrew Sabl (2001, 323), who defends the acceptance of punishment for civil disobedience as akin to payment of an 'entry-fee', and as testing the sincerity of the protester by deterring 'frivolous' acts of disobedience.

20. Edmundson adds that 'only those who have tried unsuccessfully to get arrested can know how frustrating this tactic can be'. Others have stressed that many civil disobedients would welcome an appearance in court. See Turenne (2004, 379); Greenawalt (1987, 240).

6. MOVING FORWARD

1. As I explain below, my account draws significantly on William Edmundson's defence of a 'virtue of law-abidance' (2006).

2. Delmas does not envisage the possibility of the protesters being wrong.

3. On this point, Richard Bellamy (1999, 101) has argued that the Rawlsian model constitutes an attempt 'to keep the ship of state on an even keel by steering clear of the winds of controversy'.

4. On political stability, see Vallier (2017).

5. See also Barbalet (2000).

6. For a critical commentary of virtue ethical accounts of state legitimacy, see LeBar (2013).

7. On deontology, see Darwall (2003b).

8. For the original discussion of 'inside-out' versus 'outside-in' accounts of morality, see McDowell (1979).

9. For a related analysis of law from a virtue ethical perspective, see Brownlee (2015).

10. In the last part of this chapter, I will interpret this idea in light of a civil disobedient's duty to answer to her fellows for the breach of the law, but not to necessarily accept the punishment.

11. As noticed in chapter 1, even supporters of associative accounts of political obligation acknowledge that the moral credentials of the law and/or of the underlying regime cannot be entirely ignored in assessing whether the citizen has a duty to obey.

12. For the opposite view that the state is incompatible with individual autonomy, see Wolff (1998).

13. One major exception is Dworkin (1985, 105), who suggests that, by engaging in civil disobedience, agents might 'acquit rather than challenge . . . their duty as citizens', a suggestion I endorse below.

14. Lefkowitz (2007) and Smith (2013) agree that civil disobedience constitutes a form of political participation. They, nonetheless, also contend that civil disobedience requires accepting the punishment.

15. In the next section I elaborate on an argument I have presented in Moraro (2014).

16. This is not to say that someone who chooses evil over good is not acting autonomously. The point is that we do not have an obligation to provide her with the evil options. Compare Raz (1986, 411–12).

17. Once again, the requirements of the duty cannot be identified without considering the specific circumstances under which the agent is to act.

18. 'Just as ethics calls for non-compliance with, indeed rejection of, immoral beliefs and desires, so political theory, if brought to bear upon the question of what the virtuous man should do in certain circumstances, seems to support the conclusion that disobedience of bad laws and decrees may well be called for' (Rosler 2005, 237).

19. In this section, I draw on material from Moraro (2018b).

20. 'Punishment is an apt response only to unjustified and unexcused wrongdoing' (Gardner 2007, 197).

Bibliography

Ackerman, Bruce. 1989. 'Why Dialogue'? *Journal of Philosophy* 86 (1): 5–22.

Adams, N. P. 2018. 'Uncivil Disobedience: Political Commitment and Violence'. *Res Publica* 24 (4): 475–91.

Aitchison, Guy. 2018. 'Coercion, Resistance and the Radical Side of Non-Violent Action'. *Raisons Politiques* 69 (1): 45–61.

Allen, Michael. 2009. 'Civil Disobedience and Terrorism Testing the Limits of Deliberative Democracy'. *Theoria: A Journal of Social and Political Theory* 56 (118): 15–39.

Anderson, Joel, and Axel Honneth. 2005. 'Autonomy, Vulnerability, Recognition, and Justice'. In *Autonomy and the Challenges to Liberalism: New Essays*, edited by Joel Anderson and John Christman, 127–49. Cambridge: Cambridge University Press.

Applbaum, Arthur Isak. 2010. 'Legitimacy without the Duty to Obey'. *Philosophy & Public Affairs* 38 (3): 21–239.

Archard, David. 2001. 'Political Disagreement, Legitimacy, and Civility'. *Philosophical Explorations* 4 (3): 207–22.

Arendt, Hannah. 1958. *The Human Condition*. Chicago: University of Chicago Press.

Aristotle. 2004. *The Nicomachean Ethics*, edited by J. A. K. Thomson, Hugh Tredennick and Jonathan Barnes. Further revised edition, Penguin Classics. London: Penguin.

Bakan, Joel. 2004. *The Corporation: The Pathological Pursuit of Profit and Power*. New York: Free Press.

Barbalet, Jack. 2000. 'Vagaries of Social Capital: Citizenship, Trust and Loyalty'. In *Citizenship, Community and Democracy*, edited by E. Vasta, 91–106. Basingstoke: St Martin's Press.

Barber, B. 2003. *Strong Democracy: Participatory Politics for a New Age*, 20th anniversary ed. Berkeley: University of California Press.

Baron, Marcia W., Philip Pettit, and Michael Slote. 1997. *Three Methods of Ethics: A Debate*. Oxford: Wiley-Blackwell.

Bauer, Steven M., and Peter Eckerstrom, J. 1987. 'The State Made Me Do It: The Applicability of the Necessity Defense to Civil Disobedience'. *Stanford Law Review* 39: 1173–1537.

Bedau, Hugo A. 1961. 'On Civil Disobedience'. *Journal of Philosophy* 58 (21): 653–65.

Bedau, Hugo A., ed. 1991. *Civil Disobedience in Focus*. London: Routledge.

Bellamy, Richard. 1999. *Liberalism and Pluralism: Towards a Politics of Compromise*. London: Routledge.

Beran, H. 1987. *The Consent Theory of Political Obligation*. London: Croom Helm.

Berofsky, B. 2007. *Liberation from Self: A Theory of Personal Autonomy*. Cambridge: Cambridge University Press.

Blake, Michael. 2016. 'Civil Disobedience, Dirty Hands, and Secession'. In *The Theory of Self-Determination*, edited by Fernando R. Tesón, 166–83. Cambridge: Cambridge University Press.

Bolinger, Renee Jorgensen. 2017. 'Revisiting the Right to Do Wrong'. *Australasian Journal of Philosophy* 95 (1): 43–57.

Boot, Eric. 2017. 'Classified Public Whistleblowing: How to Justify a Pro Tanto Wrong'. *Social Theory and Practice* 43 (3): 541.

Bratman, Michael. 1987. *Intention, Plans, and Practical Reason*. Cambridge, MA: Harvard University Press.

Brennan, Geoffrey, and Loren Lomasky. 1993. *Democracy and Decision: The Pure Theory of Electoral Preference*. Cambridge: Cambridge University Press.

Brownlee, Kimberley. 2012. *Conscience and Conviction: The Case for Civil Disobedience*. Oxford: Oxford University Press.

Brownlee, Kimberley. 2015. 'What's Virtuous About the Law'? *Legal Theory* 21 (1): 1–17.

Brownlee, Kimberley. 2016a. 'The Civil Disobedience of Edward Snowden: A Reply to William Scheuerman'. *Philosophy & Social Criticism* 42 (10): 965–70.

Brownlee, Kimberley. 2016b. 'Reply to Critics'. *Criminal Law and Philosophy* 10 (4): 721–39.

Brownlee, Kimberley. 2018. 'Two Tales of Civil Disobedience: A Reply to David Lefkowitz'. *Res Publica* 24 (3): 291–96.

Buchanan, Allen E. 2003. *Justice, Legitimacy, and Self-Determination: Moral Foundations for International Law*. Oxford: Oxford University Press.

Bufacchi, V. 2007. *Violence and Social Justice*. Basingstoke: Palgrave Macmilllan.

Bulman-Pozen, Jessica, and David E. Pozen. 2015. 'Uncivil Obedience'. *Columbia Law Review* 115 (4): 809–72.

Calhoun, Cheshire. 2000. 'The Virtue of Civility'. *Philosophy & Public Affairs* 29 (3): 251–75.

Carter, Alan. 1998. 'In Defence of Radical Disobedience'. *Journal of Applied Philosophy* 15 (1): 29–47.

Cavallaro, James. 1993. 'The Demise of the Political Necessity Defense: Indirect Civil Disobedience and *United States vs. Schoon*'. *California Law Review* 81 (1): 351–85.

Celikates, Robin. 2016. 'Democratizing Civil Disobedience'. *Philosophy & Social Criticism* 42 (10): 982–94.

Cervera-Marzal, Manuel. 2013. 'Désobéissance civile et libéralisme'. *Canadian Journal of Political Science* 46 (2): 369–96.

Ceva, Emanuela. 2015. 'Why Toleration Is Not the Appropriate Response to Dissenting Minorities' Claims'. *European Journal of Philosophy* 23 (3): 633–51.

Ceva, Emanuela, and Michele Bocchiola. 2018. 'Personal Trust, Public Accountability, and the Justification of Whistleblowing'. *Journal of Political Philosophy* (forthcoming).

Chenoweth, E., and M. J. Stephan. 2013. *Why Civil Resistance Works: The Strategic Logic of Nonviolent Conflict*. Paperback ed. New York: Columbia University Press.

Christiano, Thomas. 2008. *The Constitution of Equality: Democratic Authority and Its Limits*. Oxford: Oxford University Press.

Coady, C. A. J. 1986. 'The Idea of Violence'. *Journal of Applied Philosophy* 3 (1): 3–19.

Cohen, Jean L., and Andrew Arato. 1992. *Civil Society and Political Theory: Studies in Contemporary German Social Thought*. Cambridge, MA: MIT Press.

Cohen, Marshall. 1972. 'Liberalism and Disobedience'. *Philosophy and Public Affairs* 1 (3): 283–314.

Cooke, Maeve, ed. 1998. *On the Pragmatics of Communication / Jurgen Habermas Studies in Contemporary German Social Thought*. Cambridge, MA: MIT Press.

Cooke, Maeve. 2016. 'Civil Obedience and Disobedience'. *Philosophy and Social Criticism* 42 (10): 995–1003.

Corlett, J. Angelo. 1997. 'What Is Civil Disobedience'? *Philosophical Papers* 26 (3): 241–59.

Crisp, Roger, ed. 1996. *How Should One Live? Essays on the Virtues*. Oxford: Clarendon Press.

Dagger, R. 1997. *Civic Virtues: Rights, Citizenship, and Republican Liberalism*. Oxford: Oxford University Press.

Dagger, Richard. 2000. 'Membership, Fair Play, and Political Obligation'. *Political Studies* 48 (1): 104–17.

Dahl, Robert Alan. 1989. *Democracy and Its Critics*. New Haven: Yale University Press.
Darwall, Stephen L. 2003a. *Consequentialism*, edited by Stephen L. Darwall. Oxford: Blackwell.
Darwall, Stephen L., ed. 2003b. *Deontology*. Oxford: Blackwell.
Darwall, Stephen L. 2006. *The Second-Person Standpoint: Morality, Respect, and Accountability*. Cambridge, MA: Harvard University Press.
Davidson Sorkin, Amy. 2015. 'Don't Blame Edward Snowden for the Paris Attacks'. *New York Times*, 19 November.https://www.newyorker.com/news/amy-davidson/dont-blame-edward-snowden-for-the-paris-attacks.
Delmas, Candice. 2016a. 'Civil Disobedience'. *Philosophy Compass* 11 (11): 681–91.
Delmas, Candice. 2016b. 'That Lonesome Whistle'. *Boston Review*, 14 June 2018.http://bostonreview.net/editors-picks-world-us/candice-delmas-lonesome-whistle.
Delmas, Candice. 2017. 'Disobedience, Civil and Otherwise'. *Criminal Law and Philosophy* 11 (1): 195–211.
Delmas, Candice. 2018a. *A Duty to Resist: When Disobedience Should Be Uncivil*. New York: Oxford University Press.
Delmas, Candice. 2018b. 'Is Hacktivism the New Civil Disobedience'? *Raisons Politiques* 69 (1): 63–81.
Dewey, John. 1916. 'Force and Coercion'. *International Journal of Ethics* 26 (3): 359–67.
Dimock, Susan. 2014. 'Contractarian Criminal Law Theory and Mala Prohibita Offences'. In *Criminalization: The Political Morality of the Criminal Law*, edited by Antony Duff, Lindsay Farmer, Sandra Marshall, Massimo Renzo and Victor Tadros, 151–81. Oxford: Oxford University Press.
Driver, Julia. 2002. 'Human Nature. The Virtues and Human Nature'. In *How Should One Live? Essays on the Virtues*, edited by Roger Crisp. Oxford: Clarendon Press.
Driver, Julia. 2011. 'Promising Too Much'. In *Promises and Agreements: Philosophical Essays*, edited by Hanoch Sheinman. Oxford: Oxford University Press.
Duff, Antony. 2001. *Punishment, Communication, and Community*. Oxford: Oxford University Press.
Duff, Antony. 2007. *Answering for Crime: Responsibility and Liability in the Criminal Law*. Portland: Hart.
Duff, Antony. 2008. 'The Incompleteness of "Punishment as Fair Play": A Response to Dagger'. *Res Publica* 14 (4): 277–81.
Dworkin, Gerald. 1988. *The Theory and Practice of Autonomy*. Cambridge: Cambridge University Press.
Dworkin, R. M. 1985. *A Matter of Principle*. Oxford: Clarendon.
Dworkin, R. M. 1986. *Law's Empire*. London: Fontana.
Dworkin, R. M. 2013. *Taking Rights Seriously*. London: Bloomsbury. Original edition, 1977.
Eckersley, Robyn. 1996. 'Greening Liberal Democracy'. In *Democracy and Green Political Thought*, edited by B. Doherty and M. de Geus, 212–36. London: Routledge.
Edgar, H. 1973. 'The Eespionage Statutes and Publication of Defense Information'. *Columbia Law Review* 73 (5): 930–1087. doi: 10.2307/1121711.
Edmundson, William A. 1998. *Three Anarchical Fallacies: An Essay on Political Authority*. Cambridge: Cambridge University Press.
Edmundson, William. 2004. 'State of the Art: The Duty to Obey the Law'. *Legal Theory* 10 (4): 215–59.
Edmundson, William A. 2006. 'The Virtue of Law-Abidance'. *Philosophers' Imprint* 6 (4): 1–21.
Fabre, Cécile. 2002. 'Good Samaritanism: A Matter of Justice'. *Critical Review of International Social and Political Philosophy* 5 (4): 128–44.
Falcon Y. Tella, Maria Jose. 2004. 'Civil Disobedience and Test Cases'. *Ratio Juris* 17 (3): 315–27.
Feinberg, Joel. 1965. 'The Expressive Function of Punishment'. *The Monist* 49 (3): 397–423.
Feinberg, Joel. 1984. *The Moral Limits of the Criminal Law Volume 1: Harm to Others*. New York: Oxford University Press.

Feinberg, Joel. 1989a. 'Autonomy'. In *The Inner Citadel: Essays on Individual Autonomy*, edited by John Philip Christman, 27–53. Oxford: Oxford University Press.

Feinberg, J. 1989b. *The Moral Limits of the Criminal Law Volume 3: Harm to Self*. Oxford: Oxford University Press.

Fischer, John Martin, and Mark Ravizza. 1998. *Responsibility and Control: A Theory of Moral Responsibility, Cambridge Studies in Philosophy and Law*. Cambridge: Cambridge University Press.

Fischer, John Martin, and Neal A. Tognazzini. 2011. 'The Physiognomy of Responsibility'. *Philosophy and Phenomenological Research* 82 (2): 381–417.

Fishkin, James S. 2009. *When the People Speak: Deliberative Democracy and Public Consultation*. Oxford: Oxford University Press.

Fortas, Abe. 1968. *Concerning Dissent and Civil Disobedience*. New York: New American Library.

Frankfurt, H. G. 1988. *The Importance of What We Care About: Philosophical Essays*. Cambridge: Cambridge University Press.

Frankfurt, H. G. 1999. *Necessity, Volition, and Love*. Cambridge: Cambridge University Press.

Fredman, Sandra. 2008. *Human Rights Transformed: Positive Rights and Positive Duties*. Oxford: Oxford University Press.

Fung, Archon. 2005. 'Deliberation before the Revolution: Toward an Ethics of Deliberative Democracy in an Unjust World'. *Political Theory* 33 (3): 397–419.

Galston, William A. 1991. *Liberal Purposes: Goods, Virtues, and Diversity in the Liberal State*. Cambridge: Cambridge University Press.

Gardner, John. 2007. *Offences and Defences: Selected Essays in the Philosophy of Criminal Law*. Oxford: Oxford University Press.

Gaus, Gerald F. 1999. *Social Philosophy*. Armonk: Sharpe.

Gellman, Barton. 2013. 'Edward Snowden, after Months of NSA Revelations, Says His Mission's Accomplished'. *Washington Post*, 23 December.https://www.washingtonpost.com/world/national-security/edward-snowden-after-months-of-nsa-revelations-says-his-missions-accomplished/2013/12/23/49fc36de-6c1c-11e3-a523-fe73f0ff6b8d_story.html?noredirect=on&utm_term=.ff1ffa5b51bb.

Gilabert, P. 2018. *Human Dignity and Human Rights*. Oxford: Oxford University Press.

Goodin, Robert E. 2000. 'Democratic Deliberation Within'. *Philosophy & Public Affairs* 29 (1): 81–109.

Goodin, Robert E., and Simon J. Niemeyer. 2003. 'When Does Deliberation Begin? Internal Reflection versus Public Discussion in Deliberative Democracy'. *Political Studies* 51 (4): 627–49.

Green, Leslie. 2003. 'Civil Disobedience and Academic Freedom'. *Osgoode Hall Law Journal* 41 (2/3): 381–405.

Green, Leslie. 2010. 'Two Worries about Respect for Persons'. *Ethics* 120 (2):212–231

Greenawalt, Kent. 1987. *Conflicts of Law and Morality*. Oxford: Oxford University Press.

Gunther, Klaus. 1998. 'Communicative Freedom, Communicative Power, and Jurisgenesis'. In *Habermas on Law and Democracy: Critical Exchanges*, edited by M. Rosenfeld and A. Arato, 234–54. Los Angeles: University of California Press.

Gutmann, Amy, and Dennis F. Thompson. 1996. *Democracy and Disagreement*. London: Belknap Press of Harvard University Press.

Habermas, Jürgen. 1985. 'Civil Disobedience: Litmus Test for the Democratic Constitutional State'. *Berkeley Journal of Sociology* 30: 95–116.

Habermas, Jürgen. 1987. *The Theory of Communicative Action*. Cambridge: Polity.

Habermas, Jürgen. 1990. *Moral Consciousness and Communicative Action*. Cambridge: Polity.

Habermas, Jürgen. 1992. 'Citizenship and National Identity: Some Reflections on the Future of Europe'. *Praxis International* 12 (1): 1–19.

Habermas, Jürgen. 2009. *Between Facts and Norms: Contributions to a Discourse Theory of Law and Democracy*. Translated by William Rehg. Cambridge: Polity Press. Original edition, 1996.

Haksar, Vinit. 2003. 'The Right to Civil Disobedience'. *Osgoode Hall Law Journal* 41 (2/3): 407–26.

Hall, Matthew R. 2007. 'Guilty But Civilly Disobedient: Reconciling Civil Disobedience and the Rule of Law'. *Cardozo Law Review* 28: 2083–2829.
Hardimon, Michael. 1994. 'Role Obligations'. *Journal of Philosophy* 91 (7): 333–63.
Hare, R. M. 1998. *Essays on Political Morality*. Oxford: Clarendon Press.
Harel, Alon. 2002. 'Unconscionable Objection to Conscientious Objection: Notes on Sagi and Shapira'. *Israel Law Review* 36 (3): 219–26.
Hart, H. L. A. 1955. 'Are There Any Natural Rights'? *Philosophical Review* 64 (2): 175–91.
Hauptmann, Emily. 1999. 'Review: Deliberation = Legitimacy = Democracy'. *Political Theory* 27 (6): 857–72.
Haworth, L. 1986. *Autonomy: An Essay in Philosophical Psychology and Ethics*. New Haven: Yale University Press.
Herr, William A. 1974. 'Thoreau: A Civil Disobedient'? *Ethics* 85 (1): 87–91.
Herstein, Ori J. 2012. 'Defending the Right to Do Wrong'. *Law and Philosophy* 31 (3): 343–65.
Higgins, R. C. A. 2004. *The Moral Limits of Law: Obedience, Respect, and Legitimacy*. Oxford: Oxford University Press.
Hindkjaer Madsen, Tine. 2018. 'On a Belief-Relative Moral Right to Civil Disobedience'. *Res Publica*. doi: 10.1007/s11158-018-9404-7.
Hohfeld, Wesley. 1919. *Fundamental Legal Conceptions as Applied in Judicial Reasoning*, edited by Walter Cook. New Haven: Yale University Press.
Horton, John. 2010. *Political Obligation*. Basingstoke: Palgrave Macmillan.
Horton, John. 2012. 'Political Legitimacy, Justice and Consent'. *Critical Review of International Social and Political Philosophy* 15 (2): 129–48.
Humphrey, Mathew. 2006. 'Democratic Legitimacy, Public Justification and Environmental Direct Action'. *Political Studies* 54 (2): 310–27.
Hurka, Thomas. 1993. *Perfectionism*. New York: Oxford University Press.
Hursthouse, Rosalind. 2001. *On Virtue Ethics*, 2nd ed. Oxford: Oxford University Press.
Kamath, M. V. 2007. *Gandhi, A Spiritual Journey*. Mumbai: Indus Source Books.
Katz, Barbara. 1985. 'Civil Disobedience and the First Amendment'. *UCLA Law Review* 32: 904–19.
Kavka, Gregory S. 1995. 'Why Even Morally Perfect People Would Need Government'. *Social Philosophy and Policy* 12 (1):1–18.
Kingwell, M. 1995. *A Civil Tongue: Justice, Dialogue, and the Politics of Pluralism*. University Park: Pennsylvania State University Press.
Kirkpatrick, Jennet. 2008. *Uncivil Disobedience: Studies in Violence and Democratic Politics*. Princeton: Princeton University Press.
Klosko, George. 2004. *The Principle of Fairness and Political Obligation*. Lanham, MD: Rowman & Littlefield.
Klosko, George. 2011. 'Are Political Obligations Content Independent'? *Political Theory* 39 (4): 498–523.
Knowles, Dudley. 2012. 'Good Samaritans and Good Government'. *Proceedings of the Aristotelian Society* 112: 161–78.
Kormann, Carolyn. 2018. 'The Divestment Movement to Combat Climate Change Is All Grown Up'. *New York Times*, 14 September.https://www.newyorker.com/news/dispatch/the-divestment-movement-to-combat-climate-change-is-all-grown-up.
Kramer, Matthew H. 2005. 'Legal and Moral Obligation'. In *The Blackwell Guide to the Philosophy of Law and Legal Theory*, edited by Martin P. Golding and William A. Edmundson, 179–90. New York: Blackwell.
Kymlicka, Will. 1995. *Multicultural Citizenship: A Liberal Theory of Minority Rights*. Oxford: Clarendon Press.
Kymlicka, Will. 2002. *Contemporary Political Philosophy: An Introduction*. Oxford: Oxford University Press.
Kymlicka, Will, and Wayne Norman. 1994. 'Return of the Citizen: A Survey of Recent Work on Citizenship Theory'. *Ethics* 104 (2): 352–81.
Larmore, Charles E. 1987. *Patterns of Moral Complexity*. Cambridge: Cambridge University Press.

LeBar, Mark. 2013. 'Virtue and Politics'. In *The Cambridge Companion to Virtue Ethics*, edited by Daniel C. Russell, 265. Cambridge: Cambridge University Press.

Lefkowitz, David. 2005. 'A Contractualist Defense of Democratic Authority'. *Ratio Juris* 18 (3): 346–64.

Lefkowitz, David. 2007. 'On a Moral Right to Civil Disobedience'. *Ethics* 117 (2): 202–33.

Lefkowitz, David. 2016. 'Should the Law Convict Those Who Act from Conviction? Reflections on a Demands-of-Conscience Criminal Defense'. *Criminal Law and Philosophy* 10 (4): 657–75.

Lefkowitz, David. 2018. 'In Defense of Penalizing (But Not Punishing) Civil Disobedience'. *Res Publica* 24 (3): 273–89.

Levine, Matthew S. 2004. 'Punishment and Willingness to Pay'. *Gonzaga Law Review* 40: 329.

Lewis, Paul. 2013. 'Edward Snowden Inflames US-Russian Tensions with Moscow Meeting'. *The Guardian*, 13 July.https://www.theguardian.com/world/2013/jul/12/edward-snowden-russian-moscow-meeting.

Livingston, Alexander. 2017. 'Fidelity to Truth: Gandhi and the Genealogy of Civil Disobedience'. *Political Theory* 46 (4): 511–36. doi: 10.1177/0090591717727275.

Loesch, Martin. 1991. 'Motive Testimony and a Civil Disobedience Justification'. *Notre Dame Journal of Law, Ethics and Public Policy* 5 (4): 1069–119.

Louden, Robert B. 2011. *Kant's Human Being: Essays on His Theory of Human Nature*. Oxford: Oxford University Press.

Lovell, J. S. 2009. *Crimes of Dissent: Civil Disobedience, Criminal Justice, and the Politics of Conscience*. New York: New York University Press.

Lyons, David. 1998. 'Moral Judgment, Historical Reality, and Civil Disobedience'. *Philosophy and Public Affairs* 27 (1): 31–49.

MacCallum, Gerald C. 1993. 'What Is Wrong with Violence'? In *Legislative Intent and Other Essays on Law, Politics, and Morality*, edited by Marcus Singer and Martin Rex, 235–56. Madison: University of Wisconsin Press.

Macedo, Stephen. 1990. *Liberal Virtues: Citizenship, Virtue, and Community in Liberal Constitutionalism*. Oxford: Clarendon Press.

MacIntyre, Alasdair. 2007. *After Virtue*, 3rd ed. Notre Dame: University of Notre Dame Press. Original edition, 1981.

Manin, Bernard. 1987. 'On Legitimacy and Political Deliberation'. *Political Theory* 15 (3): 338–68.

Marcuse, Herbert. 1965. 'Repressive Tolerance'. In *A Critique Of Pure Tolerance*, edited by Barrington Moore, Herbert Marcuse, and Robert Paul Wolff, 95–137. Boston: Beacon Press.

Markovits, Daniel. 2005. 'Democratic Disobedience'. *Yale Law Journal* 114: 1897–1952.

Mason, Andrew. 2012. *Living Together as Equals: The Demands of Citizenship*. Oxford: Oxford University Press.

May, T. 2015. *Nonviolent Resistance: A Philosophical Introduction*. Cambridge, UK: Polity Press.

McArthur, Tom, Jacqueline Lam-McArthur and Lise Fontaine. 2018. *Oxford English Dictionary*. Oxford: Oxford University Press.

McCarthy, Thomas. 1994. 'Kantian Constructivism and Reconstructivism: Rawls and Habermas in Dialogue'. *Ethics* 105 (1): 44–63.

McDowell, John. 1979. 'Virtue and Reason'. *The Monist* 62 (3): 331–50.

McEwen, Stephen J. Jr. 1991. 'The Protester: A Sentencing Dilemma'. *Notre Dame Journal of Law, Ethics and Public Policy* 5 (4): 987–93.

Mendus, S. 1989. *Toleration and the Limits of Liberalism*, edited by Peter Jones and Albert Weale, *Issues in Political Theory*. Houndmills: Macmillan.

Mill, John Stuart. 1975. *On Liberty*. Edited by David Spitz. New York: Norton.

Milligan, Tony. 2013. *Civil Disobedience: Protest, Justification and the Law*. London: Bloomsbury Publishing.

Milligan, Tony. 2017. 'Animal Rescue as Civil Disobedience'. *Res Publica* 23 (3): 281–98.

Möller, Kai. 2009. 'Two Conceptions of Positive Liberty: Towards an Autonomy-Based Theory of Constitutional Rights'. *Oxford Journal of Legal Studies* 29 (4): 757–86.

Moraro, Piero. 2012. 'A Dilemma for the Civil Disobedient: Pleading "Guilty" or "Not Guilty" in the Courtroom'. In *The Public in Law: Representations of the Political in Legal Discourse*, 99–111. Farnham: Ashgate.

Moraro, Piero. 2014. 'Respecting Autonomy through the Use of Force: The Case of Civil Disobedience'. *Journal of Applied Philosophy* 31 (1): 63–76.

Moraro, Piero. 2018a. 'Is Bossnapping Uncivil'? *Raisons Politiques* 69 (1): 29–44.

Moraro, Piero. 2018b. 'On (Not) Accepting the Punishment for Civil Disobedience'. *Philosophical Quarterly* 68 (272): 503–20.

Moraro, Piero. 2019a. 'The Costs of Disobedience: A Reply to Delmas'. *Res Publica: A Journal of Moral, Legal and Political Philosophy.* https://doi.org/10.1007/s11158-019-09422-7.

Moraro, Piero. 2019b. 'Punishment, Fair Play and the Burdens of Citizenship'. *Law and Philosophy.* https://doi.org/10.1007/s10982-019-09346-6.

Morris, C. W., ed. 2000. *The Social Contract Theorists: Critical Essays on Hobbes, Locke, and Rousseau.* Lanham, MD: Rowman & Littlefield.

Morris, Herbert. 1968. 'Persons and Punishment'. *The Monist* 52 (4): 475–501.

Mouffe, Chantal. 2005. *On the Political.* London: Routledge.

Murphy, Liam B. 2001. 'Beneficence, Law, and Liberty: The Case of Required Rescue'. *Georgetown Law Journal* 89 (3): 605–65.

Nozick, Robert. 1997. *Socratic Puzzles.* Cambridge, MA: Harvard University Press.

Nozick, Robert. 2013. *Anarchy, State, and Utopia*, edited by Thomas Nagel. New York: Basic Books. Original edition, 1974.

O'Neill, Onora. 1983. 'Kant after Virtue'. *Inquiry* 26 (4): 387.

O'Neill, Shane. 1997. *Impartiality in Context: Grounding Justice in a Pluralist World.* Albany: State University of New York Press.

O'Sullivan, Siobhan, Clare McCausland and Scott Brenton. 2017. 'Animal Activists, Civil Disobedience and Global Responses to Transnational Injustice'. *Res Publica* 23 (3): 261–80.

Olick, R. S. 2001. *Taking Advance Directives Seriously: Prospective Autonomy and Decisions Near the End of Life.* Washington, DC: Georgetown University Press.

Oshana, M. 2006. *Personal Autonomy in Society.* Aldershot: Ashgate.

Parekh, Bhikhu. 1993. 'A Misconceived Discourse on Political Obligation'. *Political Studies* 41 (2): 236–51.

Parsons, Nick. 2013. 'Legitimizing Illegal Protest: The Permissive Ideational Environment and "Bossnappings" in France'. *British Journal of Industrial Relations* 51 (2): 288–309. doi: 10.1111/j.1467-8543.2012.00899.x.

Pepitone, Julianne. 2011. 'Why Occupy Wall Street Isn't about a List of Demands'. *CNN Money.*https://money.cnn.com/2011/10/12/technology/occupy_wall_street_demands/index.htm.

Percival, J. 2008. 'Climate Activists Held after Stansted Runway Protest'. *The Guardian*, 8 December.https://www.theguardian.com/environment/2008/dec/08/stansted-runway-protest.

Perry, Lewis. 2013. *Civil Disobedience: An American Tradition.* New Haven: Yale University Press.

Petherbridge, Danielle. 2016. 'Between Thinking and Action: Arendt on Conscience and Civil Disobedience'. *Philosophy & Social Criticism* 42 (10): 971–81.

Pettit, P. 2012. *On the People's Terms: A Republican Theory and Model of Democracy.* Cambridge: Cambridge University Press.

Plamenatz, John Petrov. 1968. *Consent, Freedom and Political Obligation.* Oxford: Oxford University Press.

Pukas, Serge. 2007. 'Waldron's Defence of the Natural Duty of Justice Revisited'. *Ethical Perspectives* 14 (1): 29–51.

Putnam, Robert D. 2000. *Bowling Alone: The Collapse and Revival of American Community.* New York: Simon & Schuster.

Quong, Jonathan. 2004. 'The Rights of Unreasonable Citizens'. *Journal of Political Philosophy* 12 (3): 314–35.

Railton, Peter. 1984. 'Alienation, Consequentialism, and the Demands of Morality'. *Philosophy and Public Affairs* 13 (2): 134–71.
Rawls, John. 1993. *Political Liberalism*. New York: Columbia University Press.
Rawls, John. 1997. 'The Idea of Public Reason Revisited'. *University of Chicago Law Review* 64 (3): 765–807.
Rawls, John. 1999. *A Theory of Justice*. Cambridge, MA: Harvard University Press.
Rawls, John. 2000. *Lectures on the History of Moral Philosophy*. Edited by Barbara Herman. Cambridge, MA: Harvard University Press.
Raz, Joseph. 1979. *The Authority of Law: Essays on Law and Morality, Authority of Law*. Oxford: Clarendon Press.
Raz, Joseph. 1986. *The Morality of Freedom*. Oxford: Oxford University Press.
Raz, Joseph. 1999. *Practical Reason and Norms*. Oxford: Oxford University Press. Original edition, 1975.
Raz, Joseph. 2001. *Value, Respect, and Attachment*. Cambridge: Cambridge University Press.
Renzo, Massimo. 2011. 'State Legitimacy and Self-Defence'. *Law and Philosophy* 30 (5): 575–601.
Renzo, Massimo. 2012. 'Associative Responsibilities and Political Obligation'. *Philosophical Quarterly* 62 (246): 106–27.
Renzo, Massimo. 2013. 'Responsibility and Answerability in the Criminal Law'. In *The Constitution of the Criminal Law*, edited by R. A. Duff, L. Farmer, S. Marshall, M. Renzo, and V. Tadros, 209–36. Oxford: Oxford University Press.
Rosen, Michael. 2012. *Dignity: Its History and Meaning*. Cambridge, MA: Harvard University Press.
Rosler, Andrés. 2005. *Political Authority and Obligation in Aristotle*. Oxford: Oxford University Press on Demand.
Rostbøll, Christian F. 2005. 'Preferences and Paternalism: On Freedom and Deliberative Democracy'. *Political Theory* 33 (3): 370–96.
Rostbøll, Christian F. 2008. *Deliberative Freedom: Deliberative Democracy as Critical Theory*. Albany: State University of New York Press.
Rousseau, Jean-Jacques. 1968. *The Social Contract*. Harmondsworth: Penguin.
Sabl, Andrew. 2001. 'Looking Forward to Justice: Rawlsian Civil Disobedience and Its Non-Rawlsian Lessons'. *Journal of Political Philosophy* 9 (3): 307–30.
Sandel, Michael J. 1998. *Liberalism and the Limits of Justice*, 2nd ed. Cambridge, UK: Cambridge University Press.
Sandel, Michael J. 2005. *Public Philosophy: Essays on Morality in Politics*. Cambridge, MA: Harvard University Press.
Santoro, Daniele, and Manohar Kumar. 2018. *Speaking Truth to Power: A Theory of Whistleblowing*. Berlin: Springer.
Schaffler, Samuel. 2001. *Boundaries and Allegiances: Problems of Justice and Responsibility in Liberal Thought*. Oxford: Oxford University Press.
Schauer, Frederick F. 2015. *The Force of Law*. Cambridge, MA: Harvard University Press.
Scheuerman, William. 2014. 'Whistleblowing as Civil Disobedience: The Case of Edward Snowden'. *Philosophy and Social Criticism* 40 (7): 609–28.
Scheuerman, William E. 2015. 'Recent Theories of Civil Disobedience: An Anti-Legal Turn'? *Journal of Political Philosophy* 23 (4): 427–49.
Scheuerman, William E. 2018. *Civil Disobedience*. Medford, MA: Wiley.
Schlossberger, Eugene. 1989. 'Civil Disobedience'. *Analysis* 49: 148–56.
Schroeter, François. 2004. 'Endorsement and Autonomous Agency'. *Philosophy and Phenomenological Research* 69 (3): 633–59.
Shapiro, I., and C. Hacker-Cordón. 1999. *Democracy's Values*. Cambridge, UK: Cambridge University Press.
Shelby, T. 2016. *Dark Ghettos: Injustice, Dissent, and Reform*. Cambridge: Harvard University Press.
Shue, H. 1996. *Basic Rights: Subsistence, Affluence, and U.S. Foreign Policy*. Princeton: Princeton University Press.
Sidgwick, H. 1874. *The Methods of Ethics*. London: Macmillan.

Simmons, A. John. 1979. *Moral Principles and Political Obligations*. Princeton, NJ: Princeton University Press.
Simmons, A. John. 2001. *Justification and Legitimacy: Essays on Rights and Obligations*. Cambridge: Cambridge University Press.
Simmons, A. John. 2007. 'Civil Disobedience and the Duty to Obey the Law'. In *A Companion to Applied Ethics*, edited by R. G. Frey and C. Wellman, 50–61. Malden: Blackwell.
Simmons, A. John. 2010. 'Disobedience and Its Objects'. *Boston University Law Review* 90 (4): 1805–31.
Singer, Peter. 1991. 'Disobedience as a Plea for Reconsideration'. In *Civil Disobedience in Focus*, edited by Hugo A. Bedau, 122–29. London: Routledge.
Slote, Michael. 2001. *Morals from Motives*. Oxford: Oxford University Press.
Smart, Brian. 1978. 'Defining Civil Disobedience'. *Inquiry* 21 (1–4): 249–69.
Smith, M. B. E. 1973. 'Is There a Prima Facie Obligation to Obey the Law'? *Yale Law Journal* 82 (5): 950–76.
Smith, William. 2010. 'Reclaiming the Revolutionary Spirit: Arendt on Civil Disobedience'. *European Journal of Political Theory* 9 (2): 149–66.
Smith, William. 2013. *Civil Disobedience and Deliberative Democracy*. Oxon: Taylor & Francis.
Smith, William. 2016. 'The Burdens of Conviction: Brownlee on Civil Disobedience'. *Criminal Law and Philosophy* 10 (4): 693–706.
Smith, William. 2017. 'Civil Disobedience as Transnational Disruption'. *Global Constitutionalism* 6 (3): 477–504.
Smith, William. 2018. 'Disruptive Democracy: The Ethics of Direct Action'. *Raisons Politiques* 69 (1): 13–27.
Smith, William, and Kimberley Brownlee. 2017. 'Civil Disobedience and Conscientious Objection'. *Oxford Research Encyclopedia of Politics*. Accessed 18 December 2018. doi:10.1093/acrefore/9780190228637.013.114.
Solove, D. J. 2008. *Nothing to Hide: The False Trade-Off between Privacy and Security*. New Haven: Yale University Press.
Soper, Philip. 2002. *The Ethics of Deference: Learning from Law's Morals*. Cambridge: Cambridge University Press.
Starr, A., L. A. Fernandez and C. Scholl. 2011. *Shutting Down the Streets: Political Violence and Social Control in the Global Era*. New York: New York University Press.
Steiner, Hillel. 1974. 'Individual Liberty'. *Proceedings of the Aristotelian Society* 75: 33–50.
Stilz, Anna. 2009. *Liberal Loyalty: Freedom, Obligation, and the State*. Princeton, NJ: Princeton University Press.
Storing, Herbert J. 1991. 'The Case Against Civil Disobedience'. In *Civil Disobedience in Focus*, edited by Hugo A. Bedau, 91–108. London: Routledge.
Strawson, Peter Frederick. 2008. *Freedom and Resentment and Other Essays*. Oxon: Routledge.
Swan, Kyle. 2012. 'Republican Equality'. *Social Theory and Practice* 38 (3): 432–54.
Swanton, C. 2003. *Virtue Ethics: A Pluralistic View*. Oxford: Oxford University Press.
Talisse, Robert B. 2005. 'Deliberative Responses to Activist Challenges: A Continuation of Young's Dialectic'. *Philosophy and Social Criticism* 31 (4): 423–44.
Tamir, Yael. 1993. *Liberal Nationalism: Studies in Moral, Political, and Legal Philosophy*. Princeton, NJ: Princeton University Press.
Taylor, Charles. 1989. *Sources of the Self: The Making of the Modern Identity*. Cambridge, MA: Harvard University Press.
Thomassen, Lasse. 2007. 'Within the Limits of Deliberative Reason Alone'. *European Journal of Political Theory* 6 (2): 200–18.
Turenne, Sophie. 2004. 'Judicial Responses to Civil Disobedience: A Comparative Approach'. *Res Publica* 10 (4): 379–99.
Vallier, Kevin. 2017. 'Three Concepts of Political Stability: An Agent-Based Model'. *Social Philosophy and Policy* 34 (1): 232–59.
Vossen, Bas van Der. 2011a. 'Associative Political Obligations'. *Philosophy Compass* 6 (7): 477–87.

Vossen, Bas van Der. 2011b. 'Associative Political Obligations: Their Potential'. *Philosophy Compass* 6 (7): 488–96.
Waldron, Jeremy. 1993a. *Liberal Rights: Collected Papers 1981–1991*: Cambridge, UK: Cambridge University Press.
Waldron, Jeremy. 1993b. 'Special Ties and Natural Duties'. *Philosophy and Public Affairs* 22 (1): 3–30.
Walker, A. D. M. 1988. 'Political Obligation and the Argument from Gratitude'. *Philosophy & Public Affairs* 17 (3): 191–211.
Wall, Steven. 1998. *Liberalism, Perfectionism and Restraint*. Cambridge, UK: Cambridge University Press.
Walzer, Michael. 1970. *Obligations: Essays on Disobedience, War, and Citizenship*. Cambridge, MA: Harvard University Press.
Walzer, Michael. 1974. 'Civility and Civic Virtue in Contemporary America'. *Social Research* 41.
Watson, Gary. 2004. *Agency and Answerability: Selected Essays*. Oxford: Clarendon Press.
Weinar, Leif. 2017. John Rawls. In *Stanford Encyclopedia of Philosophy*, edited by Edward N. Zalta. Stanford: Stanford University Press.
Weingartner, Hans. 2006. *The Edukators*. Moore Park, NSW: Twentieth Century Fox Home Entertainment distributor.
Weinstock, Daniel. 2016. 'How Democratic Is Civil Disobedience'? *Criminal Law and Philosophy* 10 (4): 707–20.
Welchmann, Jennifer. 2011. 'Is Ecosabotage Civil Disobedience'? *Philosophy and Geography* 4 (1): 97–107.
Wellman, Christopher H. 1996. 'Liberalism, Samaritanism, and Political Legitimacy'. *Philosophy and Public Affairs* 25 (3): 211–37.
Wellman, Christopher H., and A. John Simmons. 2005. *Is There a Duty to Obey the Law?* New York: Cambridge University Press.
Wendt, F. 2018. *Authority*. Cambridge: Polity Press.
Wolff, R. P. 1998. *In Defense of Anarchism*. Berkeley: University of California Press. Original edition, 1970.
Wood, A. W., ed. 2008. *Groundwork for the Metaphysics of Morals / Immanuel Kant*. New Haven, CT: Yale University Press.
Young, Iris Marion. 1996. 'Communication and the Other: Beyond Deliberative Democracy'. In *Democracy and Difference: Contesting Boundaries of the Political*, edited by Seyla Benhabib, 120–36. Princeton, NJ: Princeton University Press.
Young, Iris Marion. 2000. *Inclusion and Democracy*. Oxford: Oxford University Press.
Young, Iris Marion. 2001. 'Activist Challenges to Deliberative Democracy'. *Political Theory* 29 (5): 670–90.
Young, Robert. 2017. *Personal Autonomy: Beyond Negative and Positive Liberty*. London: Routledge.
Zinn, Howard. 1991. 'Law, Justice, and Disobedience'. *Notre Dame Journal of Law, Ethics and Public Policy* 5 (4): 899–920.
Žižek, Slavoj. 2008. *Violence: Six Sideways Reflections*. London: Profile Books.
Zwiebach, Burton. 1975. *Civility and Disobedience*. New York: Cambridge University Press.

Index

Printed in Great Britain
by Amazon

42698078R00108